Guerrilla Gambling

How to Beat the Casinos
at
Their Own Games!

Frank Scoblete

Bonus Books, Inc., Chicago

97 96 95   5   4   3   2

Library of Congress Catalog Card Number: 93-72147

International Standard Book Number: 1-56625-027-7

Bonus Books, Inc.
160 East Illinois Street
Chicago, Illinois 60611

Composition by Point West, Inc., Carol Stream, IL

Printed in the United States of America

*This book is dedicated to
the George Baileys of the world*

Contents

Illustrations

Chance favors those minds which are prepared.
—*Louis Pasteur*

Introduction

I believe that the book you are holding is the most complete and comprehensive review of casino table games to be published in over 30 years. It contains excellent and sometimes unusual playing strategies for the traditional table games of blackjack, craps, roulette, and baccarat; strategies that will decidedly improve your chances of going home a winner; strategies I use myself. In blackjack, I have outlined and explained how to play the new variations and rules that are coming into vogue. I have given a complete strategy for double-exposure blackjack, a game that is currently being widely promoted in Atlantic City. In craps, I have offered two new methods of play, the *oddsman's bet* and the *best buys,* which were developed by the Captain, the individual I wrote about in my previous book on craps for Bonus Books *(Beat the Craps Out of the Casinos: How to Play Craps and Win!).*

I have covered the two most popular casino poker games, seven card stud and Texas hold'em, in such a way as to give the non-professional, non-expert player a shot at the big boys (and girls) of the casino poker rooms.

The book you are holding has information on most of the new games currently being introduced into the casinos: pai gow poker, Caribbean stud, Hickok's six card, Hickok's aces and eights, super pan nine, California aces, red dog, double down stud, pokette and sic bo. I have tried to cover every table game that I found on my 1993 tour of America's casinos and riverboats. Some of the newer games can only be found in one or two casinos. Others are being introduced widely.

Finally, no comprehensive gambling book would be complete without a look at slots and at the incredible and ever-growing phenomenon of video poker. Today's slot machines certainly represent the cutting edge of gaming technology and are as related to yesterday's one-armed bandits as birds are distantly related to dinosaurs. For video poker buffs, and they are legion, I have detailed general strategies of attack that can be used for the three most popular games: jacks or better, deuces wild, and joker's wild (joker poker). I have also pointed out which machines are preferable to play and offer the good players a better bang for their bucks.

I have included a chapter—the last one—about a "typical" day in my life as a casino gambler. This particular day took place in Las Vegas. Quite often strategy books don't capture the "feel" of what it is like to actually wager sums in casinos on a regular basis. Chapter 21 is my attempt to let you experience what I myself experience.

I realize that my readership is like Gaul—divided into three parts: those of you who have little experience in casinos and want to get information before you spend your money pursuing Lady Luck; those of you who have casino playing experience but are looking for stronger playing strategies for the particular games, old and/or new, that you are interested in; and those of you who enjoy reading about your favorite pastime—gambling. For all of you, I hope I have given you what you want.

Many people have contributed to the creation of this book. Now is the time to thank them for their help and advice. First

I'd like to thank the Captain, the living legend of craps, who has once again allowed me to write about his ideas and methods of play. Thank you to Albert Ross and to Howard T. Mann, who never seems to stop going. To Roger Gros of *Casino Player Magazine*, Chuck Di Rocco of *The Sports Form*, and Howard Schwartz of the Gambler's Book Club—thank you for reading an advance copy of the book. Also, another thank you to Howard Schwartz for helping me with my bibliographical information and recommendations. I would like to thank the staff of the Gambler's Book Club for always helping me locate the exact information I was looking for. A thank you to my good friends KF and Alan Tinker for sharing the adventure with me and for suggesting the framework for Chapter 21. A special thank you to my publisher at Bonus Books for knowing a good bet when he sees it. To my sons Greg and Mike—the biggest "wins" in my career. Lastly, to AP, "my dearest partner in greatness," who threw her lot with me—it's been some trip so far, hasn't it?

CHAPTER ONE

The Guerrilla Gambler

Despite their extensive and slick advertising to the contrary, the casinos are not your friends and their CEOs and other honchos do not want to see you win. The casinos exist to destroy you economically while simultaneously making you feel good about it. They would prefer that their patrons be economic sheep, quietly led to monetary slaughter, your wallets having been fattened on the grassland of impossible dreams. The casinos make meals of their players! They are wicked witches and many of their players are naive Hansels and Gretels happily stoking the fires of their own destruction with stupid play and unreal expectations.

Of course, no losing gambler feels *good* about losing (unless that person is mentally unbalanced), so the casinos have created a propaganda machine that uses the *Big Lie* techniques so adroitly exploited in World War II in order to make losing more palatable for the victims. Many casino habitués have unfortunately bought into one or more of these *Big Lies* and many gambling authorities, some of whom work for the very casinos they pretend they want you to beat, have spread them far and wide. These ideas constitute a good-time gospel of giddy defeat that lures still more losers into the temples of chance where they are quickly slaughtered.

To have any hope of becoming a winning casino gambler, not only must you know the games, the various percentages, strategies and so forth, you must also know how the casinos "play with your head," the kind of psychological warfare they wage against their unwary patrons, the mind games they get you into. Some of the most knowledgeable computer statisticians and players are big losers because they get caught in the illusion and hype. When you enter the lists with the casinos you are fighting two battles—one between you and the casino, and the other between you and yourself. It is the latter that you must win consistently to come out ahead. To do so you must be able to separate what is true and what is false, strategically and psychologically.

The Big Lies and the Truth

The following are some of the *Big Lies* that the casinos use in their psychological war against you. I have phrased them exactly as I've heard them from the lips of my fellow players. If you should ever hear yourself saying these things—bite your tongue!

I only play for fun, I don't care if I win or lose.

People who spout this line of propaganda have never watched their own faces as they lose bet after bet, session after session. I have yet to *see* a person who is losing *look* happy about it. I've *heard* them say losing doesn't bother them but that's not what their demeanors or countenances reveal. Despite their protestations of joy, their faces betray them. They are not smiling. The sweat drips down their foreheads. Their eyes have the look of shock victims. Losing is not fun, period. Winning is fun. True, you can't win *all* the time, and losing sessions and streaks will occur, but you must play the strongest possible strategies and you must play to win—or why bother?

Nobody can win. The casinos have the edge so I just go to make a donation and hope to get lucky.

The greatest myth in casino gambling is the myth that *you can't win*. This discourages a lot of otherwise intelligent people from investigating the odds and strategies of the games they choose to play. The casinos want to encourage people to play but they want them to play stupidly.

Are you so certain that you can't win? Then why did you buy this book? Certainly, there are better and worse ways to play even games with a negative expectancy. Knowledge is power for the player. Unfortunately, some 80 million Americans gamble. How many of them have bothered to research their pastime? How many of them have even read *one* book on the subject? Very few indeed. The casinos have propagandized heavily in this area. They have pushed the notion that you have to get lucky (they also push the notion that you *will* get lucky) and that there is no skill involved whatsoever. This is only a partial truth.

Now here are the facts. There are some casino games that if played over an extended period of time will inevitably lead to losses. Some of these games give the casinos a slight edge over time; some of them give the casino a huge edge. Such games you don't play over extended periods of time. There are other casino games that with proper money management and playing strategies can be beaten in the long run. These you will play for extended periods of time. None of my strategies will make you rich, so if thoughts of making a living at gambling are free-floating in your consciousness—then find a book that promises you the moon, the sun and the stars. I can't deliver those.

I can deliver this message: The casinos can be beaten by astute, controlled and disciplined players who are willing to be patient and to settle for small victories. The casinos want you to think it is only *dumb* luck that makes the difference between a winner and a loser. I disagree. It is a combination of *luck* and *skill* that makes for winning. The casinos want you to think big—bet big—hope big (and lose big). I want you to think (period), bet in proportion to your bankroll and your strategy, and get away a winner. Be it big or small, a win is a win.

I only play to break even.

When you entered the casino you *were* even, so why play at all? Just *pretend* to play. Stand by a machine or a table and play the game mentally. Pretend to be betting real money. If you lose your mental money, you will still be even.

So how come people who claim they only play to break even don't settle for the *pretend* game I just outlined above? Because obviously that's not why they play!

It is equally obvious that these people want to win, but they are just too timid to admit it for fear of sounding silly. Just listen to people who are standing in line for their room reservations, or for a buffet, or for a show, or to cash in their chips. You will rarely hear any of them say something to the effect that they come to the casinos to win and are quite serious about what they are doing. Most make jokes about the amount of the donations they have made over the years. A few will talk about their good luck. You will almost never hear them say that they are serious about their gambling and that they are skillful and play to win. Somehow or other, people who are serious about casino gambling are anathema to many other casino gamblers. They are looked upon as if they were crazy. For some reason you shouldn't be serious when you put your hard-earned money at risk. You should be frivolous. For some reason you should feel embarrassed because you seriously *don't* want or *expect* to lose.

Don't fall for this nonsense. You are going to the casinos to win money and don't be ashamed to admit it. You want to play the best you can.

I go to the casinos to relax and unwind.

Casinos are anything but relaxing. In fact, they are high energy places that exhaust their patrons. That is part of the psychological warfare. Individuals will play for 20 straight hours and brag about their lack of sleep. Then they'll claim that this is how they unwind. Nonsense. Very few people leave casinos more refreshed than when they entered. Unless you know how to pace yourself and dictate your own rhythms, you will not find a vacation at a casino resort relaxing. Taxing, yes, both financially and emotionally; relaxing, no.

If you truly want to relax and unwind, go to a spa, or a beach. Better yet, stay home and take a nap. Again, you just have to look at the faces of the people checking out of the casinos on any given day. You will be hard pressed to see a person whose face evinces any evidence of a relaxing and unwinding stay. More than likely the people checking out will be weary, bleary and puffy-eyed, tired and somewhat cantankerous. Either that or they'll be supercharged and hyper. But they will look nothing like people who have just spent several days meditating transcendentally.

I go to the casinos for their shows, restaurants, and ambience.

For non-gamblers married to gamblers this could very well be the case. For the player, however, fine shows and fine dining are of secondary importance to the action. Indeed, the shows tend to pump you up for the action in the casinos. That is intentional, and it's another part of the psychological warfare waged by the casinos against the players. The comedians get you to laugh about your losses. The singers and dancers get you to feel upbeat. When you are released from the showroom, you make a mad dash for the tables because *now* you feel lucky. Very few people make a mad dash for their rooms after the shows to go to sleep!

Now, I don't dismiss the enjoyment inherent in a good meal or a good show. I don't dismiss the comfort of a gorgeous hotel room with a spectacular view of an ocean, a river, or a city. I just don't think they are the main reasons why a player goes to a casino hotel. I know I don't hop a plane to go to Vegas as often as I do just to have gourmet meals and a room with a view. I go specifically to play and *beat* certain games—many of which are not in the better hotels. Nor do I go to Atlantic City on weekdays because of the superstar entertainment—there isn't any superstar entertainment mid-week. But there are better games in some of the casinos. And I certainly do not go on the riverboats to soak up the smoke-filled atmosphere! But many of them do have excellent blackjack games.

So the good meals and the exciting shows are secondary inducements and are essentially irrelevant to the player who wants to win. If my main object on a given evening is a gourmet meal, I'll just stay in New York and choose from hundreds of such restaurants. If my main object is to see a superstar entertainer or a great show, I'll do likewise. When I go to a casino I go to win money, period. And when you're winning, the shows and meals are just that much better.

I go to the casinos for the free food and drinks.
I like to be comped.

There is no such thing as "free" food and drink in a casino. It is mere appearance. The high rollers who seemingly get everything for "free" usually pay a very dear price for their complimentaries. Yes, the casinos will "comp" you to a meal or a room as their way of saying: "Thank you for playing at such and such a level!" What they are really saying is something slightly different: "Thank you, sucker, for playing at such and such a level for such and such a period of time because we have such and such an advantage over you and the longer you play the more we win from you and sure we'll give you a little something back in the form of a meal and a room to fatten you up for your next visit."

Now, if you aren't a high roller, during the course of play scantily-clad cocktail waitresses will bring you "free" alcoholic drinks for which you'll pay a heavy price once they kick in and loosen you up to bust out your bankroll and play like a demon *rummy*. The casinos don't give anything away. To get something, you have to take it! I'd rather win a thousand dollars and pay for my room and food and go home with some cash in my pocket than get everything for "free" and go home broke. Better yet, I'd rather get some comps *and* go home with cash in my pocket.

I just enjoy playing. Winning or losing doesn't matter.

This is one of the more dangerous concepts in casino mythology because it smacks of truth. I have fallen prey to this "enjoyment-of-playing" syndrome. The games are fun, no doubt about it. The contest between you and the mighty casino is riveting. There is pleasure in the mere exchange between yourself and the gods of chance.

But if the only reason for playing is fun, and not the winning of money, why not just play the *pretend* game as previously described? Why risk real money? Better yet, why not just buy some of the layouts of your favorite games and play at home? Play with your friends for match sticks. You won't even have to travel to a casino.

So why don't we do this, we who enjoy the sheer joy of playing? Because there is no excitement involved unless there is something at risk. I really don't care if I win or lose match sticks. I care enormously if I win or lose my money. Thus, it is the fear of losing, mingled with the hope of winning, that gets the adrenaline pumping and the heart beating. It is not the mere fact of a card being dealt you or a ball being spun or a pair of dice being rolled that causes such a thrill—it's what's at stake on the turn, the spin, the roll.

I bet with my head, not over it.

Any bet that you do not have a reasonable chance of winning is a bet that is over your head. Although there is a small range of dispute over what can be considered a reasonable chance of winning, no one will dispute that wagers and/or games that favor the house by three, six, 10, 20 and 50 percent are not reasonable bets. And just because a losing bet doesn't leave you economically destitute doesn't mean that you should make it. A gambler with a big bankroll is much like a swimmer with a strong stroke—when he swims with the sharks, he might not drown, but he sure as hell stands a good chance of being devoured.

Casinos are fun places and everyone is having such a good time.

Winners are having a good time. Shareholders in the casino are having a good time. Losers are not having a good time. Just watch them slam their fists on the tables; listen to them curse and mutter obscenities to themselves; see them glare balefully at the players currently being favored by Dame Fortune. Do they seem to be having such a wonderful time? I think not.

The above are merely a few of the myriad mindsets that mislead and ultimately betray the casino gambler. If you are a casino gambler or want to be one, then you had better know yourself and your motivation for playing. If it is anything other than having a reasonable chance at winning, then find some other way to spend your money. Collect rocks or other material objects, build models in your den, do anything that will give you something to show for your efforts and your financial and emotional investment. A losing gambler has nothing to show for his time, tension, and torment except a few war stories that bore his hearers in the telling.

However, if you want to be a winning casino gambler, if you want to take your best shot at those glittering, glitzy and garish monsters, then I say—go for it. It can be done. The casinos can be beaten. You do have a chance. You are not *fated* to lose at every game offered. You are not just relying on dumb luck. There are ways to cut the casinos' edge to a minimum and at times to zero. There are even ways to get a slight edge for yourself. Win or lose, however, you will not be one of the legion of the doomed who are merely throwing their money away on a handle and a hope. You can mentally and strategically play to win. In casino gambling it is *how* you play the games that counts! How you play them is often the determining factor in whether you win or lose.

Fellow players, we are in a war against the casinos. It might be a civilized war, where chips substitute for blood, but it is a war nevertheless. And it is a war against a supreme opponent who has superior resources and, more importantly, all the time in the world to take you out. Add to this that our superior opponent has set the venue and rules for the struggle, and has even stacked the deck in its favor, and you get some idea of the nature of the struggle you have chosen to participate in.

As you know, and as I shall describe and explain throughout this book, the casinos have attempted to structure each game so that the more "action" the game gets, the better the casinos' chance to win. With an arsenal of money and scores of competent generals, all skilled in the art of gambling's psychological warfare, the casinos have perfected techniques for subtly yet inexorably destroying unwary and unwitting opponents.

And what do we, the players, have going for us against such formidable competition? Only our knowledge of the odds, probabilities and strategies of the games we choose to play—*and* the all-important fact that we choose the time, place and game we wish to play. It is left to our discretion when, where and how to place a bet. While we do face a mighty antagonist, we face that antagonist when we choose to do so. We are the Davids in the war against the Goliaths, but we are the Davids who can pick our shots. Thus, it is our skill and our timing that we must rely on to turn the tide of victory in our direction.

I absolutely believe that the players' overall strategic decisions are the long-range determining factors in winning and losing at certain select games.

That.

And luck.

For what is true of any war, or any endeavor in life for that matter, is also true of gambling—winning is a combination of timing, skill and luck. But luck favors those who have the skill and timing. Luck favors the prepared. So in our war against the casinos, we must be totally armed with the best strategies and the proper mental attitude.

Please don't think I'm being facetious or disingenuous when I say that you need luck to help you win your war against the casinos. You do. However, you are not relying on luck as the sole weapon in your confrontation with the casinos. Rather, you are skillfully going to take advantage of the opportunities presented to you when, where, and if you choose to play. You are going to be mentally precise, strong-willed, strong-minded, and disciplined so that when luck comes your way you will be able to take advantage of it.

Sad to say, I can't give you luck. Besides, I'm not a particularly lucky person myself. I've never won a lottery (not even a minor prize), I've never won a single prize in all the chances I've bought for charity. When I flip a coin to determine something or other, I invariably call the wrong side. When I plan a picnic, it rains. In fact, in any purely *random* game, I've lost more times than I've won; much more than probability theory would suggest. I'm not a lucky guy that way.

But I beat the casinos regularly and I even beat them in games that are *supposedly* random! I don't beat them for millions and I don't earn my primary living from casinos. But I'm a winner in the war against the casinos. I take their "free" food and "free" rooms and, because I'm ahead at the tables over the years, my comps are truly complimentary. I remember one pre-dawn last summer when AP, my playing partner, and several of my friends, KF and Alan Tinker (all long-term winning players), and I were on the corner of Flamingo and Las Vegas Boulevard, looking down the Strip towards downtown. The eastern sky was starting to lighten. On the right was the Flamingo Hilton, on the left Caesar's Palace, and farther down on our left, the towering, golden Mirage. I turned to them and, being the dramatic type, I held out my arm like Caesar to his troops, and indicating the Strip and by extension all of Las Vegas, I said: "We own this town!" We all laughed, partly because of my dramatic view of things, partly because—*it was true!* We were winners—all of us—and had been for a long time. Someday, I hope you get the chance to say that and to feel what it is like to really know and believe—"I am a winner!"

With proper application of the techniques espoused in this book, there is a very good chance that you too will become a winner at the games you choose to play. Craps and roulette are two fine examples of *seemingly* random games that can be exploited by skill and perception. Blackjack is primarily a game that can be won by skill in the short run, and even more so by skill extended over time. Poker is skill and knowing the psychology of the people you are playing against. While I can't give you luck, I can share with you the secrets I've learned from my own experience as a successful gambler and the experiences and research of others whom I respect. I can give you the weaponry necessary to become a successful casino gambler. That in and of itself is a major step towards winning. The rest is up to you.

Consider this book, then, as a manual in the art of guerilla warfare against the casinos. Consider yourself a guerrilla fighter... a guerrilla gambler.

Guerrilla gambling has two components—attitude and technique. The attitude necessary to be a successful guerrilla gambler I have already touched upon. Here are the major principles. This is your credo, your Ten Commandments of attitude, if you will. Digest them and make them a part of yourself. Think of yourself as a latter-day Moses, leading the Israelites against the heart- hardened casino-pharaohs. Take the spoils.

The Ten Commandments of the Guerrilla Gambler

1. I gamble to win, period.

2. I never gamble to impress the house or my friends or anyone else.

3. I am going to be absolutely honest with myself and others when it comes to my wins, losses, and reasons for gambling.

4. I am going to keep accurate records of all my sessions at whatever games I play.

5. I am going to count all complimentaries as a part of my overall statistics. Thus, if I lost $25 at the tables but was given a $100 meal, I am ahead $75.

6. I am going to take advantage of every possible casino promotion. If the casino is giving away a free pen, I am going to accept the free pen, even if I own a pen factory.

7. I will not be shy or self-effacing towards casino hosts, pit bosses, or floormen and floorwomen. No matter how long or short my sessions of play are, I will always ask for a free breakfast, lunch, dinner or snack based upon my play. I'll always ask for a free room or "consideration" on the room bill after my stay. Every "consideration" the casino gives me, I will count in my record keeping.

8. I will never *ever* point out a mistake in my favor during a game. This is not cheating but common sense. I don't want the dealer who made the mistake to be embarrassed in front of his superiors. The dealer isn't going to think to himself:"Wow! What an honest guy!" Instead, he's going to be saying to himself: "That schmuck! He made me look like an idiot!" or, worse, "I did him *a favor* because he tipped me and he makes me look like an idiot in front of the boss!" The casinos never give back the money of a player who makes stupid mistakes in his play, do they?

9. The casinos are my enemy. I am a cold-blooded killer of casinos. I give no quarter, no mercy, but I ask for everything I can get.

10. I must remember at all times that the true contest is often not me against the casinos but *me against myself!*

Guerrilla Gambling Techniques

Guerilla gambling techniques must all fall into one philosophical framework owing to the nature of casino games. To wit, the following logical proposition:

> 1. Because the casinos have given themselves long range advantages in most games...

> 2. Because the casinos have a virtually unlimited bankroll with which to grind the players down...

> 3. Because the casinos use psychological warfare to lure players into playing stupidly and carelessly...

I, the guerrilla gambler, must...

> 1. only play in short-run bursts when the likelihood of winning is greatest...

> 2. only play against games where the casino has a small edge or no edge...

> 3. use strategies designed to turn the tables quickly in my favor...

> 4. have a sufficient bankroll that is reserved only for gambling...

> 5. never allow myself to lose an entire session stake at one table or one game...

> 6. learn techniques of extending my *body-time* at the table but not my *risk-time* in order to win complimentaries from the casino...

> 7. be prepared to leave precipitously if things go against me early.

Your passion as a guerrilla gambler is to outwit the casinos. By playing for short-run bursts, especially in games such as baccarat and roulette, and learning techniques of extending *body-time* but not *risk-time* in such games as blackjack and craps, you can increase not only your chances of winning but also your chances of being comped. Every victory helps in the war against the casinos and there are no small wins. A comp for a sandwich is worth its value in chips!

So my design for this, your guerrilla manual, is quite simple. I shall outline how each game is played, and the percentages for and against the players if these are easily digestible. Then I shall give what I consider to be the best techniques, be they short-run guerrilla strikes, long-run trench warfare, or some combination of both that will allow you potentially to come home victorious. Although I shall offer strategies for most games offered in the casinos, I shall not do this for all of them. Some games just aren't worth playing. Of the ones that I do cover in some detail, not all are equal in winning potential. Some casino games are not worth the effort to play. For example, sic bo, an Asian game played in Vegas and recently incorporated into Atlantic City, has such a heavy house edge on most bets that short of stealing chips from the dealer's rack, there is no way to successfully approach this game. So I won't even attempt it.

Games such as sic bo, keno, the big wheel (or wheel of fortune), and other essentially losing propositions I shall cover in one chapter. None of these games will really be worth playing, but each has a certain popularity among certain customers. So, if you are going to play them, at least you'll know what you are facing. These are, of course, suicide games but there are better and worse ways of killing oneself, I guess. So if you are determined to play the wheel of (mis)fortune or sic bo, you'll be able to make the best of the bad bets being offered.

Finally, at the end of each section devoted to a given game, I shall recommend further reading and comment on the books and journals concerning that particular game. Some games, such as blackjack, have literally hundreds of books written about them and quite a bit of time, effort, and knowledge has gone into sifting the wheat from the chaff. Other games have very few books written about them: Baccarat, for example, is a game that can easily be handled by progressive betting systems or other wagering devices and does not require too many decisions on the part of the players or too many words on the part of us writers. Many of the books I'll recommend won't be books about strategies *per se* but about the authors' experiences in the lands of chance. These I think you'll enjoy for the sheer adventure.

In the concluding chapters I shall have some words on money management and the mental edge necessary to pursue gambling as a pastime or hobby. In the appendix, I shall list recommended general-interest gambling books, magazines, newsletters and journals that might be of interest to you. I would like to say that I will exhaust the literature for you, but so many little newsletters come and go throughout the country, some good, some atrocious, that all I can do is alert you to those journals that have some kind of track record of success. If you are anything like me, you will probably enjoy reading about gambling almost as much as doing it. When I'm not playing or writing about gambling, I'm reading about it. Thus, I have included a list of publishers that deal primarily in gambling books and journals in the appendix. Contact them and ask for a list of their books. Many of these publishers will be delighted to handle book orders through the mail. One of your best bets for gambling books, and a must visit when you are in Las Vegas, is the Gambler's Book Club at 630 S. 11th St., Las Vegas, NV 89101. Just about every book I recommend can be ordered by mail through this club. Additionally, don't be put off by the fact that many of the books I'm recommending are self-published. All of them are worth reading. For some reason, major publishers, especially in New York, have not updated or improved their gaming inventories, and when they attempt to, the books are not always the best. Many are not well-written and show no real grasp of casino conditions. Sometimes I think gambling books are apportioned by the major publishers thus:

"Hey," says the publisher, "you think we should have a gambling book?"

"Sure," says the editor.

"Who should write it?"

"Well, my brother-in-law has been playing for years. He's lost millions. I'll get him to write it," says the editor.

Every book I recommend, be it self-published, published by a small press, or put out by a big corporate giant, is worthy of your time.

I truly believe this—a well-read gambler is a well-armed gambler. I think this book will give you plenty of ammunition.

To conclude this chapter:

I don't know about love, but all *is* fair in war. Remember this: No casino has ever returned money to a player who lost more than he could afford to. There is a wonderful moment in the movie *Lost in America* when a husband, played by Albert

Brooks, discovers that his wife, played by Julie Haggerty, has caught gambling fever and has lost every penny they had during the night while he was peacefully sleeping in their hotel room. When he confronts the casino manager, he begs for his money back, saying his wife didn't know what she was doing. He tells the manager that it would be good publicity for the casino to give back their nest egg. "You'll be known as the friendly casino!" he opines. The casino manager looks at him coldly and states simply: "We don't return money."

Fellow players, fellow guerrilla gamblers, the casinos are in business to take *your* money. They want to rip your economic head off. They are economic vampires and your wallets are their collective lifeblood. We, in turn, are in the business of ambushing them—hitting them hard and fast and running with the money. Take them for everything you can get. Stake them in their hearts, bleed them, and enjoy the sunrise as a winner!

CHAPTER TWO

The Fundamentals of Roulette

Roulette is perhaps the oldest casino game, having been played for generations in Europe among the nobility. Many a nobleman has lost his lands, fortune and family because of an obsession with beating the little round ball and the spinning wheel. Myriad, ingenious, and ultimately futile betting systems have been devised in an attempt to outfox and outbet the wheel. There is unfortunately no way to beat roulette in the long run *if the wheel is perfectly balanced and there are no imperfections, however small, in the mechanism*. Luckily, however, many roulette wheels are imperfect and can be exploited by intelligent players and certain long and short-term betting and playing strategies. These I shall cover in the next chapter.

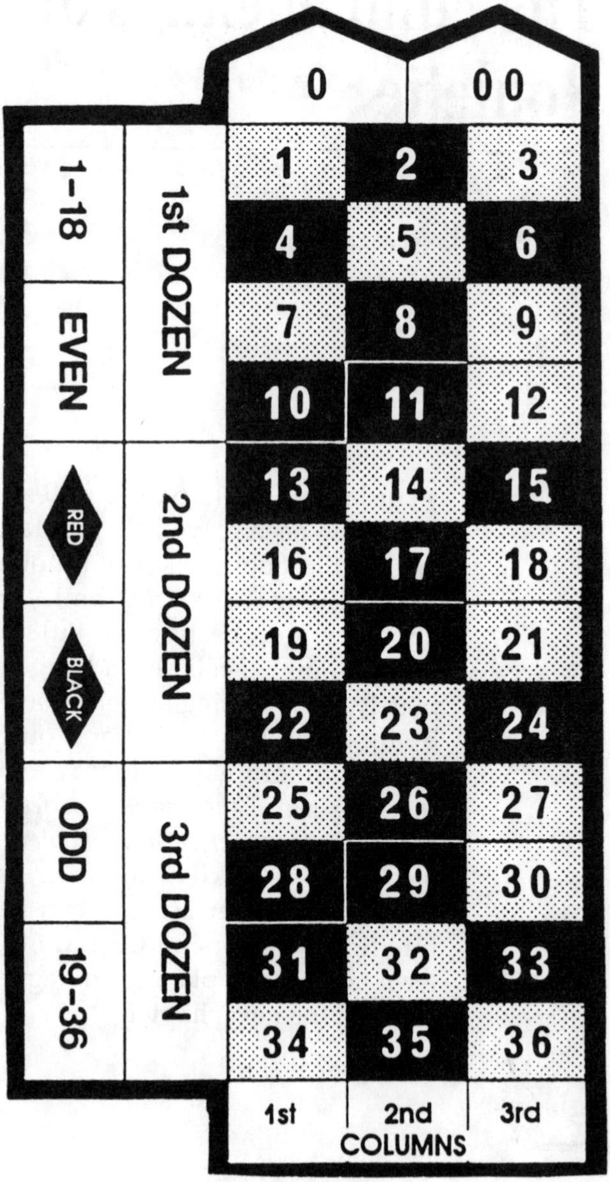

FIGURE 1
American Roulette Layout

The Setup of Roulette

The typical roulette setup is composed of the layout and the wheel. The layout is where you place your bets and is arranged in numerical order from left to right in columns of three, beginning with one, two, and three and ending with 34, 35, and 36. At the top of the layout will be a 0 and a 00, if it is an American wheel, and a 0 if it is a European wheel (sometimes referred to as a French wheel). The American wheel is called a double-zero wheel and the European wheel is called a single-zero wheel. The majority of American casinos use the double-zero wheel because it gives them more of an edge over the player. This I'll discuss shortly.

Any bet placed directly on a number or on a line between numbers is called an *inside bet*. Any bet placed in the boxes and columns on the outside of the layout is called, cleverly enough, an *outside bet*. (Figure 1-Roulette Layout)

If you take a look at the wheel in Figure 2, you will notice an interesting fact. It has no correlation with the layout. The reason for this is simple. Not all roulette wheels are perfectly balanced and some sections will tend to come up more often than other sections if the wheel is even slightly unbalanced. In addition, some roulette wheels have long and short-term biases, not directly attributable to unbalancing, which nevertheless cause certain numbers and sectors to come up more frequently than probability theory would indicate.

Now, most roulette players are *layout* players and thus do not pay much attention to the positioning of the numbers on the wheel itself. The layout player might enjoy betting groups of numbers, but these groups exist only on the layout, not on the wheel. For example, if you wanted to bet the numbers one, two, three, and four on the layout, it would not be very hard because they are all together on the board. However, take a look at the wheel and you'll notice that they are fairly far apart. Although they form a continuous section of the layout, they do not form a continuous section of the wheel. Thus, a player betting one, two, three and four would not be able to exploit a sector bias with those numbers since those numbers don't form a sector of the wheel. The casinos know that by positioning the numbers on the wheel as they do, players will not inadvertently be able to exploit wheel biases by betting sectors of the layout.

The Wheel

Since most American casinos use the double-zero wheel, we shall use this as our primary model. Take a look at the wheel. You will notice that the single zero is on top and that directly across from it is the double zero.

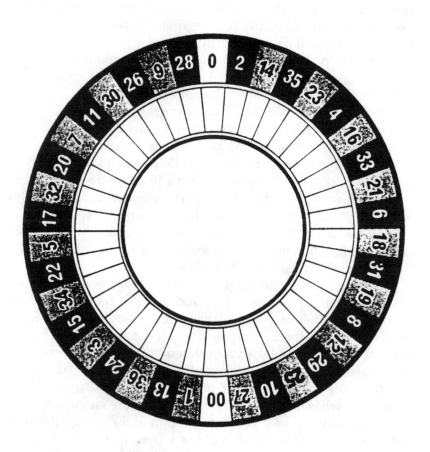

FIGURE 2
The American Roulette Wheel

Now, going clockwise you will notice the following:

1. There are 38 numbered grooves for the ball to fall into.

2. Half the numbers are red, half are black.

3. The 0 and the 00 are green.

4. Almost directly across from each even number is the next odd number (and vice versa). Thus, two is almost directly across from three.

5. Pairs of even numbers alternate with pairs of odd numbers except when split at the poles by 0 and 00.

6. The colors of the numbers on the wheel correspond to the colors of the numbers on the layout, the only correspondence between the two.

The Percentages

When you buy into a roulette game, the dealer will more than likely hand you one or more stacks of colored chips. You will notice that each player has his or her own color. This is to avoid the confusion so common in Europe where quite often players and dealers alike don't know whose bet is whose when it comes to payoff time. Thus, to avoid flaring tempers and flying fists, the casinos in America have decided to do away with the European same-chips tradition and give every player his or her own chips. (Another blow to colonialism!)

Once you have your chips, you are free to bet in a host of ways. Unfortunately, and with very few exceptions, most roulette bets give the house a substantial 5.26 percent advantage at the double-zero wheel and a 2.70 percent advantage on the single-zero wheel. The casinos have structured the game to favor themselves, naturally.

Here's how they do it.

On a double-zero wheel there are 38 possible decisions on a given spin of the ball (39 if you count the possibility of the ball flying off the wheel as it's spun and hitting a customer, as I've seen happen on a number of occasions—but the casino doesn't book this bet!). The *true odds* on such a bet are 37 to one because according to probability theory, if you were to bet the number 12, it would *theoretically* hit once every 38 spins and *theoretically* miss 37 times every 38 spins—thus giving you true odds of 37 to one. This is called a *fair game*, where neither the casino nor the player has the edge. *Theoretically*, in such a game, the casino would break even and the player would break even in the long run. I have italicized *theoretically* because in the real world of short-term play it would be almost unheard of for each number to hit exactly once in 38 spins.

In a fair game, if you bet one dollar on that 12 and it hit, you would receive 37 dollars in return. But the casino does not offer a fair game. In the real world of casino roulette, a winning bet on a number pays off at 35 to one. Thus, in the real world you would only receive a $35 payoff. In essence, the casino took a tax of two dollars out of your win of $37 and kept it for itself. This constitutes a 5.26 percent edge or tax. (The casino keeps two dollars for every $38 bet. Thus, 38 divided into two equals .0526315 to be exact.) Put another way, for every dollar you bet at roulette, the house taxes you 5.26 cents. This is also what you can expect to lose in a random, non-biased roulette game—5.26 percent of all your *action*. (Action is defined as the total amount of money you bet during the course of your play.)

Now, on the European, single-zero wheel, the player has a somewhat more advantageous game. There are 37 numbers and thus the odds of hitting any one are reduced to 36 to one. The casino still pays 35 to one, however, so the player only pays a tax of one dollar per win as opposed to two dollars in the double-zero game. This gives the house a smaller edge or tax base—2.70 percent. (Thirty-seven divided into one equals .027027 to be exact.) Some American casinos do offer the single-zero game and it behooves any roulette player to check out whether or not the casino he's planning to play in has one.

There are two exceptions to the 5.26 edge of the casino in the double-zero game, and these I'll explain when I cover the various types of bets you can place in roulette. Since many of you who will play roulette might do so in foreign countries where the game dominates, or on cruise ships or riverboats, quite often the bets and calls will be made in French, the classic language of roulette. Thus, in the following I shall give the English and French terms (in parentheses) for the various bets. If you are going to be playing roulette in Europe, beware: Since the players don't have individually colored chips you have to keep a sharp eye on your bets. There are quite a few roulette cheats who work European casinos looking for unwary players and lazy *croupiers* (dealers) to hoodwink. In addition some of these bets have more than one name in English and whenever possible I've given you the various names they are known by.

Inside Bets

The Straight Up Bet (En Plein)

You bet one or more numbers by placing your wager directly on the number or numbers. If your number or one of your numbers hits, you will be paid off at 35 to one. The house edge is 5.26 percent.

Split Bet (A Cheval)

You place your wager on a line between two numbers. If either of these two numbers comes up, you are paid off at 17 to one. A split can also be made between 0 and 00 by placing a single wager between them. However, if you are too far away to split the top 0 and 00, most casinos will accept a split of these numbers by placing your wager on the line between the Second Dozen Box and the Third Dozen Box. This house edge on this bet is 5.26.

The Street Bet, The Three Number Bet, or the Trio (Transversale)

This is a single bet on any one of the three numbers hitting. You make this bet by placing your wager on the outside border of the three numbers you wish to bet on. If you win, you are paid off at 11 to one. This bet carries a 5.26 edge for the house.

The Corner or Four Number Bet (Carre)

You are betting that one of four numbers will hit on the next spin of the wheel. However, this bet can only be accepted on those numbers that form a square. You place your wager on the intersection where all four numbers meet. If you win, the bet pays off at eight to one. This bet carries a 5.26 house edge.

The Five Number Bet

This bet only appears on the double-zero layout (thus it doesn't have a French equivalent) and is a single bet that one of the top five numbers (0, 00, one, two or three) will win on the next spin. You make this bet by placing your wager where the line between the 0 and the three meets the border of the layout. This bet pays off at six to one. This bet carries a large 7.89 percent edge in favor of the house and is the worst bet in roulette. Some roulette writers call this "the beast with five numbers."

The Line Bet or Six Number Bet (Sixain)

This bet is placed on the outside borders of the numbers at the line that separates the two sets of numbers. You are betting that one of those six numbers will hit on the next spin of the wheel. This bet pays off at five to one. The house has its usual 5.26 advantage on this bet.

Outside Bets

The Column Bet (Colonne)

This is a single bet that one of the columns of numbers on the layout will contain the number that hit. You place this bet at the bottom of the column in the area that says two to one. This wager pays off at two to one. Zero and 00 are not considered a part of any column and thus the house continues to maintain its 5.26 percent edge over the player.

The Dozens Bet (Douzaine)

You are betting that within a dozen consecutive numbers on the layout the lucky hit will be made. (Remember this is *not* a dozen consecutive numbers on a section of the wheel!) You make this bet in the areas labeled either First Dozen, Second Dozen, or Third Dozen. If one number in your dozens bet hits, you are paid off at two to one. The house edge is 5.26.

Odd and Even Bets (Impair et Pair)

This bet is placed in the section of the layout that says, naturally enough, Odd or Even. There are 18 odd numbers and 18 even numbers. There are therefore 18 ways to win and 20 ways to lose because you also lose this bet when 0 or 00 is the number hit. The bet pays off at even money and is one of a number of even-money bets in roulette. The house still has a 5.26 percent edge on this bet. However, in Atlantic City and in casinos using Atlantic City rules, casinos will return half your losing bet should the 0 or 00 be the number hit. This effectively reduces the house edge to 2.63 percent. In English, returning half your bet is called *surrender*; in French it is called *en prison* and the player has the additional option of either accepting half his wager back or letting the full bet ride on the same proposition on the next decision. The house has the same edge either way—2.63 percent.

High or Low Bets (Passe et Manque)

This bet goes in the boxes marked either one to 18 or 19 to 36 and is a wager as to whether the high numbers or the low numbers will contain the winning hit. This is an even money bet and again there are 18 ways to win and 20 ways to lose. The house has a 5.26 percent edge unless the casino is following Atlantic city rules and returns one-half of the losing the bet when 0 or 00 is the winning number, in which case the house edge is reduced to 2.63 percent.

Red or Black Bets (Rouge et Noir)

Another even money bet with the same percentages as above. This bet is placed in the area indicating Red or Black and is a wager that the winning number will be either a red one or a black one. Once again, if the casino follows Atlantic City rules, half this bet is returned should 0 or 00 appear.

Okay, so much for the details. Because of the high house percentages, roulette would be a game to avoid if it weren't for the fact that it can be beaten—if you know what to look for and how to play it.

CHAPTER THREE

Guerrilla Roulette

As you can see from the previous chapter, the casinos have structured every bet in roulette in such a way that, if all goes as planned, the patron will face heavy odds and sooner or later lose his entire bankroll. But not all is hopeless and we players are not hapless in the face of such a prospect. *Theoretically*, roulette is an unbeatable game *if* the mechanism of the roulette wheel is flawlessly balanced, *if* the grooves are uniformly structured and surfaced, *if* the dealers are incapable of controlling consciously or unconsciously the fall of the ball to hurt the players, and *if* the players are unable to anticipate by sight where the ball will land.

Those are quite a few *ifs* and because of them roulette has given rise to several wonderful strategies designed to exploit potentially beatable *wheels*. I stress *wheels* because to win at roulette you must beat the mechanism itself, not the layout. The layout is merely where you place your bets.

There is only one sure way to beat a wheel and that is to *clock* it. This is a time-consuming, tedious task. It requires the recording of thousands upon thousands of spins of a given wheel and the analysis of the results based on probability theory. For those of you who are interested in becoming clockers, I will recommend two marvelous books at the end of this chapter that contain all you need to know in order to become a proficient wheel clocker.

However, most roulette players aren't interested in spending long hours clocking and analyzing wheels. Actually, most roulette players have only a passing interest in winning at all. That is why they play their favorite numbers time after losing time—momma's birthday, Elvis's stamp day, etc. That is why they play layout strategies and use disastrous, progressive betting strategies such as the Martingale and the Grand Martingale which call for doubling bets after losses. These roulette players can only "get lucky" on occasion by playing this way. They have no long term expectations or even hopes that they can come out winners.

Not so with the guerrilla gambler.

While the guerrilla gambler also rejects the laborious task of clocking wheels, he recognizes that there are several strategies that can be used in short term play to increase his possibility of exploiting a potentially biased wheel. As a guerrilla gambler, you want to hit, win, and run with the money. There are two roulette strategies that fit the bill, both designed to take advantage of potentially biased wheels.

Neither of these strategies can *guarantee* that you will definitely be playing a biased wheel; but if you are, then you will be able to take full advantage of it. If you aren't? So what? You will only be playing for 38 spins, unless you are winning truckloads of money, and 38 spins cannot cripple your bankroll. (I'll cover bankroll requirements at the end of this section.) In addition, in short term play at roulette, numbers tend to repeat. It would defy all logic and probability if in 38 spins of a roulette wheel each number was selected once. The worst case scenario of the strategies I'm about to discuss is simply that you won't be playing a biased wheel and the casino will have its normal edge on you.

Big Number Roulette

A BIG number in roulette is any number that has hit with a frequency greater than its probability. If you were to observe 38 spins of the wheel and you noticed that several numbers had hit several times each, these numbers would be considered BIG numbers. You would bet them. Of course, the more spins of a wheel that you observe, the greater confidence you can have in the repeatability of certain numbers.

For the purposes of guerrilla gambling, you must observe 10 spins of a wheel before you place any money at risk. In 10 spins, whatever numbers had repeated you would bet. Thus, if the numbers 12, 18, and 33 had hit twice each, you would place a bet on these three numbers. If only one number repeated, you would only bet this one number.

Now, as you are playing, BIG numbers will change. Taking our three number example above: On the 11th spin of the wheel, let us suppose that 33 had hit again. Thirty-three had now hit a third time. This would be the BIG number and you would bet it.

That is a conservative BIG number strategy. You only bet the number or numbers that have hit the most times. However, more aggressive players might desire more action. If you are aggressive, then bet the BIG number(s) and any number(s) that repeated somewhat less frequently. Keep in mind that you are only playing 38 spins of a given wheel. If after 38 spins, you are ahead enough to play 38 more spins and *still* be able to walk away with a profit should you lose every one of those subsequent spins, then you would plunge in for another session at that particular wheel. However, if you are down, even slightly, you will call it a session at that wheel and either move on to another wheel or on to another game.

There is an even better way to ascertain BIG numbers in certain casinos. Recently many casinos in Atlantic City and Las Vegas have erected scoreboards over their roulette wheels that record the last 20 numbers and colors that have hit. This is a wonderful gimmick and quite helpful to the guerrilla gambler. When you come to one of these tables, simply record the last 20 numbers that came up, determine which to bet, and work from there. You'll have to keep a running tally just as you would without the scoreboard after you record the initial 20 numbers because the scoreboard drops the earliest number in favor of the latest one.

The BIG number strategy is designed to take advantage of short term fluctuations in probability; that is, certain numbers repeating simply due to randomness. It is also a wonderful strategy for taking advantage of biased wheels. If the numbers that are repeating actually do represent a bias, they will keep on repeating. Thus, 38 spins will lead to 38 more spins which will lead to 38 more spins and so on—with you winning something on each 38-spin session. It's a marvelous short-range strategy for the guerrilla gambler and the one I recommend most highly.

Sector Slicing

The second strategy that I recommend for short-term guerrilla roulette play requires a little more effort. In addition to keeping track of the numbers as they hit, you must locate them on the wheel. What you are looking for is a slice of the wheel where numbers are hitting in bunches. These numbers may not necessarily be repeating individually, but their section or slice contains the majority of the hits. Simple rules of thumb will suffice to establish a sector slice to bet on after 10 spins.

> 1. Have four or more numbers hit in six or seven consecutive grooves?
> 2. Have six or more numbers hit in nine or 10 consecutive grooves?
> 3. Have eight or more numbers appeared in 11 to 19 consecutive grooves?

To implement sector slicing, you must have a diagram of the wheel upon which to record the hits. This is a simple thing to get as most casinos offer players a scorecard with a picture of the wheel on it.

If you notice that a given sector has recorded a sufficient number of hits based on our three principles above, then you will place a bet on every number in that sector—even the numbers that have not as yet hit. You will now play 38 spins of the wheel.

With each spin, you must analyze the sector you are betting on. If you have selected, for example, a sector that has nine numbers, you have a slice that is one-fourth of the wheel. If it only hits one-fourth of the time, you will lose money because the house edge is taking its cut from your winnings. On a fourth of the wheel, you should give yourself only eight to 10 spins before abandoning that slice and either picking a new one (if one presents itself) or moving to a new wheel.

It is not unusual, as the spins progress, to see several small slices appear. If you are a conservative player, then you bet the slice that is smallest but has the greatest density of hits. If you are an aggressive player, you can bet all the slices.

However, after 38 spins you must once again assess your situation. If your slices have not produced a profit, you must abandon that wheel and seek a new one. It is conceivable that on those initial 10 spins an area of the wheel predominated due to random fluctuations. As you started betting, this "slice" tended to crumble, as hits were made everywhere but within it. I strongly caution you that when you are using Sector Slicing as the betting principle, you be ready to abandon the wheel if the slice is not giving you sufficient promise of reward. You are risking four or more bets on every spin of the wheel and it can get quite costly if your slice doesn't hit consistently.

Bankroll Requirements for Guerrilla Roulette

You want to be able to play 10 sessions of roulette. I base this assumption on a simple idea—most people visit casinos for two to four days. That can give you anywhere from two to five sessions of roulette play per day. Therefore, you must have sufficient capital on hand to weather a losing streak of 10 straight sessions at the roulette wheel.

Let us take a worst-case scenario. You play at 10 different wheels and you do not win a single bet. How much would you lose? Since I don't know what your capital is, let me discuss betting in terms of units. The definition of *a unit* is this: A unit is the smallest amount you will bet when you gamble. For some of you a unit will be whatever the table minimum is— $.50, $1, $2 or $5. For others, it can be $10 or $100 or more. You determine what your unit is based upon your ability to play at that level without getting the cold sweats, without mortgaging your house, without losing your comportment when you lose your unit.

For the BIG number method of play, betting only one unit per spin and losing every spin, you would lose 38 units. Therefore a conservative BIG number player would need 380 units to play 10 sessions. However, very few players will stick to the one-number principle because quite often two, three and sometimes four or more numbers have hit exactly as many times in short-term play. Thus, a bankroll of at least 760 units is needed to play BIG number roulette, if the player intends to bet more than one number at certain times.

Of course, there is a slight difficulty with establishing a precise number of units for *inside* roulette betting, because if you are betting more than one number you don't have to bet the table minimum on *each* number. Rather, you can spread it around. Let us say that the table minimum is $10 and you have five BIG numbers that have hit the exact same number of times. You can bet $2 on each number and thus you have bet the table minimum ($2 \times 5 = 10$). The same holds true for a person betting his own unit denomination. If you are a $100 bettor, you can spread the $100 over two or more numbers. But as a general rule of thumb, a bankroll of 760 units would be appropriate for playing BIG number roulette.

What are the chances of losing 10 BIG number sessions in a row in such a disastrous way—not winning a single bet? Remote, to say the least.

For the Sector Slicing strategy, you have to have a bigger bankroll because you will definitely be betting four or more numbers on every spin of the wheel. A disastrous Sector Slice session would be 10 losses in a row without a hit on a four number slice. That's 40 units. If you were only to play four-number slices, you would need 400 units to sustain an horrendous losing streak. However, to truly play Sector Slices, you need to have the flexibility to bet the size of the sectors that are actually showing, and not the sectors you wish were showing. Remember, four hits could be in six or seven grooves after 10 spins and you would have to bet those six or seven grooves to cover the sector properly. That means six or seven units or the spreading of your minimum unit over these numbers if your unit is large enough to cover the totality.

As you can see, there is a lot of guesswork in determining bankroll requirements for guerrilla roulette. To be safe, I would estimate that *conservatively* you'll be playing six to 10 slices on every spin of the wheel—for 10 spins per session. As stated previously, if you don't win after 10 spins, that session at that wheel is terminated. Thus, you need 60 to 100 units per session, and 600 to 1,000 units over 10 sessions in order to play Sector Slices at roulette.

Of the two strategies outlined above, the Big Number and Sector Slicing, I am decidedly partial to the former. This is no doubt due to the fact that it is easy to play, whereas sector slicing requires a little effort, and also that I have personally been successful with it. In fact, I am developing a deep and abiding affection for Big Number roulette play as it has given me an incredible year at the roulette tables since I started playing it. In fact, Chapter 21, *A Day in the Life of A Guerrilla Gambler*, details a wonderful session of guerrilla Big Number roulette. So far I have found it to be a very strong strategy, especially in casinos with electronic scoreboards. But let me caution you. I never play more than the 38 spins, unless I'm truly winning big time. In fact, most times, if my number hits early, I leave with my winnings right away.

Whether I have actually found biased wheels, or whether I have just been lucky, is irrelevant to me. I'm winning with it. But I don't stay very long at the roulette dance, that's for sure, because that giant casino edge hovers in the background waiting to slice my bankroll to ribbons.

Recommended Reading

The Julian Strategies in Roulette by John F. Julian. Paone Press, Box 610, Lynbrook, NY 11563. ($16.95) An excellent book on roulette. This is a clear, intelligent analysis of the game and the many approaches for beating it. Fully develops a method for clocking wheels and *clocking players*, as well as *BIG number* strategies, *Slice* strategies, and betting strategies for layout play. Includes a thoughtful analysis of the supposedly "even" money bets. Julian's various strategies are excellent and his style is lively and to the point.

Beating the Wheel by Russell T. Barnhart. Carol Publishing Company, 600 Madison Ave., New York, NY 10022. ($12.95) Another excellent book, especially for those of you who are interested in wheel clocking, as it is an exhaustive analysis of both its history and theory. It is very heavy on the mathematics, sometimes unnecessarily so, but Barnhart's stories of successful roulette players are worth the price of the book.

The Eudaemonic Pie by Thomas A Bass. Vintage Books, 201 E. 50th St., New York, NY 10022. ($5.95) This book chronicles the often hilarious, often serious, but never dull adventures of a group of computer wizards as they try to beat the wheel using a hidden computer in their shoes. They aren't fully successful, although they show that it can be done, but it's a great story and a good read. You won't learn any strategies from this book but you will go on a great adventure.

CHAPTER FOUR

The Fundamentals of Blackjack

Without question, the most popular casino game is blackjack. It is also the most written about, debated, and analyzed game offered by the casinos. It has the greatest number of experts playing it—and an even greater number of idiots. It is a game made for the computer buffs and mathematicians because, unlike most casino games, blackjack is dynamic—the true odds of the game are constantly shifting from moment to moment and from hand to hand.

At any given moment, the player may have an edge; the next moment, the casino will have it. Because of this dynamism, proper blackjack play, that is basic strategy and card counting, can theoretically result in a slight overall, long-run advantage for the player. It is the possibility of gaining this slight advantage that has caused a cottage industry of books, newsletters, and scholarly conferences to spring up in the past 25 years. It has also caused quite a few people, who have no business playing the game, to saunter to tables and face casino edges in the double digits owing to their poor and uninformed play.

Blackjack Myths

Unfortunately, there are quite a few myths about blackjack that should be laid to rest before venturing any further.

Myth #1: All blackjack players have an edge over the casino and can win in the long run.

Sorry. Most blackjack players are so poorly prepared for their sorties into casinoland that blackjack makes more money for the casinos per bet than any other table game. Stupid players think that they can beat the game because they have heard or read somewhere that brilliant players have done so. So they play and lose, lose, lose. Brilliant players, on the other hand, never tire of warning neophytes to be careful and not to expect too much too soon, that blackjack is a roller coaster.

Myth #2: If a player learns the proper basic strategy for playing the hands, he will win in the long run.

(Note: Basic strategies have been developed by computers for the playing of each hand you receive against the dealer's up card. These basic strategies are considered the optimal way to play each hand in the long run.)

Not so. The basic strategy for both single- and multiple-deck blackjack games cannot give you an edge over the casino (except in rare single-deck games with extraordinary rules where the player might have a 0.10 percent edge off the top). At best, you can play even or almost even in a single-deck game, and face a 0.35 percent to 0.61 percent house edge in multiple-deck games, depending on the number of decks and the rules. Basic strategy is the best way to play, except for card counting, but it can't give you a long range advantage over the casinos. Basic Strategy can only make you a tough player, a good player, and a non-sucker.

Myth #3: Card counting guarantees that in the long run I will be a winner at blackjack and make a fortune in the bargain.

This is the myth that causes the most misery for unwary and uninformed would-be card counters. Card counting can give you a theoretical edge over *certain* blackjack games in the long run. However, card counting cannot give you an edge over *every* blackjack game. So many other factors have to be considered *in addition to the skill of the player* when establishing the beatability of a blackjack game. These I shall go into in Chapters 5 and 6. Suffice it to say that just because you learn how to count cards, and can do so proficiently, is not a guarantee that you will beat the casinos in the long run. Indeed, more card counters have gone broke faster than have basic strategy players because card counting calls for tremendous escalation of bets in certain situations and this causes wild swings in a player's bankroll. An under-financed card counter is courting economic disaster.

As far as getting rich from playing blackjack is concerned, this is another myth that has been propounded over and over by some of my fellow gambling writers. I know of no one who has *gotten* rich from playing blackjack. I know individuals who have won large sums of money over their blackjack playing careers. These individuals, however, started with large sums of money. A great card counter wins in proportion to the bets he can afford to make over an extended period of time, and the fluctuation he is willing to experience in his bankroll without getting a heart attack. There are no $5 blackjack bettors who become millionaires solely from playing blackjack. In fact, there are very few blackjack professionals who actually make good livings from playing. For most experts, writing about playing is more profitable than actually playing.

Why?

First, the casinos tend to look with disfavor on card counters and will readily ban anyone who is the least threat, be it real or imagined, to the casino's bankroll. Second, anyone betting big money is watched closely and, if he is considered a good player, the casinos will take measures against him. Even

in states where the banning of card counters is illegal, such as
New Jersey, the casinos simply use more decks, cut more cards
out of play, stop mid-shoe entry, and limit the kinds of bets that
can be made in games where mid-shoe entry is allowed. When
all else fails—the casinos simply shuffle the cards when they
think an individual player is betting big enough and is expert
enough to take advantage of a given situation to the casino's
detriment.

So card counting is not an absolute road to riches. It is
however a necessary technique for players who wish to spend
a significant amount of time at the blackjack tables with some
confidence that they can take the laurels of victory from the
casino in the long run.

But the good news is this. If you know the right games to
play and the right techniques to employ while playing them,
you can win at blackjack in the long run. You won't be able to
quit work or lounge around a pool all day in friendly casinoland but you will be able to get the edge.

How the Game is Played

Blackjack appears to be a simple game and, indeed, its
structure is quite easy to follow. All the cards have their face
value. An eight equals an eight, a two equals a two, and so
forth. All picture cards equal 10, as does, naturally, a 10. An ace
equals either an 11 or a one. It is up to the player to decide how
he is using the ace. Hands with an ace as one of the first two
cards are called *soft hands*. Hand without an ace as one of the
first two cards are called *hard hands*.

The objective of a blackjack game is to beat the dealer. This
can be done in one of two ways. You can beat the dealer
because you have a better hand or you can beat the dealer
because he has gone over 21 and *busted*. If either the player or
the dealer has an ace and a 10 value card as his first two cards,
this is called a blackjack or *natural* and is usually paid off at
three to two for the player. If the dealer has a blackjack and the
player has a blackjack, the hand is a standoff or *push* and
nobody wins. In fact, any time the dealer and the player have
the same valued hand it is a *push*. Never play in a blackjack

DEALER

FIGURE 3
Blackjack Layout

game where the dealer wins the pushes, unless it is a face-up or double-exposure game, the strategy for which is quite different than for regular blackjack.

Blackjack tables generally seat six to seven players. Each player places a bet in the betting area in front of him. The dealer deals each player two cards. In single-deck games, the cards are dealt face down to the players from a hand-held deck. In multiple-deck games, the cards are usually dealt face up from a shoe, which is a box that contains cards. The dealer also deals himself two cards, one face up and one face down. All your playing decisions will be based on the face-up card of the dealer.

Once the player is dealt his first two cards, he must decide whether to ask the dealer to *hit* him, that is, to give him another card; or, he must indicate that he is content with his first two cards and will *stand*.

The player can also decide to do any of the following:

1. If he has a pair of the same number, the player can *split* it and make each card the first card of a new hand. The dealer will then deal him a second card on the first hand and the player will play out that hand. When he is finished, the dealer will deal him a second card on the second hand and the player will play out that one.

2. The player can *double down* on his first two cards (when allowed). This means that the player is placing a bet equal to or less than his initial bet and will now receive only one card.

3. In some casinos, the player can *surrender* his hand. That means he gives up playing the hand in exchange for losing only half his bet.

4. The player can *insure* his hand against a dealer's face-up ace. He would put out a bet that can be as much as half his original bet in the area of the layout marked *insurance.* The insurance bet pays two to one. This bet is a side bet where the player who is insuring is wagering that the dealer indeed has a blackjack—thus, the dealer has a 10 in the hole with the ace on top. This is a very poor bet and should never be made, unless the player is counting cards and has a reasonable assurance that the 10 is underneath.

If the player should bust his hand (go over 21), the dealer will immediately remove both the player's bet and his cards. If the dealer should subsequently bust, the player who has busted first still loses. This is the casino's biggest edge—the player must play his hand first and if he busts, regardless of what the dealer does, the player loses.

Once all the players have played their hands, the dealer plays his. However, the dealer does not have any individual discretion in the playing of the hands but must play according to a prearranged set of rules. These rules are usually posted at the table for everyone to see and there is very little variation from casino to casino. The dealer must hit all hands that total 16 or less, and stand on all hands that total 17 or more. The only area where casinos differ in the application of these rules concerns the soft hand of 17 (ace + six). Some casinos have their dealers stand on soft 17. Some casinos have their dealers hit a soft 17. It is to the player's advantage if the casino's rule is to stand on a soft 17.

When the dealer has finished playing his hand, he pays off

the winners and takes the bets from the losers who didn't bust beforehand.

Simple? Quite. Yet, there are many rules variations within the structure of blackjack that can make the game more or less favorable for the players. These I shall discuss in Chapter 5.

Basic Strategy

Knowing how the game of blackjack is played is not the same as knowing how to play the game. For every set of rules, there are distinct basic strategies designed to optimize one's chances of winning. This does not mean that you have to memorize dozens of basic strategies since the overwhelming majority of decisions that you will have to make are the same in all strategies. However, basic strategy has two major categories— single-deck and multiple-deck—and if you intend to play blackjack, you must decide which strategy to memorize. Those of you who decide to play single- *and* multiple-deck games should seriously consider first mastering one and then mastering the other.

The best way to decide which one to memorize (or which to memorize first) is to check out the casinos that you intend to play in. If you are going to be a regular in Atlantic City, then you should memorize the multiple-deck basic strategy since all the blackjack games in Atlantic City are of this variety. If you are going to play in Las Vegas, you should memorize the single-deck strategy first because Las Vegas has quite a number of casinos offering single-deck games. Would it hurt a Las Vegas player to use a single-deck strategy against a multiple-deck game or vice versa? Only marginally, since the strategies usually differ most on hands that don't occur with great regularity. But if you want to be the best player that you can be, you should know both strategies. In the war against the casinos, it's best to be fully armed.

At first it might seem a daunting task, memorizing the several pages of material that are coming up, but don't let that stop you. In fact, if you spread your learning out over several weeks, doing a little at a time, you will readily assimilate the basic strategy you've selected. If you are the lazy type and only want to learn a single discrete guerrilla tactic to use against blackjack, then skip this part and go to Chapter 7 for information on *scanning for blackjacks*.

A friendly caution is hereby given—don't play blackjack without learning a basic strategy because players who trust their own instincts and ideas are giving the casino a monumental edge. You are better off skipping the game of blackjack altogether and playing one of the other, less complex casino games than playing improperly at blackjack. The casinos make a fortune from poor blackjack players. Do not join their regiment.

Since there are more multiple-deck games in the world than single-deck games, I have decided to give the multiple-deck basic strategy first. In the pages that follow, the left hand column will contain the player's hand; the right hand column will contain the decision you should make based on the dealer's up card. How many cards compose a given hand is essentially irrelevant except for splitting or doubling down purposes. For example, if you had a nine composed of two cards—a four and a five, or a three and a six, etc.—you would double down against any dealer up card of three through six. If you had a nine composed of three cards—say, a four, a two and a three—you would hit until you had 12 or more and then follow the basic strategy for that hand. Thus, if the dealer showed a six and you had a three-card nine, you would hit it. If you received a three, you would now have 12. The basic strategy calls for standing with a 12 against a dealer's up card of six. Hit any hand that is 11 or under, no matter how many cards compose it, until you reach 12 or more and then follow the basic strategy for that hand. You never hit hard hands of 17 or more against anything.

If you have played blackjack before, but you haven't employed a basic strategy, some of these moves will seem strange. For example, many players blanch at hitting a hand of 12 against the dealer's two or three. Many players cringe when having to split a hand of 8,8 against a dealer's 10. Many of these moves do seem almost suicidal but in fact they are the proper strategies. Remember that millions of hands have been generated by computer to establish these basic strategy rules. And many of these rules are designed to *lose you less* in bad situations. Having 8,8 against a dealer's 10 is a losing hand. By splitting them, you decrease the total amount of your losses in this situation than if you hit or stood. So follow these basic strategies perfectly and don't allow any fools at the table to intimidate you into not hitting that 12 against a dealer's two, or splitting those 8,8s against a dealer's 10. Also, keep in mind that all soft hands become hard hands when the ace can no longer be used as an 11.

Basic Strategy for Multiple Deck Games

Player's Hard Hand:	*Decision based on dealer's up card:*
8	Hit against everything.
9	Double against 3 through 6. Hit against everything else.
10	Double on 2 through 9. Hit on 10 and ace.
11	Double on 2 through 10. Hit on ace.
12	Hit against 2 and 3. Stand against 4, 5, 6. Hit against 7 through ace.
13	Stand against 2 through 6. Hit against all else.
14	Stand against 2 through 6. Hit against all else.
15	Stand against 2 through 6. Hit against all else.
16	Stand against 2 through 6. Hit against all else.

(If surrender is allowed, you will surrender a hand of 15 or 16 against a dealer's 10. You will surrender a 16 against a dealer's 9, 10 or ace.)

17, 18, 19, 20, 21	Stand against everything.

Player's Soft Hand:	*Decision based on dealer's up card:*
A2	Double against 5 and 6. Hit against all else.
A3	Double against 5 and 6. Hit against all else.
A4	Double against 4, 5, 6. Hit against all else.
A5	Double against 4, 5, 6. Hit against all else.
A6	Double against 3, 4, 5, 6. Hit against all else.
A7	Double against 3, 4, 5, 6. Stand on 2, 7, 8, ace. Hit against 9 and 10.
A8,A9	Stand against everything.

Player's Pair:	*Decision based on dealer's up card:*
A,A	Split against everything.
2,2	Split against 2 through 7. Hit against all else.
3,3	Split against 2 through 7. Hit against all else.
4,4	Split against 5 and 6. Hit against all else.
5,5	Double 2 through 9. Hit against all else.

6,6	Split against 2 through 6. Hit against all else.
7,7	Split against 2 through 7. Hit against all else.
8,8	Split against everything.
	(If surrender is allowed, surrender 8,8 against a dealer's 10.)
9,9	Split 2 through 6; 8 and 9. Stand against 7, 10, ace.
10,10	Stand against everything.

If you are playing multiple-deck games, the overwhelming majority of casinos will allow you to double down after splitting pairs. For example, if you had 2,2 and the dealer was showing a five, you would split your twos. Now, the dealer deals you a nine on the first two. You have 11. You would double down your 11 in this situation. The rule of thumb is to treat either half of a split the way you would a regular hand and follow the basic strategy tables as indicated. Some casinos will allow you to resplit pairs up to four times. Thus, if you received a 2,2 and split and received another two, you would resplit and so forth. If the casino has not posted whether or not you can double after splits or resplit pairs, don't hesitate to ask. These options are favorable to the player and should be taken advantage of.

Basic Strategy for Single Deck Games

The single-deck game is the best game for the blackjack player to play, if the rules are liberal when it comes to doubling down and splitting. If you have the option of playing single- or multiple-deck games, you would be foolish to choose the latter. A single deck offers so many more opportunities for the basic strategy player and the card counter alike. For the guerrilla gambler, it can be a gold mine if approached properly, as you will see in Chapter 7.

Player's Hard Hand	Decision based on dealer's up card:
8	Double against a 5 and 6. Hit against all else.
9	Double against 2 through 6. Hit against all else.
10	Double against 2 through 9. Hit against all else.
11	Double against everything.
12	Hit against 2 and 3. Stand against 4, 5, 6. Hit against all else.

13	Stand against 2 through 6. Hit against all else.
14	Stand against 2 through 6. Hit against all else.
15	Stand against 2 through 6. Hit against all else.
16	Stand against 2 through 6. Hit against all else.

(If surrender is allowed, surrender a 15 or 16 against a dealer's 10.)

| 17,18,19,20,21 | Stand against everything |

Player's Soft Hand	**Decision based on dealer's up card:**
A,2	Double against 4, 5, 6. Hit against all else.
A,3	Double against 4, 5, 6. Hit against all else.
A,4	Double against 4, 5, 6. Hit against all else.
A,5	Double against 4, 5, 6. Hit against all else.
A,6	Double against 2 through 6. Hit against all else.
A,7	Double against 3 through 6. Hit against 9 and 10. Stand against 2, 7, 8, ace.
A,8	Double against a 6. Stand against all else.
A,9	Stand against everything.

Player's Pair:	**Decision based on dealer's up card:**
A,A	Split against everything.
2,2	Split against 3 through 7. Hit against all else.
3,3	Split against 4, 5, 6, 7. Hit against all else.
4,4	Double against 5 and 6. Hit against all else.
5,5	Double against 2 through 9. Hit against all else.
6,6	Split against 2 through 6. Hit against all else.
7,7	Split against 2 through 7. Hit against 8, 9, ace. Stand against a 10.

(If surrender is allowed, surrender 7, 7 against a dealer's 10.)

| 8,8 | Split against everything. |

(If surrender is allowed, surrender 8, 8 against a dealer's 10.)

| 9,9 | Split against 2 through 6; 8, 9. Stand against 7, 10, ace. |
| 10,10 | Stand against everything. |

Additional Single-Deck Strategies

The single-deck blackjack game is quite different from the multiple-deck game because the composition of a given hand is actually an important factor in your decisions. For example, in a multiple deck, any player's hand of 12 is to be treated as an equal to any other hand of 12. Not so with a single deck. A 10, 2 is to be handled differently than, say, a 5, 7 when facing a dealer's up card of four. In the former situation, you would hit; in the latter situation, you would stand. Now, on the basic strategy for single deck, I have not added any of the refinements that follow because they will not drastically alter your long-run expectations. However, if you want to get an extra edge, I recommend you incorporate the following variations of play into your single-deck strategy.

1. Hit 10, 2 against a dealer's 4. Stand on all other hard 12s.

2. Hit 10, 3 and 9, 4 against a dealer's 2. Stand on all other hard 13s.

3. Stand on any three or four card total of 16 against a dealer's 10.

4. Stand on a 9, 7 against a dealer's 10. If surrender is allowed, however, you would surrender this hand as you would any 16 against a dealer's 10.

5. If you can double after splitting pairs:

   a.) Split 2, 2 against a dealer's 2.
   b.) Split 3, 3 against a dealer's 2 or 3.
   c.) Split 4, 4 against a dealer's 5 or 6.

CHAPTER FIVE

Rules Variations and Their Impact on the Player

There are good blackjack games and bad blackjack games and you should be able to distinguish between them. Basic strategy players and card counters alike benefit from liberal rules, and are hurt by tight games with few options for the players. Even if the option is only marginally helpful to a player, it is better to play at a table with this option, all other things being equal. The world of blackjack is an ever-changing landscape and new rules come and go. However, for good or ill, the following rules can be found often enough in casinos that it is worth knowing their impact on your expectations.

Doubling on any first two cards: A good rule for the basic strategy player when used properly. For basic strategy players, follow the doubling strategies for the single and/or multiple decks as detailed in the previous chapter. For the card counter, this is an even better rule since a card counter will find many more opportunities to double. If the dealer should have a blackjack, you only lose your initial bet on any double down.

Doubling on Nine, 10, and 11 only: This is not a good rule for single- deck basic strategy players since there are times when you will double on eight. This rule is primarily aimed, however, at card counters in order to diminish their opportunities for doubling in advantageous situations.

Doubling on 10 and 11 only: Awful rule and any game that stipulates this should be avoided if better games are available.

No Doubling: Don't play this game—at all.

Splitting Aces: Good rule, especially if the casino allows you to resplit aces. When you split aces you can receive only one card on each ace; thus you cannot double down after splitting aces. If the dealer has a blackjack, you lose only your initial bet.

Splitting Pairs: Favorable rule for the player, especially if you can double down after splitting and if you can resplit pairs.

Insurance: If the dealer has an ace as his up card, you can insure your hand for up to half its value. Bad rule for basic strategy players. Never insure anything, even your own blackjack. However, insurance is a wonderful rule for card counters who will know exactly when to take it. Quite often the difference between a winning or losing session for a card counter, especially in single-deck games, is proper use of the insurance option.

Doubling Down on Three or More Cards: Good option for basic strategy players if used correctly. However, any casino that allows this option usually has a lousy game for card counters. (Some games are better for basic strategy players than for card counters!)

Early Surrender: The player has the option of surrendering his hand when he sees his first two cards. In exchange, he gets back half his bet—even if the dealer has a blackjack. Very good option for basic strategy players. Great option for card counters.

Late Surrender: Same as above except...and this is a BIG except...if the dealer has a blackjack, you lose your entire bet. Good option for both basic strategy players and card counters.

No Hole Card Blackjack: You won't find this option in America. However, if you travel to foreign casinos, you'll run into it. Dealer doesn't take a hole card until all the players have played their hands. Bad rule for the player because the casino will take all double downs, splits and resplits if the dealer gets a black-jack.

Six Card Winner: You won't find this rule much anymore, even though it is only marginally favorable to the player. It is only slightly more favorable to card counters. You win if you get 21 or less with six cards.

Five Card Charlie: If you receive 21 with five cards, you win a bonus from the casino—usually two to one. This favors the player but doesn't occur very often.

Seven-Seven-Seven 21: In some eight-deck games, the casino will pay a handsome bonus if you can get three sevens of the same suit. Don't hold your breath waiting for this, as it happens rarely. However, some casinos will pay a small bonus if the player gets three sevens of any suit. This is favorable to the player if...

      1. You don't deviate from basic strategy when you get two sevens in an attempt to get a third.
      2. You don't have to put up a side bet to get the payoff.

Six-Seven-Eight Suited: Another extremely rare hand that many casinos will pay a bonus for—usually two to one. Favorable to the players if you don't change your basic strategy in an attempt to suit up, except in the case of a six-seven suited against the dealer's two.

Over-Under: This option is beginning to be seen more and more in Las Vegas and Atlantic City. You make a side bet that the next hand dealt you will be either over 13 or under 13 on the first two cards. Aces count as one for this and the dealer takes all hands of 13. Very unfavorable rule for basic strategy players. Marginally helpful rule for certain card counters.

Dealer Hits A, 6 (Soft 17): Bad rule for all players. Helps the dealer improve an otherwise bad hand for the house.

Blackjack Jackpot: A large progressive jackpot that climbs as play continues. This option is starting to catch on. You win it if, on the first hand out of the shoe, you receive an ace and jack of a specified suit. Good for players as long as you don't play an otherwise inferior game in order to go for the bonus.

Red or Black: This is a bet where the player guesses what the color of the dealer's face-up card will be by placing a bet on a separate betting area. At first this would seem like an even game off the top, but the house stipulates that if the two of the color you chose shows up, your bet is a push. This gives the house an advantage over the basic strategy player. For the card counter keeping track of the colors, this is a phenomenal game.

Number of Decks: The greatest single variable in determining the viability of a given game is the number of decks. As a general rule of thumb, the fewer the decks, the better it is for the players—if the rules are similar. For the guerrilla gambler, the single-deck game offers opportunities for card counters, basic strategy players and the relatively unknowledgeable alike. A single-deck game can range from a +.15 percent in favor of a player to a –.10 percent (sometimes more) against the player, depending on the rules. Multiple-deck games tend to have somewhat more liberal rules because of the advantage to the casino of using more decks. Thus, a double-deck game with good rules will have approximately a 0.31 to 0.35 percent advantage in favor of the house; a four-deck game will have approximately a 0.41 to 0.52 advantage in favor of the house; a six-deck game will have approximately a .58 percent advantage for the house; and an eight-deck game will have approximately a .61 percent advantage in favor of the house. The assumption on all these house edges is that the player is playing perfect basic strategy. For non-basic strategy players, the house edge can be as much as eight percent or more depending on how foolishly a person plays.

DEALER

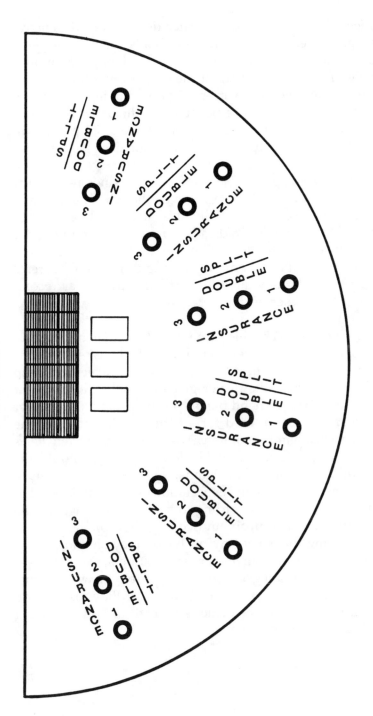

FIGURE 4
Multiple Action Blackjack Layout

Penetration: How many cards a dealer deals is called penetration. If a game deals all the cards out, that's 100 percent penetration. For the basic strategy player, the depth of penetration is of little significance. However, for the card counter the depth of penetration is another key variable in determining whether to play a given game. The more penetration, the better the game. The minimum necessary for a decent game is 75 percent in multiple-deck games and 66 percent in single-deck games.

Face-Up or Double Exposure Blackjack: More casinos in Atlantic City are starting to offer this game, even though it never really caught on in Las Vegas. Generally, dealt from a shoe of six to eight decks, this game is a radically different one from regular blackjack since *both* the dealer's cards are dealt face up. The basic strategy charts for it are also quite different. Chapter 8 contains a basic strategy table for this game as well as recommendations for further reading.

Multiple Action Blackjack: This game is getting tremendous publicity in Las Vegas and I even found it on the Mississippi riverboats. The player plays three hands against the dealer's face-up card. The rub is this—the dealer gives himself three different hole cards, one for each hand the player has played. (The dealer keeps the same face-up card for all three of his hands.) The dealer plays each hand separately. The player has played *all his hands*, however, before the dealer does anything. Should the player bust on any one of his hands, he loses all three hands. This game has the exact same expectation as regular blackjack if all the hands are played according to basic strategy against the dealer's up card. The problem occurs when players are so afraid of busting that they stay on hands they shouldn't. The casino eats these people alive. For card counters, this is a good option because they can get more money into play without suspicion. For basic strategy players—beware! Play just as you would normally against the dealer's up card or you are asking for "multiple" losses over the long haul.

CHAPTER SIX

Card Counting

Card counting is not difficult to learn. In fact, I think learning the theory of card counting is much easier than memorizing basic strategy. By the end of this chapter, you will know *how* to count cards. Whether you will actually be able to *do* it is an entirely different matter. The actual counting of cards in a casino—with lights flashing, people talking, slot machines jingling and clanging, waitresses asking you if you want something to drink, with music blaring in the background—is not that easy.

The difference between a card counter starting out and a basic strategy player starting out is this: The basic strategy player must put in quite a bit of time memorizing at home because he plays by rote, but once he has mastered the strategy, he can play it mechanically; the card counter, on the other hand, cannot master the art at home. He must go to a casino and see if he can concentrate amid the din and do in a casino what he did so well at home.

But learning how to count cards is an important weapon in the arsenal of a guerrilla gambler and, if you wish to be able to fully attack blackjack in the guerrilla style, then by all means learn how to count cards.

The theory of card counting is quite simple: Big cards favor the players, small cards favor the dealer. This is a fact backed up by tens of millions of computer runs over four decades of blackjack study. Thus, as the game is progressing, if the deck contains more big cards (10s and aces) because more little cards have been played, it will be to the player's advantage, whereas if the deck contains more little cards (twos through sixes), it will favor the dealer. Of course, having a deck favor you is not the same as a guaranteed win, nor is having an unfavorable deck a guaranteed loss. However, in the long run analysis of blackjack, the player will win more hands when the decks contain high cards than he will lose, and he will lose more hands when the decks contain low cards than he will win.

Card counting systems take advantage of this fact in four ways:

1. All card counting systems keep track of the relationship of small cards to big cards in the remaining deck.

2. When the cards remaining in the deck favor the player, the player will bet larger sums of money. When the cards remaining in the deck favor the casino, the player will bet smaller amounts or the minimum amount allowed.

3. Certain changes in basic strategy are made based on the "count" that increase a player's advantage or decrease his disadvantage when playing certain hands.

4. The use of the insurance option now becomes viable at certain times.

If you have decided to learn how to count cards, you have another big decision to make. What card counting system will you use? There are literally dozens of different counting systems on the market, some selling for upwards of $295. To make matters worse, most of the card counting systems are good! There are card counting systems that keep track of every card in the deck; there are systems that are four-level systems—that is, cards are assigned a value of +1 to +4 (and −1 to −4); there are three- and two-level systems. Some are so difficult and so elaborate that only a genius could play them. Some are so simple that mere mortals (you and I) can play them.

You are lucky, for, unlike me, you don't have to attempt to play a representative sampling of all these systems before deciding which to choose. I did. I've played three-level counts, two-level counts and one-level counts with side counts of aces and fives. They all work.

Unfortunately, for me, they all work about as well as the simplest and easiest to learn and use—a one-level count, called the Hi-Lo Count, that only follows certain cards. Recent research, and blackjack is a well-researched game, has shown that there isn't much difference in performance between a good one-level count and a good multi-level count. The only real difference is the level of difficulty in learning and executing the multi-level as opposed to the single-level counts. So why bother wasting time learning a more difficult count when its advantage over a simpler count is miniscule?

So the count we'll deal with will be Hi-Lo.

Here are the card values in the Hi-Lo counting system.

$2 = +1$	$7 = 0$	$10 = -1$
$3 = +1$	$8 = 0$	$ace = -1$
$4 = +1$	$9 = 0$	
$5 = +1$		
$6 = +1$		

As you are playing, if more small cards are coming out of the deck, you have what is called a *positive count*. If more large cards are coming out of the deck, you have what is called a *negative count*. After a round of play, if the count is positive, the next round should theoretically favor the player because a greater proportion of the large cards remain in the deck to be played. If the count is negative after a round of play, the next round favors the casino because a greater proportion of the small cards remain to be played.

Why do the large cards favor the player and small cards favor the house?

> 1.) Large cards make a blackjack more likely. Although the player and the dealer have an *equal* chance of getting a blackjack, the player is paid off at three to two. Thus, if a player gets one blackjack in one round of play and the dealer gets one blackjack in another round of play, the player comes

out ahead, assuming his bets were the same in both rounds. The converse is also true. With small cards remaining in the deck, a blackjack is less likely.

2.) Although the dealer will get slightly better hands in a positive count (as will the player), when the dealer has a bust hand (12 to 16), he is more likely to actually bust. The dealer has to hit his bust hands, the player doesn't. In a negative count, the dealer will hit his bust hand and is more likely to make a good hand because small cards are more likely to come out.

I want to reinforce what I said earlier. The fact that something is *more likely* to happen doesn't *guarantee* it *will* happen every time. When you count cards, you will have very high positive counts where the dealer will draw to his bust hands and still get small cards. You will have negative counts where blackjacks appear—one after another. Over time, over the long run (whatever that is), what is more likely to happen will happen more often than what is less likely to happen. But sometimes that long run is a long time coming—especially when you are losing hand after hand.

That's why many counters prefer to use guerrilla tactics against blackjack, rather than play a traditional game that demands countless hours in order to get into the long run. Guerrilla gambling can save time, money, and aggravation.

Now that you know the values of the cards, you have to hit upon a workable method for counting them. You have to keep a *running count* of the cards as they come out of the deck.

In games where every player has his cards dealt face up (usually multiple-deck shoe games), you can wait until every player receives his hand and then count as the dealer hits them or passes them by. For example, if the player in the first baseman's seat (the seat closest to the dealer's left) has a 10 and a two, the count is neutral. If he hits his 12 and gets a six, the count is now +1. Now, you would move onto the next player. He has two 10 cards. The count is now –1. Thus, you would follow the dealer around the board. This is only one method of counting in a face-up game. You could, for example, scan the table and cancel out conflicting pairs. Thus, a player with two 10s and a player with two fives cancel each other out immediately and the count is neutral. You will have to practice at home to decide what counting procedure is best for you.

In single-deck and double-deck hand-held games, the cards are usually dealt face down. Thus, you have to wait until the player busts or the dealer turns the player's cards over at the end of the round to count them.

To become proficient, you have to put the practice in. Card counting is, as you have just seen, easy to understand, hard to actually do at first. However, once you master card counting, you never forget how to do it. Like riding a bike, counting cards and playing basic strategy can become second nature.

What should also become second nature are the variations in basic strategy required based on the count. There are literally hundreds of variations both for single- and multiple-deck games. However, much like the numerous card counting systems, memorizing hundreds of strategy variations will not yield you much value for your time. You are better off simply memorizing the few strategy variations for certain hands that occur with some regularity and in count ranges that you are more often likely to have. Thus, the following variations should be incorporated into your arsenal.

Variations in Single-Deck Basic Strategy

All strategy variations in single-deck games are based on the running count.

Running Count	Variation in Strategy
–1 or less	hit 13 against the dealer's 2 or 3
+1 or more	stand on 12 against the dealer's 2 or 3 stand on 10, 2 against dealer's 2, 3, or 4 insure all hands against a dealer's ace double on 10 against a dealer's ace
+2 or more	stand on all 16s against a dealer's 10 double A, 8 against a dealer's 5

These few variations in strategy will help you considerably in playing certain hands. Remember that at a +1 or more, you insure all your hands against the dealer's ace—even the hands 11 or 10 that you are doubling down. The correct use of the insurance option in a single-deck game is probably the key variation to employ.

Variations in Multiple-Deck Basic Strategy

Counting into a multiple-deck game is slightly more complicated than counting into a single-deck game because you have to keep track of two different counts—the *running count* and the *true count*. The running count is the count you keep as the game is progressing. Thus, if the following cards appear: 4, 8, 6, ace, 10, 5, 3, 2, 7, 4—you have a running count of +4 (4 = +1; 8 = 0; 6 = +1; ace = –1; 10 = –1; 5 = +1; 3 = +1; 2 = +1; 7 = 0; 4 = +1). But what if this were the first round of play in an eight-deck game—would you have an edge over the casino? No.

To establish whether a count actually means you have an edge over the casino (or whether the casino has an edge over you), you must divide the number of decks remaining to be played into your running count—this is your *true count* because it gives you a true indication of what is actually happening.

Say you have a running count of + 8 with four decks remaining to be played in an eight-deck game, your true count would be +2. You divided the decks remaining to be played, four, into your running count of +8, which gives you a true count of +2.

Now, exactly what does this mean in terms of an edge? As a general rule of thumb, any positive true count equals a half percentage point in favor of the player. Thus, a true count of + 2 equals one percent in favor of the player. However, the casino has approximately a half percent on the player in a multiple-deck game, so the above situation would give the player a one-half percent edge over the casino.

With four decks remaining to be played in an eight-deck game, you ask yourself the question: Is a one-half percent edge worth very much? The answer is somewhat ambiguous. If you were playing millions of hands just like this—four decks remaining to be played with a one-half percent edge—then, yes, that one-half percent would be a viable edge. But if you were playing only a hundred hands in this situation, you probably wouldn't notice anything at all—you'd win some and lose some. That's because in a multiple-deck game with four decks remaining and a one-half percent edge, many of the cards can be clumped behind the shuffle point (the shuffle point is the area of the shoe where the dealer places the plastic card that indicates how many cards have been cut out of play).

For a true count to be significant in a multiple-deck game, it should give you an edge of at least one percent or more. Thus, your true count should be approximately +3 before you consider any severe escalation of bets. In fact, many blackjack pros don't even bother playing the first two decks of an eight-deck shoe but prefer to count *outside* (that is, behind the players) until the true count is +3 or more. If the count reaches this with six or fewer decks remaining, the player jumps in and begins to place bets. This guerrilla technique of jumping in on positive decks only is called *Wonging* and is named after Stanford Wong, the pseudonym used by a very popular and astute blackjack author who originated the idea. Wonging is an excellent, though boring, way to beat the six- and eight-deck game.

There is no magic formula for estimating decks other than practice. You have to get a visual feel for what composes one deck, two decks, three decks, etc. The best way to do this is to buy enough decks so that you can practice estimating at home before you try to do so in a casino. Getting a reasonably accurate true count is a necessary skill if you wish to have a chance against the multiple-deck games.

In a single-deck game, you do not need to be able to get a true count in order to know whether you or the casino has the edge. Any negative count favors the casino and any positive count favors the player. You can, if you want, get a true count for a single-deck game as well. This can be done by dividing the fraction of the deck remaining to be played into the running count. Thus, a running count of +3 with a half deck remaining would be a true count of +6 because 0.5 divided into three equals six. However, in a multiple-deck game, the true count is the basis of all decisions and must be ascertained at all times.

True Count	*Variation in Strategy*
–2 or less	sit out and don't play
–1 or less	hit 13 against the dealer's 2 or 3
+2 or more	stand on 12 against a dealer's 2 or 3 double down on 11 against an ace stand on 16 made with three or more cards against a dealer's 10

+3 or more   insure every hand against the dealer's ace
                                    double down on 10 against the dealer's ace
                                    double down on 9 against the dealer's 2

Betting in Blackjack

The key to winning money in traditional blackjack play is
to bet more when the count favors you, bet less when it doesn't.
Theoretically, the best procedure would be to bet the table minimum when the count is negative and bet the table maximum
when the count is positive. However, do this in today's casinos
and you'll be asked to leave the premises in Las Vegas and the
dealer will shuffle up on you in Atlantic City. Also, very few
people can afford the staggering fluctuations in bankroll that
can occur when your bets vary so dramatically. You'll be sky
high one moment—economically and emotionally—and lower
than Hades the next.

But to win at traditional blackjack, you must escalate your
bets in positive counts; otherwise, the casino's slight edge will
grind you down.

Most current blackjack authors recommend a betting
spread of one unit to four units (some go as high as six units)
based on the true count. Thus, in a neutral or negative deck,
you would bet your minimum of one unit. If the true count
were +1 in a single deck or +3 in a multiple deck, you would
bet two units. If the count were respectively +2 or +4, you
would bet three units; if the count were +3 or +5, you would
bet four units. The total bankroll for a traditional card counter
should be somewhere between 800 and 1,000 units. Such a
bankroll should help you weather the sometimes rather long
but inevitable losing streaks. An under-financed card counter
will invariably get wiped out because the swings of fortune are
so great owing to the escalation of bets in high counts.

Unfortunately for the card counters, most casino pit people
have read most of the same blackjack authors and are on the
lookout for the one to four unit spread, especially if the bet is
bumped directly from one unit to four units. They are on the
lookout for proper use of the insurance option and the surrender option. They are also on the lookout for anyone who varies

his strategy with the count. Many of the casino pit people know as much as card counters because many casino people *are* card counters.

I spoke to a very astute Las Vegas pit boss whose casino offers good single- and double-deck games with liberal rules. He had this to say about the traditional method of card counters:

"A single card counter can't really hurt the casino's bottom line in any significant way unless he's playing for tens of thousands of dollars over an extended period of time. However, hundreds of card counters can hurt us by taking up the spaces at the table that would otherwise be occupied by inferior players and by winning small amounts consistently. That's why we ban them. Every trick they use to fool us, we know about because we've read the same books they have. The first thing you look for is bet spread and proper use of insurance—especially in a single-deck game. I mean anyone who insures a stiff hand against the dealer's ace when a big bet is out is probably counting cards. The casinos that are offering the better games usually hire people who are good counters in order to catch good counters."

I remember when I was playing at the Golden Nugget in downtown Las Vegas and the casino pit crew had clipboards with the words COUNTER CATCHERS stenciled on them. They were especially on the lookout for players who bet green ($25) and varied their bets upwards with the count. The red chip players ($5) didn't seem to concern them and several counters were varying their bets from $5 to $30 in gradual stages right under their noses. I would recommend that if you are going to play the traditional blackjack games, and not the guerrilla kind, that you escalate your bets only by doubling the previous bet and preferably only after a win. This tends to resemble what many players do when they feel that they are on a hot streak—they escalate their bets by doubling their previous bets. You can also consider taking insurance when you have the *smallest* possible bet out so that when you take it with a big bet out, it will seem natural. Don't do this too often, however, because your edge is slight at best and you can wipe it out by making too many foolish plays.

Apropos of this, I will have several recommended books at the end of the blackjack section that show you how to camouflage your counting activities and blend in with the mass of losers.

But there are ways of playing blackjack other than spending endless hours at the tables, varying your bets with the count, and playing cat and mouse games with the pit crew. If you want to win at blackjack and sock it to the casinos simultaneously, then guerrilla blackjack might be the game for you.

CHAPTER SEVEN

Guerrilla Blackjack

Blackjack is a game that is made for hit-and-run guerrilla techniques such as Wonging described in the last chapter. There are several strategies that the guerrilla blackjack player can employ—some of which will actually give you a mathematical edge over the casino. Most of these strategies will require some card counting and almost all will necessitate an understanding of basic strategy for any reasonable chance of success. Card counters will, of course, have the better of it because they have a reasonable certainty of playing a favorable game. The basic strategy player, on the other hand, is hoping for a quick win and then out. All of these strategies require that you have cash or preferably chips ready to be laid down at a moment's notice and it is a good idea for all guerrilla gamblers to have a ready supply of chips handy when hitting the casino for a session. To get chips, cash in big at one game, even though you don't intend to stay very long.

Guerrilla Scanning Techniques

The best blackjack game to play is the single deck, and the best way to play it is to hit when the deck favors you and drop out when it doesn't. Most casinos will not allow you to do this over and over, especially if the tables are crowded and, most especially, if the casino thinks you're only playing the positive hands.

Still, the ultimate guerrilla tactics fall into what John F. Julian calls *scanning techniques* (see *Julian's No-Nonsense Guide to Winning Blackjack* at the end of the next chapter). Here the guerrilla blackjack player scans a table for specific situations and plays only one or two hands before leaving and going to another table, and ultimately to another casino and so forth. Scanning works best in single- and double-deck games where the guerrilla player can get a good edge rather quickly.

Scanning techniques can be used by card counters and basic strategy players alike. Of course, the card counter will be better armed and better able to fully assess the battle than will the non-counter.

Bombing for a Blackjack

The first scanning technique is called *Bombing for a Blackjack* and can be employed against a single or double deck. First we'll discuss single deck.

You scan the first round and if the count is +1 or more and no aces have been dealt, you come in with a bet of four units on the next round. If you are not a counter, you would scan the first round and if no aces appeared, you would come in with a bet of two units. (If the dealer should shuffle up on you, the next time you jump in reduce the size of your bet in half and see what happens. Some casinos are very leery of scanners and quick to shuffle up if the size of the four-unit bet is substantial—say, four $100 chips.)

In a single-deck game, approximately 16 to 22 cards are dealt to a full table in a round. If no aces appeared, the remaining deck (from 30 to 36 cards) would have four aces. The chances of a blackjack on the next round are comparatively quite high—especially if the count is in the positive zone. If you don't get a blackjack, as most times you won't, you play the hands according to established basic strategy and/or variations based on the count. Regardless, the chances of a winning hand or a desirable winning of a doubling down are quite good.

For non-counters who do not wish to learn basic strategy, you can scan for a blackjack and place a two-unit bet also. But you must follow these simple rules of play:

1. Hit all hands that you can't bust on against all dealer hands.

2. Stay on all your stiff hands (less than 17) against a dealer's 2 through 6.

3. Do not hit any hand that is a hard 17 or more

4. Hit all your stiff hands against a dealer's 17 or more

By following these simple rules, you can make strikes against the single deck when no aces appear on the first round. I don't recommend this technique, since it is preferable that you employ correct basic strategy; nevertheless, you can get in the action with a decent chance of winning your bet. I caution you, however, that prolonged play—even against a single-deck game and even using guerrilla bombing for blackjacks—without a full knowledge of basic strategy will ultimately be a losing proposition.

The strategy is essentially the same for the double-deck game, except that the initial bet after a first round with no aces appearing will be half the amount. Thus, the card counter with a positive count would only bet two units and the basic strategy player would only bet one unit. Should the second round yield no aces (or one ace), the counter would increase his bet in a positive deck to four units; the non-counter would increase his bet to two units.

The advantage to card counting here is evident. The card counter will not play after scanning, regardless of whether or not aces have appeared, if the deck is negative. Thus, the counter will always be bombing for a blackjack in decks highly favorable for such an occurrence. The basic strategy player is somewhat at a disadvantage as he will have to play in both negative and positive decks since he can't distinguish between them.

When you are bombing for a blackjack, you cannot stay at the same table for more than two hands in a single deck or more than three hands in a double deck. You have to move on to another table and then another game or another casino when you have played your round(s). Remember, if you stay too long at a blackjack venue and only play a scanning game, the casino crew will catch on to you and won't allow you to bet, or the dealer will shuffle up on you every time you jump into the game. You have to scan, hit and run. Scan, hit and run. Move from table to table and then out the door to the next casino.

However, if you decide to employ guerrilla tactics in all the games that give you a decent chance of winning, then mixing up your guerrilla blackjack with guerrilla roulette and guerrilla craps and guerrilla poker, etc., will more than likely prevent the casino crew from suspecting you of counting and scanning. Consequently, you will be able to stay longer in one casino, hitting the various games and, we hope, running with the money.

Guerrilla Wonging

Stanford Wong recommends back counting (counting behind the players and only entering a game if the deck is positive) as the best method for play in multiple-deck games (see *Professional Blackjack* at the end of this chapter), but I think it is also an excellent way to play the single- and double-deck games as well.

Stroll through the casino and scan the tables. If, after a first round of a single-deck game, you notice that the count is +1 or above, put up a bet for the next round of two units. (If no aces have appeared, put up a bet of four units.) In a double-deck game, you will put up a bet of one unit if the count is +2 or more after the first round.

Let us say that after the second round the count is still positive. Then in a single-deck game you would increase your bet to four units on the third round. In a double-deck game you would increase your bet to two units if the deck remained at a +2 or more. Whether you win or lose has no bearing on your next bet.

I am assuming in all these single- and double-deck scan scenarios that there are several players at the table and that you have seen a sufficient number of cards. If there is only one other player at the table, aside from yourself, then sit down and play the traditional game because two players against the dealer is a situation you won't often see in single- and double-deck games.

Chances are that in a single-deck game, three rounds is all the dealer will allow. In the double-deck game, however, this is not so. On the fourth round, if the deck is still positive, you will spread to two hands of two units each. On the fifth round, if the deck is still positive, you will increase each hand to four units. If, at any time, the deck is negative after a round, get up and go to another table or another game.

Scanning the Multiple-Deck Game

Four-, six- and eight-deck games are much more difficult to beat, whether by scanning or by traditional play. The greater the number of decks, the fewer blackjacks you get and the greater the possibility that the cards that favor the players are all clumped behind the shuffle point. In short, you can't have as much confidence in your true count the earlier you are in a given game.

The best guerrilla attack on the multiple-deck game is a combination of *Wonging* and progressive betting.

Back count in a multiple-deck game until at least two decks have been played and the true count is a +3 or more. (If two decks have been played in an eight-deck game, you need a running count of 18; in six decks you need a running count of 12; in four decks you need a running count of six.) Place a two-unit bet. If you win, your next bet is three units. If you win that, your next bet is four units. With each successive win, you increase your betting by a unit. At any point in the progression, should you lose, you will go back to the original two-unit bet. This means that after the initial two-unit bet, you would simply place another two-unit bet should the first one be unsuccessful.

The betting ends and you move on if any of the following occurs:

1. You are down after four rounds of play and the true count is neutral or only slightly positive — +2 or less.

2. The count becomes negative and you are behind, you are even, or you have lost your last bet.

3. If the true count is +3 or more, you will continue betting two units until you lose three hands in a row.

Now, as long as you are winning you will stay at the table — even if the count becomes negative. However, you will quit the table as soon as you lose your first hand during a negative count. The reason you take a little extra risk and stay for at least one hand in a negative count is to ascertain whether you are in a player-favorable clump of high cards (which, of course, would make the count go down). If you continue to win successive hands in a negative deck, you will continue to stay and play. Otherwise, it's time to seek a new shoe or a new game.

Guerrilla Multiple-Deck Play for the Basic Strategy Player

As a basic strategy player, you are taking a greater risk than the card counter in hitting a given shoe because you don't have any idea of the composition of the decks and whether they favor you or not. So, rather than Wonging, you are going to start the shoe with a simple Martingale strategy.

The Martingale wagering system is fraught with danger if used for a prolonged period of time. Essentially what a Martingale bettor does is double his previous bet after a loss in order to recoup the loss and win the initial amount. Thus, if you were to bet one unit and lose it, you would next bet two units. If you won, you would recoup your first bet of one unit and your second bet of two units and make a one-unit profit. And so it goes. You double your previous bets until you finally win and recoup everything you lost plus one unit.

Theoretically, this form of wagering is foolproof because you have to win sooner or later—that is, *if you have an almost inexhaustible amount of capital and play in a casino that has no limit to the maximum size of your bets.* Where the danger lies in this form of betting is obvious—a string of defeats can literally wipe you out because the casinos have put a cap on the maximum amount of wagers allowed. Thus, a Martingale of between eight and 10 steps is usually enough to hit the house limit and make you a sorrowful loser. And eight to 10 losses in a row is not an unusual event for anyone who puts in time at a gambling table.

However, a limited Martingale can be a useful tool for the guerrilla basic strategy blackjack player in a multiple-deck game. You will play a simple, three-step Martingale and get out whether you win or lose.

At the opening of the shoe, you bet one unit. If you win, you leave and hit another game. If you lose, however, your next bet is two units. If you lose that, you next bet is four units. If you lose that—you say goodbye to that table and thanks for the memories and head for another game.

In this simple three-step Martingale, you are merely looking to win one of three decisions for a one-unit win. Of course, you could win more should basic strategy call for doubling or splitting. You could also lose more than the seven units should you have to double or split.

Prolonged Guerrilla Blackjack

There is another way to hit the game of blackjack. You can play 12 sessions against a single-deck game, six against a double-deck game, three against a four-deck shoe; two against a six-deck shoe, and one against an eight-deck shoe. You will either play basic strategy or count cards. At the end of the allotted sessions, you then take an inventory.

1. If you are ahead 20 or more units, you can quit, or take 10 of your 20+ units and start another round. Should you lose the 10 units, you would quit. However, should you double the 10 units, you would put aside the 10-unit win, and continue to play with the original 10 units. As long as you keep doubling those 10 units you will stay in the game, banking your win. Once you lose those 10 units, you leave.

2. After the initial sessions, if you are even or losing, you would quit the game and either take a break or play a different game.

3. After the initial sessions, if you are up less than 20 units you would quit and go to another game.

Scanning for Blackjacks

If you are going to play any prolonged session in a single- or double-deck game, you have certain advantages off the top, whether or not you are counting cards, that you don't have in multiple-deck games. In single- and double-deck games, perhaps the most important decision you will have to make is whether or not to take insurance should the dealer have an ace showing.

In a single-deck game, insurance is always called for if the deck is +1 or more. On the very first round of play, basic strategy players and card counters alike can make proper insurance bets by scanning the cards of the other players. What you are looking for is the relation of 10 value cards versus non-10 value cards.

The dealer has an ace showing. That is a non-10 value card. As you scan the other player's hands (or ask them to show their cards), you will take insurance if there is one more non-10 value card than 10 value cards. Thus, there are two more non-10s than 10s on the table because, don't forget, the dealer's ace counts as well. John F. Julian (*Julian's No-Nonsense Guide to Winning Blackjack,* see end of chapter) has developed great ways of getting players to show their cards without the casino pit personnel catching on to your expertise. It requires you to play the role of happy blackjack gambler—talkative, inquisitive, friendly, and *nosy!* In the double-deck game, you want to have four more non-10 value cards than 10 value cards in order to take insurance.

Unfortunately, you cannot use these techniques on the first round of play against a multiple-deck game because so many cards remain to be played that no scan can give you a good enough confidence rating to risk an insurance bet—which is one more reason casinos prefer the multiple-deck games and one more reason you should avoid them if you can.

Piggybacking or Backlining: Asian Guerrilla Blackjack

Years ago, I was playing at a full table in the Golden Nugget when I felt a tap on my shoulder and a very nice Japanese gentleman asked if he could place a bet on my betting square. I looked at the dealer and she shrugged. I told him it was okay by me but that I couldn't guarantee him a win, even though I had been winning consistently for a while at that table—a fact he knew.

I had a $50 bet up and this man slipped a black chip ($100) under my two greens. He said: "You play the hand."

That was my introduction to a way of playing I had read about but never really experienced, a way of playing that is common in Asian blackjack games, a way of playing that I call *piggybacking* and is commonly called *backlining*—where you can make a bet in another player's betting square where that player will play it.

This method of play is quite suited to guerrilla Wongers in multiple-deck games, especially in Atlantic City or other crowded places, where no room exists at a table where the count is positive. Simply ask a player if you can place a bet with him. You have to be willing to abide by that player's decisions, but at a crowded table it would be unusual not to find at least one player who knows basic strategy.

[Since I penned this section on blackjack, my playing partner, the beautiful AP, and I took a two-week break from writing and went to Mississippi to research the blackjack and the other games on the Mississippi riverboats. The reverse was true at these casinos—I found almost no basic strategy players. I found the worst blackjack players I have ever seen. Laughing, happy, nice people—but the worst blackjack players perhaps in the history of the world. Of course, they were so bad that the pits were totally lax when it came to watching the game for suspected card counters. I don't know if I should write this but…the beautiful AP and I had a betting spread—hold onto your basic strategy charts!—of $5 to $250. We did this by playing two hands of $10 each off the top of a six deck shoe—*where less than three-quarters of a deck had been cut out of play!*. When the counts got really negative, one of us went to the bathroom and the other played for $5. However, as soon as the true counts got to +3 we started escalating our bets to two-fold with each true count point, up to $125 per hand: thus +3 = $20; +4 = $40; +5 = 80; +6 or more = $125. All during this time, no pit person even looked at us, or made a phone call to the eye in the sky. I don't know if you card counters out there will find the same idyllic conditions as the beautiful AP and I did, but I hope you do. Of course, I also hope that the poor players I saw on these river-boats read this book, learn basic strategy and start decreasing their losses. But that will probably mean the end of the incredible games. (For a full report on Mississippi gaming, check AP's report in the Spring 1993 issue of *The Experts Blackjack Newsletter.)*]

Of course, placing a bet with another player takes a little courage and some charm but if you are the personable type, and somewhat daring, the worst that can happen is that the player so asked will tell you to take a hike. However, as you are back counting, you can size up the players at the table, determine which ones are good players, and which of these (if any) might be agreeable to such a partnership. As play is progressing, talk, discuss the game, and if you find that one of the "good" players is starting to win and the count is mounting, you might hint that you'd like to get in his game. When the true count hits +3 with two decks played, make your proposition.

Guerrilla Red and Black Back Counting

Probably the best blackjack option found in the world as I write this is the one being offered at the Four Queens in downtown Las Vegas—where you can place a side bet on whether the dealer's face-up card will be red or black. (There is talk that the Foxwoods Casino in Connecticut will have this option in the near future; indeed, by the time you are reading this it might be available in a number of locations—or nowhere.) If it is offered anywhere near you, get to the casino pronto—after first reading this section.

The fact that this game is dealt from a six-deck shoe does not lessen its attraction over regular blackjack. The reason for this is simple. The player can get a significant edge over the casino—a much greater edge than is usually available against the regular game because every point in the true count represents almost two percent in favor of the player! (Compare this with the .50 percent for every true-count point in regular blackjack.)

You have two approaches to this game. You can sit down

from the very first round of play, use basic strategy and count just the red and the black. Or you can back count the red and black and jump in when the count calls for it. You can even employ guerrilla piggybacking by placing a red or black bet on the betting square of someone who is not taking advantage of this option (if the casino will allow this). Of course, if you have a partner, as I do, one of you can count the traditional way and one can do a red-black count.

The simplest way of red-black counting is to follow traditional accounting practices—black is positive and red is negative. Thus, all black cards will be a +1, and all red cards will be –1. Any true count of two—*whether it be a minus or a plus count*—indicates that you have an even game. (You figure the true count by dividing the number of decks remaining to be played into the running count.) The reason you have an even game at plus or minus two concerns the push on the deuces that gives the casino an approximately four percent edge off the top of this game.

If you wish to add another side count to your count, you can follow how many deuces of each color have come out. For every deck played, theoretically two deuces of each color should come out. Any time more come out, you have an added advantage over the house of about .50. Keeping track of the deuces is slightly more difficult than just keeping track of the colors but for serious players it might be worth the effort.

The Four Queens limits the red-black bet to $25. If your unit of betting is $25, then any count of plus or minus three or more will call for betting the maximum since it is your lowest unit. If your unit is $5, then any plus or minus three count is a single-unit bet; any plus-minus four count is a three-unit bet; any plus or minus five count is a five-unit bet ($25). Should a casino allow a higher maximum bet, any plus or minus true count of six calls for a 10-unit bet; any true count of plus or minus seven would call for a 15-unit bet. Assuming the casino allows bets higher than $75, you would escalate in units of five with each point in the count.

If this option catches on across the country, and with the growing competition among the casinos it very well could, then a fertile field has opened for the blackjack player—be he a guerrilla player or not.

Guerrilla Blackjack Bankroll

The size of your bankroll for blackjack has to be determined by the type of play. If you intend to hit and run quickly, you will not need a large number of units. However, if you wish to play longer sessions, then a traditional bankroll is required. For blackjack, a bankroll of 200 to 400 times your minimum bet would be sufficient to sustain you for prolonged periods of play.

CHAPTER EIGHT

Face-Up or Double-Exposure Blackjack

Face-up or double-exposure blackjack has been available for many years in Las Vegas but it has never really caught on. However, recently Atlantic City casinos have begun to offer this option as have other casinos outside Nevada. In the past several months, the number of face-up or double-exposure tables has increased dramatically in Atlantic City and the game seems to be catching on there. Unlike regular blackjack, all the cards are dealt face up—including the dealer's hole card. The player makes his decisions knowing exactly what hand the dealer is playing. Just like regular blackjack, face-up or double-exposure blackjack has basic strategies for every set of rules. Since Atlantic City has taken the lead in this game, I will give you the basic strategy that fits the Atlantic City game. This strategy, with some minor modifications, can be used for the Las Vegas game also. Some of the books I'll recommend at the end of this chapter will contain the various strategies for the more obscure face-up or double-exposure games.

I have taken this strategy with permission from the charts prepared by John F. Julian in *Julian's No-Nonsense Guide to Winning Blackjack*. It is the optimum *realistic* strategy for the set of rules currently in effect in Atlantic City. The word "realistic" is the key here. The theoretically optimum play, say, of a player's six versus a dealer's 16 is to double down. However, no Atlantic city casino will allow a player to double down on a six because it gives the player too much of an advantage. Indeed, the Atlantic City rules specifically state that you can double down only on nine, 10, and 11. Atlantic City's regular blackjack games allow doubling on *any* first two cards.

In the face-up or double-exposure game many hands are automatic losers if you don't hit them. If you have a 20 and the dealer has a 20, you must hit your hand or the dealer will win the push since all ties go to the dealer. Perhaps the reason this game never caught on in Las Vegas is just the fact that for a traditional blackjack player, hitting such hands as 20, 19, 18, and 17 goes so against the grain that it is better not to play the game at all. Can face-up or double-exposure blackjack be beaten with card counting? Yes, but you must learn an entirely different system. However, for those of you who wish to face off against the face-up challenge, I'll have some recommendations for further reading at the end of this chapter.

Player's Hand	Dealer's Hand	Strategy
4,5,6,7,8	all dealer's hands	hit
9	4...7, 8, 9, 10, 11...17, 18, 19, 20	hit
	5, 6...12, 13, 14, 15, 16	double
	A,A; A,2; A,3; A,4; A,5	hit
10	9, 10, 11...17, 18, 19, 20; A,A; A,2	hit
	4, 5, 6, 7, 8...12, 13, 14, 15, 16	double
	A,3; A,4; A,5;	double
11	10, 11...17, 18, 19, 20; A,A	hit
	4, 5, 6, 7, 8, 9...12, 13, 14, 15, 16	double
	A,2; A,3; A,4; A,5	double
12	4, 5,6...12, 13, 14, 15, 16; A,5	stand
	7, 8, 9, 10, 11...17, 18, 19, 20	hit
	A,A; A,2; A,3; A,4;	hit
13	4, 5, 6...12, 13, 14, 15, 16	stand
	A,3; A,4; A,5	stand
	7, 8, 9, 10, 11...17, 18, 19, 20	hit
	A,A; A,2	hit

14	4, 5, 6...11, 12, 13, 14, 15, 16	stand
	A,2; A,3; A,4; A,5	stand
	7, 8, 9, 10...17, 18, 19, 20; A,A	hit
15	4, 5, 6...10, 11, 12, 13, 14, 15, 16	stand
	A,A; A,2; A,3; A,4; A,5	stand
	7, 8, 9...17, 18, 19, 20	hit
16	4, 5, 6...8, 9, 10, 11, 12, 13, 14, 15, 16	stand
	7	hit
	A,A; A,2; A,3; A,4; A,5	stand
17	17, 18, 19, 20	hit
	all else	stand
18	18, 19, 20	hit
	all else	stand
19	19,20	hit
	all else	stand
20	20	hit
	all else	stand
A,A	11...17, 18, 19, 20	hit
	4 to 10; 12 to 16	split
	A,A; A,2; A,3; A,4; A,5	split
2,2; 3,3	4, 5, 6...12 to 17	split
	7 to 11; 18, 19, 20	hit
	A,A; A,2; A,3; A,4; A,5	hit
4,4	12 to 16	split
	4 to 11; 17 to 20	hit
	A,A; A,2; A,3; A,4; A,5	hit
5,5	4 to 8; 12 to 16; A,3; A,4; A,5	double
	9, 10, 11; 17 to 20; A,A; A,2	hit
6,6	4, 5, 6; 12 to 17	split
	7 to 11; 18, 19, 20; A,A; A,2; A,3; A,4	hit
	A,5	stand
7,7	4, 5, 6; 12 to 17	split
	7 to 10; 18, 19, 20; A,A	hit
	11; A,2; A,3; A,4; A,5	stand
8,8	4 to 8; 12 to 17; A,3; A,4; A,5	split
	9, 10, 11; A,A; A,2	stand
	18, 19, 20	hit
9,9	4, 5, 6...8...12 to 16...18; A,5	split
	7...9, 10, 11...17; A,A; A,2; A,3; A,4	stand
	19, 20	hit
10,10	13, 14, 15, 16	split
	20	hit
	all else	stand
A,2; A,3; A,4; A,5; A,6	all dealer's hands	hit
A,7	4 to 7; 12 to 17; A,5	stand
	8 to 11; 18, 19, 20; A,A; A,2; A,3; A,4	hit
A,8	4 to 11; 17, 18; A,A; A,2; A,3; A,4; A,5	stand
	12, 13, 14, 15, 16	double

	19,20	hit
A,9	4 to 12; 17, 18, 19	stand
	A,A; A,2; A,3; A,4; A,5	stand
	13, 14, 15, 16	double
A,10	all dealer's hands	stand

Recommended Books, Magazines, and Newsletters

All the books, magazines, and newsletters that follow are recommended. However, some of the books are a little dated and although they are interesting to read for their insights into the game and the people who play and offer them, their strategies are either outdated or overrated. The simple Hi-Lo count that is offered in this book is all you need to be a proficient card counter.

Many of the older books will try to sell you on multiple-level counts with the mistaken notion that these will significantly increase your winnings. They won't. When the authors made those claims, however, they were made in good faith as the popular wisdom of the times was that the more complicated the count, the better the results. Recent thinking and research tends to show that the marginally better theoretical performance of advanced counting systems is more than offset by the difficulty in actually executing them for prolonged periods in casinos. Even a single mistake in a session would be enough to erase whatever theoretical advantage an advanced count has for a player.

So if you really want to pursue card counting seriously, master the Hi-Lo and follow the strategy indices of those more recent authors whose specialty is this particular count. All the following books are available from their publishers or from the gambling book clubs, stores and mail order firms listed in the appendix.

Books

Julian's No-Nonsense Guide to Winning Blackjack by John F. Julian. Paone Press, PO Box 610, Lynbrook, NY 11563. ($16.95) I wish Mr Julian's book had been around when I first started playing because it would have saved me a lot of aggravation. An excellent book for new and intermediate players. Contains information on all the latest games and options, plus Scan and Sprint Strategies for single- and multiple-deck games respectively. What makes the book outstanding for beginners is the wonderful method Mr. Julian lays out for memorizing the single- and multiple-deck basic strategies. In addition, he has tests at the end of each section so you can see how much you have actually learned. At the end of the book is *The Ultimate Blackjack Test*, a one hundred question test on all aspects of blackjack. This alone is worth the price of the book.

Professional Blackjack by Stanford Wong. Pi Yee Press, 7910 Ivanhoe Ave. #34, La Jolla, CA 92037. ($19.95) One of the leading theorists of the game and one of its mighty players, Stanford Wong's book is great for players who really want to dig in and get their feet wet with a host of variations for all possible rules and games. Has complete indices on Las Vegas's Double Exposure game, as well as strategy charts detailing the mathematical expectations for every kind of game. Be prepared for some detailed mathematics. In addition to this particular book, Stanford Wong has a host of other books on blackjack (all interesting and worthwhile reading), computer software, and a newsletter. Write to him at the above address and he'll send you a list of his offerings.

Fundamentals of Blackjack by Carlson R. Chambliss and Thomas Roginski. GBC Press, 630 11th St., Box 4115, Las Vegas, NV 89127. ($12.95) A must read for the advanced and expert player who isn't afraid of mathematics. It is well written, lucid, and to the point. Excellent strategies for the various single- and multiple-deck rules and variations. Examines all the major counting systems based on two criteria—playing efficiency and betting efficiency. An excellent reference book for the serious player. The two authors have another book, *Playing Blackjack in Atlantic City* (same publisher), which is worth reading although some of the advice is no longer applicable. Chambliss and Roginski are researchers first and foremost and their efforts have a somewhat scholarly bent. I use this as my first source of reference for the game.

Blackjack: A Professional Reference by Michael Dalton. Spiral Bound. Spur of the Moment Publishing, PO Box 541967, Merritt Island, FL 32954. ($29.95) This book is exactly what it says it is—a reference to everything you ever wanted to know about blackjack but didn't know you wanted to know that much. Presented in dictionary format, it is an A to Z guide covering blackjack systems, strategies, books, techniques, rules, terminology, history, videos, software, publications and more, all fully cross referenced. A great book for the serious player's blackjack library. Dalton also has a blackjack newsletter.

Blackjack for Blood by Bryce Carlson. CompuStar Press, 1223 Wilshire Blvd., Santa Monica, CA 90403. ($19.95) This is a book by a high stakes player who pushes an advanced point count system he dubs the Omega II, which is the same as Richard Canfield's "Master Count" that has been selling for $250. My advice is to stick to the Hi-Lo. But I highly recommend the book for its colorful description of what it's like to be a BIG player in today's casinos. His sections on casino comportment or how to act like a "gambler" as opposed to an "expert" as well as his advice on how to win over pit bosses, get onto junkets, etc., is needed by those of you who might want to bet big without being bounced from the casino scene. Carlson is a daring player and a good writer.

The Morons of Blackjack and Other Monsters by King Scobe. Paone Press, PO Box 610, Lynbrook, NY 11563. ($16.95) King Scobe is my favorite blackjack author because, well, because he's my alter ego. King Scobe writes about all the things a blackjack player experiences and feels. There's *more* to blackjack than count systems and strategies. This book is all about those *mores*. Deals with what it feels like to be banned; how the casinos discriminate against men and demean women; how morons and moronic play can affect your emotional expectations and your blood pressure. Essays on the New American Religion, the New American Caste System, how NOT to be a card counter. You'll meet your fellow gamblers in profiles that come alive and jump off the pages. A must read, if I do say so myself. Anything Scobe says I subscribe to 100 percent! Of course, I'm somewhat prejudiced in this.

Beat the Dealer by Edward O. Thorp. Vintage Books, 201 E. 50th St., New York, NY 10022. ($7.95) You should read this book after you have become proficient in blackjack since it is seriously outdated. This was the first book to explore the possibility of beating the casinos by counting cards. It's still a fascinatingly good read because you go back in time to the Las Vegas of old and a game that will never be again. Forget about his count systems and enjoy the nostalgia. Thorp has other excellent books on gambling which will appear in the general appendix.

The World's Greatest Blackjack Book by Lance Humble and Carl Cooper. Doubleday, 666 5th Ave., New York, NY 10103. ($9.95) A guy named *Humble* writes a book that he considers the *greatest!* As pseudonyms go I would have preferred Lance *Hubris* for a book so titled but either way the irony is evident and intended. Actually, it's quite a good book and contains an excellent count system called the Hi-Opt which can be used against regular games *and* face-up or double-exposure blackjack. Humble and Cooper have some intriguing things to say about casino cheating as well as how not to get barred. Deals with human and technical matters. Humble has a newsletter also, as well as other blackjack books, but this book is his "greatest!"

The Big Player by Ken Uston. Holt, Rinehart and Winston, 383 Madison Ave., New York, NY 10017. ($7.95)
Million Dollar Blackjack by Ken Uston. Gambling Times, Inc., 16760 Stagg St., #213, Van Nuys, CA 91406. ($14.95)
Ken Uston on Blackjack by Ken Uston. Lyle Stuart, Inc., Carol Publishing Group, 600 Madison Ave., New York, NY 10022. ($16.95)

If you are interested in reading about blackjack not only as a skill and technique but as a human adventure, then read these three books by Ken Uston, the late, great, "King of 21." Read them in the order in which they appear above because they chronicle his life, times, and evolving knowledge of the game. They are terrific reads. One of the greatest "team" players in blackjack history, Uston made a small fortune playing blackjack in Las Vegas and Atlantic City. Unfortunately,

because of Uston, casinos have tightened their rules and procedures and made it more difficult for the rest of us to win wagon-
loads of money. You will not be disappointed by "Kenny," as
his friends call him. When you're finished reading about him,
go to the casinos and watch how many men try to imitate his
playing style and personality. Imitation is the greatest form of
flattery. Very few could imitate his skill and writing ability. He
lived hard, died young and what a damn shame.

The Blackjack Formula ($10), *Blackjack for Profit* ($9.95),
Blackbelt in Blackjack ($12.95) all by Arnold Snyder. RGE
Publishing, 414 Santa Clara Ave., Oakland, CA 94610. Three
excellent books by one of the great computer blackjack buffs.
Snyder has shown quite clearly by his computer simulations
which games are beatable and which games are losing propositions for even the most skilled counter. Snyder is a prolific
writer and his columns and articles appear in a host of magazines. Also publishes his own newsletter and is author of *The
Over-Under Report*, an 18 page handbook that tackles how to
beat this option. Snyder calls himself the "Bishop of Blackjack." Amen.

Blackjack Your Way to Riches by Richard Albert Canfield. Lyle
Stuart, Inc., Carol Publishing Group, 600 Madison Ave., New
York, NY 10022. ($9.95) One of the older books. I read this
when I first started out. Loved it. Figured I'd abandon my
attempt to write the Great American Novel and concentrate on
making a few million dollars playing blackjack. I'm back to
writing that novel. Nevertheless, this book is a fascinating read,
although it does promise more than it can deliver. You'll meet
some interesting blackjack players who share their "secrets"
and very interesting it is indeed.

Playing Blackjack as a Business by Lawrence Revere. Lyle
Stuart, Inc., Carol Publishing Group, 600 Madison Ave., New
York, NY 10022. ($14.95) Another older book by one of the great
professional gamblers and...con artists? saints? shysters?
crooks? gods? of the old Las Vegas of mobsters and beatable
blackjack games. Revere (not his real name) was a blackjack
legend and was supposedly banned from every casino in
Vegas. When it was published, this book was the bible to many

players. God is dead and so is Revere. Another nostalgia piece but well worth the effort.

Blackjack: A Winner's Handbook ($8.95), *Blackjack's Winning Formula* ($8.95) by Jerry Patterson, *Break the Dealer* ($8.95) by Jerry Patterson and Eddie Olsen. Perigee Books, 200 Madison Avenue, New York, NY 10016. All three are good books. Patterson and Olsen challenge the idea of the random shuffle and offer alternative ways of thinking about the game—dealer and player biases in the shoe game, card clumping, etc. All these books heavily plug Patterson's clinics and TARGET system for selecting tables—which is a home study course that is quite costly. Patterson and Olsen are blackjack renegades and have come in for heavy fire for their "new" ideas. However, Olsen has one of the best newsletters.

Turning the Tables on Las Vegas by Ian Anderson. Random House, 201 E. 50th St., New York, NY 10022. ($10) A truly fun book that captures the pleasure and thrill of playing blackjack for high stakes in Las Vegas. The book was written in the mid-1970s as casinos were becoming increasingly more paranoid about skilled players. This is another how-to-behave book as opposed to a how-to-play book. Very few people will be able to mimic Ian Anderson because very few people have his kind of sterling money and sparkling personality. This book is a joy to read. Ian is himself a blackjack legend.

The Theory of Blackjack by Peter A. Griffin. Huntington Press, PO Box 28041, Las Vegas, NV 89126. ($9.95) This is a book for the mathematically inclined. It is scholarly, erudite and thorough. Griffin is a good writer and mixes fun with his formulas. Technical and intelligent. He's a researcher and thinker and, by his own admission, not much of a player. Griffin is refreshing, self-effacing, and sharp, and a welcome relief from the legions of blackjack "experts" who are stale, self-centered, and dull.

Blackjack Essays by Mason Malmuth. GBC, Box 4115, Las Vegas, NV 89127. ($19.95) Mason Malmuth is an intriguing theorist and he will challenge some of your sacred beliefs if you have been gambling for any length of time. However, if you are an English teacher, your skin will crawl with some of the syntax, spelling and grammar. If you are the creative type—chalk it up to genius or a vacationing editor.

Magazines and Newsletters

The Expert's Blackjack Newsletter. Published six times a year by Gambling Times, Inc., 16760 Stagg St., #213, Van Nuys, CA 91406. Usually runs 16 to 24 pages, 8½ × 11 format. Single issue: $6. Subscriptions: $30 for six issues; $60 for 12 issues. Covers all aspects of blackjack in a lively and compelling way. Name writers contribute as well as blackjack buffs. Has good updates on all the casinos and especially fine writing by the delightful AP, the Atlantic City correspondent. Excellent color-coded graphics allow you to quickly find the better games.

Blackjack Forum. Published four times a year by RGE Publishing, 414 Santa Clara Ave., Oakland, CA 94610. Runs approximately 56 pages. 5½ × 8½ format. Single issue: $10. $40 for four issues. $70 for eight issues. Covers all aspects of blackjack, from counting to camouflage, as well as side issues in gambling theory and practice. Reviews all the major casinos' games as well as books and software. Also carries a synopsis of other magazines and journals covering the gambling scene. Strong analysis by computer of many arcane and interesting blackjack questions. Name writers in each issue. Edited and inspired by Arnold "Bishop" Snyder who pours his grace on the magazine.

Robert Gates' Blackjack Monthly. Published monthly by Richard Canfield and Associates, PO Box 2830, Escondido, CA 92033. Runs approximately 12 pages. 8½ × 11 format. Single issue: $7. Subscriptions: $65 for 12 issues; $115 for 24 issues. Includes a weekly hotline number. Generally has two or more pieces by Robert Gates that are well written, challenging and informative. These can be about anything, not just blackjack. Has a thorough monthly update on all the casinos. Gives information on dealers who might be shoddy in their practices, giving the players a little better game.

Eddie Olsen's Blackjack Confidential Magazine. Published 10 times a year by Blackjack Confidential Publishing Company, Inc., 513 Salsbury Rd., Cherry Hill, NJ 08034. Runs approximately 32 pages. 8½ × 11 format. Single Issue: $10. Subscriptions: $99 for 10 issues. This magazine is loaded with information and statistics on casino wins, games, strategies. Has general interest pieces and personality profiles as well as several technical or inspirational pieces each issue. Doesn't rate every casino's games but offers the best bets. Has some of the best tournament results as well as information about upcoming tournaments. Also contains book reviews and information about other casino games.

Wong's Current BlackJack News. Published monthly, plus special editions as required, by Pi Yee Press, 7910 Ivanhoe Ave. #34, La Jolla, CA 92037. Subscriptions: $145 for one year. Can be anywhere from one page to several pages. Deals with table conditions everywhere and is always up-to-date. Any new promotions that can help a player are instantly sent in special reports. If you are a serious Nevada player, this newsletter can be a real resource. When you subscribe, you receive the "Instant Update" handbook that contains the rules for every casino in Nevada and Atlantic City. You can also call a hotline and correspond by phone or fax with the editor, Stanford Wong, one of the giants of blackjack.

Dalton's Blackjack Review. Published four times a year by Spur of the Moment Publishing, PO Box 541967, Merritt Island, FL 32954. Usually runs approximately 36 pages. 5½ × 8½ format. Single issue: $6.50. Subscriptions: $25 for four issues; $48 for eight issues. Book and product reviews, limited updates on games, plus several articles of general interest to card counters and basic strategy players in each issue. Doesn't just focus on Las Vegas and Atlantic City but gives the newly emerging Indian casinos and Mississippi casinos their due. Michael Dalton's stamp is all over the issue.

CHAPTER NINE

The Fundamentals of Baccarat

Without question, baccarat (pronounced bah-cah-rah as opposed to back-a-rat) is the most glamorous of all the casino games. It is played for high stakes, in a fashionably appointed room that is usually separated from the rest of the casino, with dealers who are invariably dressed in tuxedos, by fashionably dressed and quite beautiful female shills (a shill is a person hired by the casino to lure other people into playing) and by players who are dressed to the nines themselves. It is a high minimum game, generally $20 and up. Some of the biggest money bet in the casinos is bet at baccarat and certain baccarat players and sessions have become legendary. In fact, some of these sessions have made the national news as witnessed by the extraordinary publicity accorded one Kashiwagi, the late Japanese real estate mogul who won six million dollars one night from Trump Plaza in Atlantic City. Upon his death, the papers reported that this same individual *owed* tens of millions to casinos in Las Vegas and elsewhere. One report had him owing the Mirage 40 million dollars!

As in roulette, there are two versions of the game—the European model, where a player is the bank and all the other players at the table play against him; and the American model where all the players play against the casino whether they bet *bank* or *player*. In the American version, a winning bank bet has a five percent commission extracted since this bet has an actual edge for it that would make it a winning long range proposition for the players and a losing proposition for the casino. With the five percent commission extracted, the casino has a small 1.17 percent edge over the player on the bank bet.

Despite all the glamour, or maybe because of it, some people believe that baccarat is a difficult game to play. Steeped as it is in ritual, old world charm and wealth, the fact remains that of all the casino table games, baccarat is the easiest to play. Essentially, you are betting in baccarat the way you would bet on a coin flip. However, instead of heads or tails, you simply bet *bank* or *player*. By the way, the designation "bank" in the American game has very little meaning. If you bet bank, you do not have to pay off the players who bet "player" as you would in Europe. (There is a third bet in baccarat, the tie bet, which should be ignored since it carries a huge edge for the house.)

The Mathematics of Baccarat

As casino games go, baccarat is quite favorable for the gambler since the house edge is relatively small. Of course, unlike roulette, where a player can hope to find a biased wheel that can offset the mathematics of a game showing a large 5.26 edge for the house, a baccarat player cannot hope to find a faulty wheel or a biased game—short of stacking the deck and cheating. There is no way to overcome the mathematical probabilities of baccarat in the long run.

Unlike blackjack, there are no counting systems that have been devised that can overturn the small percentages against the players. So with baccarat, you are essentially bucking the odds and hoping for a small streak to carry you to victory. You have no choices to make, other than which square to bet on,

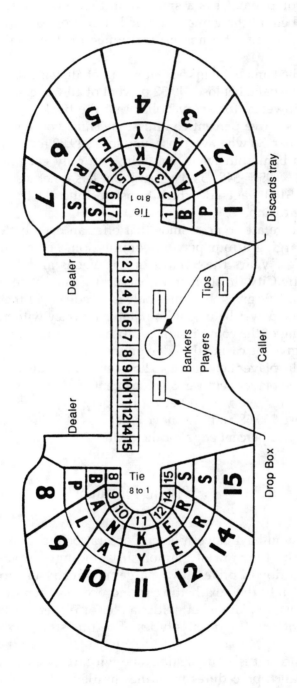

FIGURE 5
The American Baccarat Layout

bank or player. It is a smooth and simple game. Here's the math behind the game. (The tie bet is irrelevant to the mathematics since a tie has no influence on the bank or player wagers.)

The bank bet wins 50.68 percent of all wagers.

The bank bet loses 49.32 percent of all wagers.

However, for every dollar that the bank wins, the casino charges a five percent commission. Thus, you win 95 cents on the dollar. So when you lose, you lose $49.32 for every $100 you bet on bank, but when you win, you only get $48.15. (That's $50.68 × .95 = $48.15.) The bank bet has a net loss of $1.17 for every $100 wagered, which translates into a 1.17 percent edge for the casino.

There are some casinos that offer an even better bank bet by charging a four percent commission. For example, in the past few years the Sahara in Las Vegas and Tropworld in Atlantic City (in their mini-baccarat game) have offered this option. This gives the house only a .67 edge over the player.

The player bet is paid off at even money without the withdrawing of the commission because the commission isn't needed to give the casino the edge on this bet.

The player bet wins 49.32 percent of all wagers.

The player bet loses 50.68 percent of all wagers.

So for every $100 bet on the player, you will win $49.32 and lose $50.68 and thus have a net loss of $1.36. This translates into a 1.36 percent edge for the casino.

Playing Procedure

If you have never played baccarat before, don't be intimidated by the aura of glamor surrounding the playing table. Just sit down, preferably at a game already in progress, and watch until the next betting round occurs. Then decide where you wish to place a bet, with banker or player, do so and hope for a victory. (I'll discuss types of betting strategies in Chapter 10.)

Baccarat is a ritualistic game with many elaborate, almost sacrosanct, procedures from the shuffle to the dealing. During the shuffle all three baccarat dealers will mix and cut the cards.

When they are finished a player will make the final cut. Often the first card in the eight-deck shoe will be turned over. If it is, say, a six, then six cards will be taken off the top and buried. That is, they are placed in the discard pile. There is absolutely no reason to do this, except tradition, as these cards cannot affect the outcome of the game. (In blackjack, the burying of cards can affect the game because it makes the count less accurate.) The rest of the cards are then placed in a shoe with a plastic card that indicates the shuffle point.

Now the shoe is passed to the player in seat one. He will deal until a player hand wins. When that occurs the next player gets the shoe and the shoe will move counterclockwise around the table after every player win, giving each player in turn a chance to deal. The player dealing does not have to bet on bank, even though he is theoretically "the bank"; he is free to bet on player if he chooses or even to pass up the deal. When the shoe reaches seat number 15 (or whichever seat the last player is in), it moves back to seat number one.

After every bet has been placed, the dealer known as the *callman* will indicate to the shoe-player that it is time to deal a card. This first card belongs to the player hand and will be dealt face down and slid to the dealer. Then the player with the shoe will deal himself a bank card, which he will put on the side of the shoe or slightly under it. Then a second player card is given to the dealer, who will then push both cards to the individual who has made the largest bet on player. Now the player with the shoe deals himself a second bank card.

The callman now asks for the player cards, which are either flung or pushed to him. The callman will now turn them over and call out whatever hand is the player's.

Now the player with the shoe turns over the bank cards and passes them along to the caller who calls out the bank hand. From this point, the hands are played according to preordained rules that differ for bank and player. Keep this in mind, unlike blackjack, in baccarat the 10 value cards do not count in the scoring. In fact, the 10 value cards can be considered as counting zero. Indeed, the highest possible hand is a nine. Anytime you go above 10, you return to single digits. Thus, in the scoring, an initial hand of nine and nine is not 18 but eight! A hand of seven and five is not 12 but two! The player hand is played first.

Rules for Player when first two cards total:

1-2-3-4-5-10	player draws a card
6-7	player stands
8-9	this is considered a natural and player stands and bank cannot draw a card

Rules for Bank when first two cards total:

Hand	Draws when player's third card is:	Does not draw when player's third card is:
3	1-2-3-4-5-6-7-9-10	8
4	2-3-4-5-6-7	1-8-9-10
5	4-5-6-7	1-2-3-8-9-10
6	6-7	1-2-3-4-5-8-9-10
7	stands	stands
8-9	natural-stands	natural-stands

As stated, the highest possible hand is a nine. A nine dealt on the first two cards is an automatic winner and no further play is necessary. The next highest hand is an eight which is also considered a natural. Should one hand be eight and another nine, the nine wins.

Since the players have no control over the drawing of cards, knowing the rules is irrelevant.

As the game progresses those players who have won on the bank hand will be charged a commission. The dealers keep track of how much is owed and at the end of the shoe, or when the player decides to leave, he will have to pay what he owes.

In addition to baccarat, there is a game called mini-baccarat, which is handled by one dealer who deals all the hands. It is played in the main casino, for smaller stakes, but according to the regular rules. Everything is the same except for the role of the dealer and the glamor of the play.

CHAPTER TEN

Guerrilla Baccarat

A s I stated previously, you cannot hope to get a real mathematical edge in baccarat the way you can in blackjack, nor can you hope to exploit faulty equipment as you can in roulette. Baccarat is an unassailable game and you must buck the odds whenever you play it.

However, this doesn't mean you should give up all hope of wresting some money away from the baccarat tables. Before you can do this you have to decide just what level of baccarat play you wish to engage in. Can you afford the high minimums of regular baccarat? Or are your unit bets more applicable to mini-baccarat? As a guerrilla gambler engaging in various games, your betting must be in some kind of proportion. You do not want to bet larger than normal wagers in baccarat just to be able to play it. Thus, your single-unit bet must be enough to get you into the game.

In guerrilla blackjack, I recommended multiple-unit bets—particularly for card counters when they had the edge—but for baccarat a multiple-unit bet off the top would be silly since the casino always has its slight edge going for it. Thus, if you cannot get into a baccarat game with one unit, don't bother with the game. For most small bettors, regular baccarat is out of the question. However, mini-baccarat is always an option and, indeed, at times it is the more accessible game.

However, for those of you with large bankrolls, baccarat can be attacked in the guerrilla style. I recommend two approaches. The first approach I call *guerrilla streaking*. Baccarat is a game that often has long or short streaks of bank or player wins, and many a shoe has been labeled *in retrospect* a "bank shoe" or a "player shoe." Unfortunately, you cannot predict these streaks in advance.

Nevertheless, you wish to take advantage of a possible streak on either player or bank in a single shoe. Here's how to do it.

At the opening of a shoe, you do not place a bet. Wait for one round. Whichever side wins, be it bank or player, that is the side you bet one unit on for the next round. Should it win that round, you let your bet ride. You now are risking your initial one unit to win two units. Should you win your second bet, you bet only one unit on the next round. You will then alternate one- and two-unit bets until you have amassed 10 units in profit. Once you have 10 units, your next bet will be three units. Should the next bet be a win, the following bet is one unit. Now you alternate one- and three-unit bets until you have won another 10 units. Should your side continue to win, you then alternate four-unit and two-unit bets until you have amassed 30 units. Then you would go to six-unit/three-unit bets. If at any time during this procedure you lose, you sit out a round and then bet one unit on whatever side came up during the round you sat out. Chances are you won't get to the four-two or even the three-one units of betting immediately, because these would require unlikely consecutive streaks of 15 and 12 respectively right off the top. However, you could slowly build up your wins until you had 10 or 20 or 30 units.

The following chart will give you some idea of how streaking can work. I have purposely given you a long winning streak at the opening to demonstrate how the betting progresses. At the outset, the odds against a streak of nine in a row are approximately 500 to one.

Guerrilla Streaking

Hand	Unit Bet-Side	Winner	Profit
1	none	bank	none
2	one unit B	bank	one unit
3	two units B	bank	three units
4	one unit B	bank	four units
5	two units B	bank	six units
6	one unit B	bank	seven units
7	two units B	bank	nine units
8	one unit B	bank	10 units
9	three units B	bank	13 units
10	one unit B	player	12 units
11	none	player	12 units
12	one unit P	player	13 units
13	two units P	player	15 units
14	one unit P	bank	14 units
15	none	bank	14 units
16	one unit B	bank	15 units
17	two unit B	bank	17 units
18	one unit B	bank	18 units
19	two units B	bank	20 units
20	four units B	player	16 units

The above session would be an unqualified success if the player continued to win or simply maintained what he had. At the end of the shoe or at the 20-unit win mark, you would ask yourself whether you wanted to stay or whether you had a big enough win to satisfy you. If you wished to continue play, you would bet four units as I did above and continue to play the progression until you either lost six more units (giving you a net win of 10 units) or made it to 30 units. Should you make it to 30 units and desire to continue, you would play the six-three betting spread until you lost 15 units or won another 15 units. If you lost, you'd call it a session and walk away a 15 unit winner. If you won another 15 units, you'd play the six-three betting spread until you either won or lost 20 units.

Keep in mind that when you bet multiple units, you will return to a single unit at the first loss. However, when you reach a desired win plateau (20, 30 or more) then you immediately pump the bet to that level. The 20 unit level equals the four-two bet spread. The 30 unit level equals the six-three bet spread. So you would automatically go from a two-one betting spread to a three-one betting spread at a 10-unit win; you would go from a two-one spread to a four-two spread as soon as you reached a 20-unit win—even if you reached that win slowly on the two-one spread.

There is a danger to this type of progressive betting. You could have a decent run going at a lower level of betting and lose every time you pumped it up. If you find that you are consistently losing that first bigger bet when you go from a two-one unit spread to a three-one or a four-two, then stay at a lower level. Maybe the gods are telling you something.

Naturally, all the above assumes that you are winning. This doesn't always happen. Let us say that after you placed your first bet, you lost—what then? Wait another round. Then bet on the side that came up. If you lost that? Wait another round and then bet on the side that came up. And if you lost that? Go to another game because once again those baccarat gods are telling you something.

A Mini-Martingale for Mini-Baccarat

As I stated in the blackjack section, Martingale wagers can be dangerous if the bettor persists in throwing good money after bad. However, a short, explosive Martingale, a kind of do or die guerrilla ambush, is not without its merits. And in baccarat, even more so than in blackjack, a three step Martingale is a viable, one shot weapon.

You will probably not be able to do the mini-Martingale at a regular baccarat game because many casinos have stipulated that you can't sit out more than two or three hands in a row. Well, that's precisely what you are going to do. You must wait for a win of four consecutive player or bank hands. Then you place a one unit bet on the opposite. If you lose that, you place a two-unit bet. If you lose that, you place a four-unit bet. Lose that? Goodbye.

On the other hand, if you win your initial bet or any one of the three in the sequence, you wait for another run of four in a row. Then you repeat the above. If you win that, you wait for another four. When you have won four units—quit—because you are pressing your luck as it is. But a short burst like this can net you a few units in the black.

Recommended Reading

I wish I could recommend a host of books on baccarat but truthfully there isn't much out there of any worth. Aside from fully exploring the mathematics of the game, a topic I merely touched on, and the various failing attempts to discover a counting system that would give the players the edge, there really isn't much to the literature of the game. It has glamor but, unlike blackjack, poses no real challenge. It has ambience but no real thrills like craps. It has good odds but no hope for a definitive kill like roulette. In short, it's kind of a relaxed, quiet exercise in sheer guessing.

Few full length books devoted to baccarat are even worth a perusal. However, two gaming books of a general or theoretical nature contain well-written and thoughtful sections on baccarat that you might find appealing.

Of course, if you really want to pursue this particular game to the exclusion of all others, might I suggest investing in a large bankroll and an elaborate wardrobe and practice the following sentence: "My name is Bond...*James* Bond." Only substitute *your* name in the appropriate places.

The Mathematics of Gambling by Edward O. Thorp. Gambling Times Books, 16760 Stagg St. #213, Van Nuys, CA 91406. ($7.95) Has an interesting but relatively short section on attempts to discover a card counting system for baccarat.

Lyle Stuart on Baccarat by Lyle Stuart. Lyle Stuart Inc., Carol Publishing Group, 600 Madison Ave., New York, NY 10022. ($20) An enjoyable and personal book by the famous publisher and high roller. Stuart is a true gambler and you will enjoy his views and insights into the game.

CHAPTER ELEVEN

The Fundamentals of Craps

I doubt if many casino gamblers would disagree with the following statement: Craps is the single most exciting table game in the casinos. Some writers have compared it to the gambling equivalent of hitting a home run in the World Series—when you're winning. It can be exhilarating and exhausting.

When you are losing it can be the gambling equivalent of the myth of Sisyphus, whose torment for all eternity was to roll a large boulder up a mountain and then, just as he got it to the top, see it roll all the way back down, where he had to start all over again. In a word, craps can be the ultimate in frustration.

Even if you have never played it but have visited a casino, I'm sure that you have heard the cheers, moans, and mumblings coming from the craps areas. Craps lends itself to rooting and riotous reactions as those dice bounce off the back wall of Lady Luck and land to tell us if we've won, lost, or lived to play another roll. It is a game where fortunes can be won or, more

likely, lost in a split moment of time. It is a game with a cornu-
copia of betting opportunities, most of them carrying an
extremely large house edge. Just take a look at the craps layout
and you can see that craps is a bettor's paradise or hell.

Unfortunately, many otherwise astute gamblers avoid
craps for just this reason—it seems so complicated. One of my
good friends, KF, is a gifted card counter; in fact, he is one of
the best card counters in the world. Yet every time we play
craps he just watches because he feels the game is too difficult.
(Of course, I play the Captain's *Supersystem*, which I wrote
about in my previous book for Bonus Books: *Beat the Craps out
of the Casinos: How to Play Craps and Win!*, and it is somewhat
complicated for a novice to understand.) Still, here he is, a man
who uses a *four-level count system* in blackjack, one of the most
intelligent guys I know, a guy who can figure to a fraction the
exact advantage or disadvantage he has at any given moment
of a blackjack game, and he is intimidated by a game that for
the most part is played by people who have no idea of odds or
percentages. Why? The layout looks so complicated that he
reacts to it the way a vampire reacts to garlic! His reaction is
not unique. The craps layout scares many a would-be player.

But craps only *looks* complicated because of that host of
essentially irrelevant bets marked on the layout of the table.
These bets take up most of the layout's space and when you go
to a table, you'll hear people screaming out such things as:
"Give me a hard eight! I'll have a yo-eleven! Any seven for five
dollars! Give me snake eyes! Ten dollars on the 12!" And then
you'll see these same players throw chips out to the dealers
who will make the bets or indicate that these bets have been
accepted. To a novice, it looks chaotic. To a truly astute craps
player, all that activity, all that action, all those bets are meaningless. I say these bets are irrelevant or meaningless because
the guerrilla gambler, or any good craps player for that matter,
will never make them if he wishes to have any hope of wresting money from the casinos in this thrilling game. Thus, they
don't impinge upon you or affect you in any way. In Figure 6,
you will notice that I have shaded in various areas on the layout. All bets in these areas are to be avoided like the plague. In
fact, you have a better chance of surviving the plague than your
bankroll does of surviving a steady diet of these bets. They are
the junk food of gambling.

While a lot of people play craps, very few play it intelligently, and that is why it is such a big money maker for the casinos. These shaded bets are considered part of the Crazy Crapper Bets and should never be made. Why? Because the casinos have tilted the odds so much in their favor on them that the player is committing economic suicide by making them.

But aren't the odds of a bet simply the "odds?"

Unfortunately, as many of you know, there is a difference between "true odds" and "casino odds." In that difference lie the casinos' profits.

The true odds of a bet are based upon the probability of that particular event happening. For example, the number four can be made in three different ways with two dice—3:1; 2:2; 1:3—and thus it will theoretically come up once every 12 times because there are 36 possible combinations on two six-sided dice—$6 \times 6 = 36$. So the true odds against a four coming up on the next roll are always 11 to one.

The true odds of the number seven coming up (and as you know the number seven is the single most significant number in the game) are five to one because the seven can be made six ways: 6:1; 5:2; 4:3; 3:4; 2:5; 6:1. Six goes into 36 six times and thus the odds are always five to one against a seven being the next number rolled.

You always get the true odds *against something* by figuring how many times an event won't occur as opposed to how many times the event will occur. (You get the odds *for something* the opposite way!) The seven won't be rolled 30 times in 36 rolls but it *will* be rolled six times. Thus, the odds *against* a seven are 30 to six, or five to one! That's because six goes into six once and six goes into 30 five times.

Another thing to remember about probability and odds-making is this: We are talking about only the *theoretical* likelihood of an event and not the *predictive* likelihood of an event. Theoretically, the seven will show six times for every 36 rolls but in *actuality* it might show ten times, or no times, on the next 36 rolls. However, the longer the dice are rolled, as the total rolls approach the millions and billions, you will start to see numbers coming up with a frequency close to their probability. Probability theory is *indicative* and not *predictive* in the short run fluctuations of a game of chance.

Now, if the casinos were offering a *fair game*, theoretically,

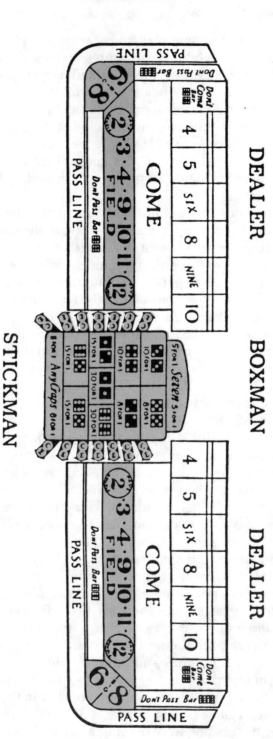

FIGURE 6
Craps Layout

at the end of an infinite number of rolls of the dice, neither the casino nor the player would be ahead. Everyone would be tied. If I bet one dollar that the next roll of the dice will be a seven, and it isn't, I lose one dollar. Theoretically, however, I will lose five times and win once on this proposition. I will lose five dollars. But I won once and was paid according to the true odds— five to one! Thus, I won five dollars when I won. I lost one dollar five times and won five dollars one time. Tie game. Fair game.

But the casinos aren't interested in giving you a fair game because they have to make money, not break even. After all, how could they pay to keep their establishments going, not to mention keeping their stockholders happy? So by slightly shifting their paybacks to favor themselves, the casinos make a great deal of money, especially on craps. Thus, on the above example of the seven, in a casino if I bet that one dollar on the next roll and the seven appears, I'll only be paid *four dollars* for my win instead of five. The casino is actually taking 20 percent of my win. The casino is a partner when you win a bet, but you are a sole proprietor when you lose.

Now, before going into the details of how the game is actually played, let me give you a chart of all the bets you *shouldn't* make. All these bets are Crazy Crapper bets where the house has altered the true odds dramatically. I'm giving them to you now instead of explaining the game to you afterwards, so that you can see them and then *forget about them.* For a fuller discussion of these bets and the fundamentals of craps, I refer you to my book: *Beat the Craps Out of the Casinos: How to Play Craps and Win!* ($9.95) Bonus Books, 160 E. Illinois St., Chicago, IL 60611.

Crazy Crapper Bets

Crapper Bet	True Odds	Casino Odds	Casino Edge
Field Bet	19 to 17	1 to 1 (2 to 1 on 2,12)	5.263%
Hard 4 or 10	8 to 1	7 to 1	11.111%
Hard 6 or 8	10 to 1	9 to 1	9.090%
11 or 3	17 to 1	15 to 1	11.111%
12 or 2	35 to 1	30 to 1	13.890%
Any 7	5 to 1	4 to 1	16.667%
Any Craps	8 to 1	7 to 1	11.111%
Big 6 or Big 8	6 to 5	1 to 1	9.090%

You can see from the above list that many craps bets are crappy, to put it in plain gamblese. What's worse, some casinos, knowing the stupidity of the players, have increased their margin of thievery on some of the above bets by playing games with the English language. Thus, in Las Vegas many casinos will pay 30 *for* one on the one roll 12 or two bet instead of 30 *to* one. What this means is the player receives 30 units back for his bet should he win, but included in this 30 units is his original one-unit bet! On the 30 to one proposition, you receive 31 units back—your 30-unit win plus your one-unit bet. This simply makes the proposition have a greater percentage in favor of the house—a whopping 16.667 percent! Still more robber-baronly, some of the Mississippi riverboats pay off at 29 *for* one—a hideous 19.44 percent in favor of the plantation... ah, I mean, the house.

Now, what does an edge of, say, 19.44 percent actually mean? Bluntly, for every $1,000 you bet on that proposition, you will lose $194.40 in the long run. Not a very attractive proposition, is it? And like most unattractive propositions in life, it must be oversold and advertised extensively using hard sell techniques in order to get people to buy it. Therefore, many of the Crazy Crapper bets are hawked unmercifully at the craps table by the stickman, one of whose jobs is to stick it to your bankroll evidently. Thus, on every roll of the dice you'll be hearing the stickman shouting: "Bet those hardways! Anyone for seven or 11? Try the 12? How about a whirl bet?" *Forget it.*

Chaos, shouting, and side bets aside, in reality, craps is a simple game—as it must be to lure all the fish who play it. It is largely a mathematically oriented game completely based on a given number's probability of appearance in 36 rolls and/or its relationship to the probability of the seven appearing. Unless there is something wrong with the dice, or the shooter can control the dice, the game is based purely on probability theory. The following chart gives the numbers that can be made from two dice, each numbered one through six; how many ways these numbers are made, and the combinations that compose them. Remember that there are six sides to each die and thus 36 possible combinations that can be made from two dice.

How the Numbers Are Made

Number	Ways to Make	Combinations
2	one	1:1
3	two	2:1, 1:2
4	three	3:1, 2:2, 1:3
5	four	4:1, 3:2, 2:3, 1:4
6	five	5:1, 4:2, 3:3, 2:4, 1:5
7	six	6:1, 5:2, 4:3, 3:4, 2:5, 1:6
8	five	6:2, 5:3, 4:4, 3:5, 2:6
9	four	6:3, 5:4, 4:5, 3:6
10	three	6:4, 5:5, 4:6
11	two	6:5, 5:6
12	one	6:6

The game begins when the stickman pushes five dice to the new shooter for the *Come Out* roll.

The shooter selects two dice and the stickman takes back the remaining three. At any time in the shooter's roll, the shooter may ask for "new dice" and the stickman will go through the above process again. The shooter now places a bet on either the *Pass Line* or the *Don't Pass Line*. He rolls and the game officially begins. Other players also may have placed bets on the Pass Line or Don't Pass Line.

If the first roll is a seven or 11, everyone who bet the Pass Line wins the equivalent amount of his bet, that is, "even money." Those on the Don't Pass Line lose their bets. However, if the shooter rolls a two or three on the Come Out roll, the Don't Pass bettors win even money, and the Pass bettors lose. Should the shooter roll a 12, the Pass bettors lose but the Don't Pass bettors push (no decision).

The shooter will keep rolling Come Out rolls until he rolls a four, five, six, eight, nine, or 10. These are called *point* numbers. Let us say the shooter rolls a six. That now becomes the *point* and the dealer will place a round, two-sided black-white puck with the white side up in the box of the number that is the point. For Pass Line bettors, the shooter must roll another six before he rolls a seven in order to win. For Don't Pass bettors, the shooter must roll the seven before a six for them to win.

Although in the long term mathematics of craps the Don't

Pass bettor has a slight edge over the Pass bettor, in reality this edge is so slight that it is essentially irrelevant. However, what is not irrelevant is the disparity of opportunity on or after a Come Out roll.

On the Come Out roll, the Pass Line bettor is in the driver's seat. That's because he wins on a seven or 11, and loses on a two, three or 12. Now, there are six ways to make a seven and two ways to make an 11, which gives the Pass Line bettor eight chances in 36 rolls for a win. However, there are four ways he can lose because the combined totals of two, three, and 12 can be made in four different ways. Thus, overall, the Pass Line shooter has a two to one advantage on the Come Out roll.

On the other hand, the Don't Pass bettor is at his most vulnerable on the Come Out because he theoretically loses eight times for every 36 rolls, but only wins three times on the two and three (remember, the Don't Pass bettor pushes on the 12—that's the casino's edge for this type of bet). Thus, the Don't Pass bettor faces odds of eight to three *against* him on the Come Out.

Once the shooter establishes his point however, the nature of the game shifts dramatically in favor of the Don't Pass bettor. That's because the seven now becomes the standard for success or failure. The Pass Bettor must buck the odds against him, while the Don't Pass bettor has the odds heavily in his favor.

The following chart shows the relationship of every point number to the seven. Since most bettors are *right bettors*, that is, they bet with the shooter and against the seven, the chart is structured *against* the Pass Bettor. For example, the point number of four is made three ways in relation to the seven's six ways. The seven will come up six times for every three times of the four. Thus, the odds are two to one against the four. However, the Don't Pass bettor has odds of two to one *in his favor!*

Number	Seven Made: Number Made	True Odds
4	six ways to three ways	two to one
5	six ways to four ways	three to two
6	six ways to five ways	six to five
8	six ways to five ways	six to five
9	six ways to four ways	three to two
10	six ways to three ways	two to one

However, the Pass Line bettor can help his cause somewhat by placing what are called *Odds* behind his Pass Line bet. This odds bet is not on the layout but is usually on a sign posted somewhere on or near the table. If the sign says, for example, "This table offers double odds," then that means you can place a bet that is two times greater than your Pass Line bet directly behind it. The odds bets are paid off at *true* odds. Thus, if the point is four, and the shooter makes his point, the odds bet is paid off at two to one. The original Pass Line bet is only paid off at even money. It is usually recommended that Pass Line bettors take the maximum odds allowed—if they can afford that much money at risk. While most casinos offer double odds, many offer triple odds or five times odds, and some few even offer 10 times odds. If you have a choice, go where the better odds are.

For the Don't Pass bettor, the situation is the reverse. Instead of taking the odds, he must *lay* the odds if he wants to get more money into action. Thus, in a double odds game, the Don't Pass bettor must lay an odds bet of $20 to win $10. I'll have a complete discussion of the efficacy of taking and laying odds in the next chapter.

There are four other types of bets of which you should be aware: *Come Bets, Don't Come Bets, Place Bets,* and *Buy Bets.* With the knowledge of the Pass and Don't Pass bets, these other four will form the framework for your guerrilla attack upon the casinos.

If you take a look at the layout, you will notice a thick rectangular area running under the boxes where the numbers are. This is called the *Come.* To the left or the right of the Come area (depending upon which end of the table you're facing), you will notice a small box marked *Don't Come.* These bets function precisely as the Pass Line and Don't Pass bets, with one exception—they must be placed after the shooter has already established his point.

Let us say that the shooter has established his point. You now place a bet in the Come area of the layout. If the shooter rolls a seven or 11, you are a winner. If the shooter rolls a two, three, or 12, you are a loser. Now, if the roll is a seven, the dealer will pay off your Come bet and return both your original bet and its payoff since the shooter has *sevened out* before making his point. However, if an 11 is thrown, you must pick up your winnings and you have the option of leaving your original

Come bet on the layout, increasing it, or taking it down. If a two, three, or 12 is thrown, your Come bet is removed by the dealer, and if you wish to have another Come working, you must place it on the layout.

Now, if and when the shooter rolls a point number (four, five, six, eight, nine, or 10), the dealer will take your Come bet and place it on the number. You will now be given the option of placing odds on it—only this time you must put the bet on the table and the dealer will pick it up and place it on your original bet, but slightly askew, to indicate that it is the odds portion of your Come bet. To win a Come bet, the shooter must roll that number again before he rolls a seven.

The Don't Come works in just the opposite fashion. When you place your bet in the Don't Come box, a two or three will win even money but a seven or 11 will lose for you. A 12 will be a push. However, should the shooter roll a point number, your Don't Come bet is placed in the lay portion of the number's box (that is, the upper portion behind the double line) and now a seven will win the bet for you. If the shooter rolls that number before rolling a seven, you lose. Like the Don't Pass, you can lay odds on the Don't Come bets as well.

The mathematics of craps gives the casinos an edge of 1.414 percent on the Pass and Come bets, and 1.402 on the Don't Pass and Don't Come bets. However, the mathematics of craps shows that when a player *takes* double odds, he can reduce the casino's edge to .606 percent on Pass-Come bets; and when he *lays* the double odds, he reduces the edge to .591 percent. However, the "mathematics" of craps is not a total and accurate story in this style of betting, as I shall demonstrate to you in the next chapter.

Finally, we come to *Place* and *Buy* bets.

You might notice that with all the previous types of bets discussed, the player had to wait for the shooter to roll a number before he got into the game and then hope that that number repeated in order to win on it. Some players just don't have the patience for this. To placate them, the casinos have Place bets for the impatient. Quite simply, with these you just put your wager on the table and tell the dealer to "Place the four (or five, or nine, or 10) for five dollars (or whatever multiple of five dollars you wish) or place the six or eight for six dollars (or whatever multiple of six dollars you wish)."

Now, like the Pass-Don't Pass and Come-Don't Come bets, the Place bets have distinct advantages and distinct drawbacks. The advantages are twofold—you don't have to wait for the number to be made twice in order to win once on it, and you have discretionary removal of the bet. The Place bets do not have to stay on the number until a decision is made as do the Pass and Come bets. (You are allowed to remove the Don't Pass and Don't Come bets but, if you do, you are quite literally insane since, once up on them, you have a terrific edge over the casino!)

The drawbacks to the Place bets are also twofold: You do not benefit by the initial rolling of winning numbers such as seven and 11 as you do on the Pass and Come and, to pay for your ability to remove your bets at will, the casino charges a tax on your wins by not giving you true odds on these bets. (Note: The odds on your Pass-Don't Pass, Come-Don't Come also have discretionary removal, and why not? The house doesn't have an edge on those bets, so it's no skin off their toothsome profits for you to call off or take down your odds!)

The following chart will show you the price you must pay for having discretionary removal of your Place bets and how this translates into the casino's edge.

Place Bet	True Odds	Casino Odds	Casino Edge
4	2 to 1	9 to 5	6.667%
5	3 to 2	7 to 5	4.000%
6	6 to 5	7 to 6	1.515%
8	6 to 5	7 to 6	1.515%
9	3 to 2	7 to 5	4.000%
10	2 to 1	9 to 5	6.667%

As you can see, with the exception of placing the six and eight, place betting can take a heavy toll on your bankroll. To lessen the impact somewhat, and to encourage more people to place the numbers, the casinos allow you to *buy* the outside numbers by paying a five percent commission. Since a dollar is usually the lowest unit at a craps table (although in Las Vegas there are tables with 25 cent minimums), you must make a place bet of the four or 10 for $20, paying a one dollar commission ahead of time. This five percent commission translates into a 4.762% advantage for the house because the house charges you one dollar to place a bet of $20. You divide that one dollar by 21 (the $20 bet plus the $1 tax) and you get a net loss of .04762 cents for every dollar bought in this way. Still, it is a better bet than the original placing of the four or 10, which carried a house advantage of 6.667 percent.

At this point you know all you need to know to play the game of craps. Naturally, like any game, you'll have to get your feet wet under actual playing conditions to fully get into the swim of things. However, once you are in the flow of the game, you can execute several guerrilla techniques compliments of the greatest craps player of all time—a man known as the Captain. So get aboard and get ready for guerrilla craps!

CHAPTER TWELVE

Guerrilla Craps

C raps can be a dangerous game emotionally because it lends itself to players "going on tilt." Going on tilt, in gambling parlance, means that the player has lost control of himself and is betting stupidly, and big, in an heroic, but idiotic, attempt to get back his losses. I have seen more players go on tilt at craps than at any other game. No wonder why. There are so many betting opportunities that offer such seemingly large payouts, that the gambler on tilt will throw his remaining bankroll onto all the wrong bets. Add to this the electricity of the game, the communal consciousness that sometimes develops at a table of whooping, rooting, anxious players, and it is easy to see why someone could overbet his bankroll and wipe himself off the gambling map in no time at all.

The guerrilla approach to craps strictly follows the fundamental principles of how to approach the game as set down by the Captain, the world's greatest craps player. I have simply taken those elements of his systems and geared them for relatively quick hit-and-run sorties into the craps pits.

You will not learn the Captain's *Supersystem* in this book because that is a method of play that requires a long run perspective. The guerrilla gambler is not interested in a war of attrition against the casinos. He is interested in getting in and getting out, hopefully with the spoils.

However, we will be using several armaments from the Captain's arsenal, including the *5-Count*, the Captain's *Best Buys*, two revolutionary Buy bets for Place bettors that will radically reduce the house's edge for the action player, and the Captain's *Oddsman's* bet that can reduce the house's mathematical edge to zero! The only other bets with which we must concern ourselves will be the Pass-Don't Pass and the Come-Don't Come bets.

The Best Buys in Craps

You saw in the last chapter the heavy *vig*, *vigorish* or tax the casino takes out of place bets, especially of the four and 10. Although buying the four and 10 for $20, and giving the casino a five percent commission ($!), reduces that load to 4.762 percent, this is still a pretty heavy tariff to pay for the opportunity to place and/or remove the bet at will.

In the past, most casinos have allowed their green chip ($25) players to buy the four or 10 for a $1 commission yet place $25 on the number instead of the usual $20. This little maneuver cut the house's edge on those buy bets to 3.846 percent. Then along came the Captain in the 1970s and he *pushed the casinos* of Atlantic City into accepting a $35 buy for a $1 commission—reducing the house edge still more dramatically—to 2.778 percent. (*Pushing the casinos* means getting the casinos to give you a better game than advertised.) If you go to Atlantic City on a regular basis you will see many craps players now buying the four and 10 for $35 each.

Now the Captain has done it again. In the past several years, the Captain and several members of the Captain's Crew have been getting the casinos to accept buy bets for $39 for that same one $1 commission. I have done this quite often in

Atlantic City. Just recently I returned from the Mississippi Gulf Coast riverboat casinos where the bet was accepted, too, albeit after several conferences in the pit with the pit boss, the floorman, boxman and whoever else wanted to analyze this seemingly radical wager. Still I was ultimately able to make it. Buying the four or 10 for $39 cuts the house's edge to 2.5 percent on a placement of these numbers. Quite a stark departure from the original edge the house had, isn't it? Just look at how you can push the casino into giving you a better game than advertised:

Bet	Payoff	Commission	House Edge
place the 4 or 10	9 to 5	none	6.667%
buy the 4 or 10 for $20	2 to 1	$1	4.762%
buy the 4 or 10 for $25	2 to 1	$1	3.846%
buy the 4 or 10 for $30	2 to 1	$1	3.226%
buy the 4 or 10 for $35	2 to 1	$1	2.778%
buy the 4 or 10 for $39	2 to 1	$1	2.500%

Of course, if you want to buy the numbers four or 10 for $40, the casino will make you pay a $2 commission and you are back to the original 4.762 percent disadvantage.

The next Best Buy bet is truly revolutionary, as it violates all the sacred shibboleths of craps thinking. In this, you are going to—(you traditional craps players, hold on to your dice!)—buy the five and nine. Now, if you take a look at the casino advantage on placing the five and nine, you'll notice that it is four percent. That's because the normal payoff for the placing of the five and nine is seven to five. However, the true odds are three to two. To find the casino advantage, let us equalize the numbers: The place bettor gets $14 for every $10 he bets on a winning roll (that's seven to five). He should have received $15 to $10 because those are the true odds. The difference between the true odds and the casino odds is one. Now just divide the total of the true odds (15 + 10) into one and you get .04 or four percent in favor of the house.

So the traditional craps thinker says to himself: Why buy the five or nine and pay a five percent commission, even if that five percent commission translates into a 4.762 percent edge? The placing of the five and nine only has a four percent edge to begin with! It's silly. Why give the casino a $1 commission and actually win less?

At first it might appear that this is an unchallengeable

argument, but at a certain level of betting, the buying of the five or nine becomes the preferred bet. The Captain has placed $39 on the table and said: "Buy the five (or nine) for $38!" and the casinos have bought the bet. For a one dollar commission, you now get true odds of three to two on your $38 dollars. This translates into a 2.564 advantage in favor of the house. A much smaller advantage than the original four percent.

At this level of betting, you are spending $39 ($38 buy plus $1 commission) to win $57. If you were the typical, traditional, place bettor, you would place the five or nine for $40 and expect a return of $56. Thus, by buying the five and nine for $38, you are betting $1 less but winning $1 more!

So for the more action oriented craps players, and those who can afford bets of this magnitude, the Best Buys along with the placing of the six and eight, will be used as your preferred method of guerrilla attack after establishing the playability of a table.

But first let me take a look at the other methods of betting we previously discussed—Pass and Don't Pass, Come and Don't Come.

Pass-Don't Pass and Come-Don't Come Betting

You will recall that by all mathematical measures, the Pass-Don't Pass and Come-Don't Come bets seem to present the least disadvantage to the player because they carry a house edge of approximately 1.4 percent. If you add to this the taking or laying of odds, you can reduce the house edge still more.

That is a traditional way to approach these wagers.

And it is an approach I dispute on the Don't Pass and Don't Come portion of the wagers and uphold on the Pass and Come portions.

Here's why.

I don't look at Pass-Don't Pass and Come-Don't Come wagers as all a part of the same game from start to finish. I consider each of these wagers to be a distinct two-wager proposition, with each segment of the proposition having merits and demerits.

The first proposition is the actual placing of your wager on the Pass or Come; Don't Pass or Don't Come. (From now on I'll refer to Pass Line and Come bets as *Do* bets and Don't Pass and Don't Come bets as *Don't* bets.) On the Do side, you have a very good chance of winning right off because there are eight winning combinations, four losing combinations, and 24 no decisions. A Do bettor during segment one has a two to one advantage on a decision but he is paid at even money! That is a big advantage! Unfortunately, those 24 no decisions will quickly get him into segment two of the game where he is at a distinct disadvantage.

Thus, the Do bettor is in the driver's seat during segment one of the game. However, once he is up on a number, this changes. He now gets paid even money but he is facing stiff odds of two to one on the four and 10, three to two on the five and nine, and six to five on the six and eight. He is in a highly negative situation since the seven is more likely to be rolled than any one of his point numbers. Yet he can only get even money for his wager, even though the odds are against him. That is why it is advantageous for the player to take the maximum odds possible. These diminish the negativity of this particular *segment* of the game. The segment two negativity far outweighs the Do bettor's segment one positivity, so anything that a bettor can afford to do to diminish the impact of the segment two position should be done. This means placing more money on the table in the form of odds to reduce the house's edge on the overall segment two proposition. (Even if it were allowed, you would never want to give odds during the segment one portion of the game because then you would be diminishing your own advantage!)

Some pundits have claimed that the odds bets are merely break even events and don't have any merit. If you were to place a five dollar Do wager and take double odds of $10, at the end of the 1980 rolls of the dice (the number necessary for every possible result) the odds bet would break even and you would lose approximately 1.4 percent of all your wagers on the Do. This is correct, but short sighted, because one individual is risking $15 on every roll once a point is established ($5 Do bet with $10 odds) while the other individual is only risking $5. And 24 out of every 36 Come Out rolls will be point numbers where the player will be taking odds. Is it the same? Hell, no.

Let the individual who is claiming that the taking of odds is the same as not taking the odds in the long run bet $15 on the Pass or Come. What happens? That's right. The house extracts its 1.4 percent from $15 instead of from five dollars but it is only extracting .6 percent from the $15 of the $5 Do player who takes $10 in odds. That is why I favor taking the odds. If you are going to bet $15, you are better off betting it as an initial $5 Pass or Come, followed by an odds bet once it is on the number.

Here are the percentages in favor of the house for Pass Line and Come bettors when they take advantage of the various odds bets:

Pass Line (Come) no odds	1.41%
With single odds	0.85%
With double odds	0.61%
With triple odds	0.47%
With five times odds	0.32%
With 10 times odds	0.18%

The reverse is not true, however. It never made sense to me for a Don't bettor to *lay* odds once he was up on a point number. At this stage he is in the driver's seat when it comes to the game because he has a significant edge — once he gets past the Come Out roll. Why water that edge down by putting a significant amount of money on the table in the form of laying odds when you have that seven working strongly in your favor? For the Pass Line bettor, taking odds makes sense. However, for the Don't Pass bettor it is silly.

The reason most traditional craps writers recommend laying the odds on Don't bets has more to do with the nature of mathematics than with the nature of reality. The mathematicians look at the Don't wagers in their *totality*. By laying odds in segment two of the game, these mathematicians reason that it will help the segment one scenario to be less negative. It will but it is irrelevant. Unfortunately, the mathematicians don't see the segmentation! But craps *is* played in discreet segments as I've stated. It is this fact that makes the laying of odds a poor proposition for the Don't bettor.

Since the Don't Pass bettor faces heavy odds of eight to three against him on the Come Out (eight chances of losing, three chances of winning, and 25 no decisions) in the overall mathematical analysis of the game, laying the odds reduces that awful edge—since the odds bet is an even money proposition between the casino and the player. It is a fair bet. And it is a fair bet for *substantial sums*—anywhere from two to 20 times greater than the original Don't Pass bet. This zero proposition must *reduce* the negative impact of the Don't Pass bettor's risk on the Come Out roll and, in conjunction with the overwhelming favorability of the actual Don't Pass bet once it is on the number, reduce the house edge significantly. But it is a *false mathematical significance* owing to the amount the odds bets entail and the fact that they are made during a segment of the game when they hurt more than help.

Certainly, anything that is a zero-win proposition is better than a negative win proposition and will theoretically improve the negative situation. After all, zero degrees is warmer than 50 below. However, the odds bet on the Don't can only be made **after** you have survived the Come Out roll. It's like you went from 50 below to 50 above. Why would you want to experience a day of zero just to reduce the impact of the day that has already vanished into the past? Once you've survived that negative Come Out roll, it makes no sense to decrease your positive expectancy by adding a zero-win proposition, even though the mathematics says otherwise. Zero degrees is a lot more negative than 50 degrees and a lot more positive than 50 degrees below. The mathematics of craps is a totality, but the playing of it is episodic and segmented and much more like the weather!

It makes sense when you are in the Do player's position, once he is up on a number and facing a highly bleak negative future, to add the zero-win scenario, since that can significantly decrease the negativity of the upcoming situations. I'd rather deal with zero degrees than 50 below. But it makes absolutely no sense to do this for the Don't bettor. I'd rather face 50 degrees than zero, which is exactly the Don't player's position once he has survived the negative Come Out segment of the game.

So are the mathematics wrong? No. The mathematics are right in theory, just as in theory the shortest distance between two points is a straight line. But there are no straight lines in reality, as Einstein proved, and because the odds bet must be placed **after** the Don't Bettor has survived the Come Out, it is only a mathematical *illusion* that it reduces the house edge—much like the straight line illusion in geometry! In reality, it waters down the Don't player's advantage just as taking the odds waters down the house's advantage against the Do player! If you think of the game in segments, you must do what is best for the segment that you are currently playing in. Thus, you do *take* the odds on the Do, and you don't *lay* the odds on the Don't.

Do on the Do. Don't on the Don't. That's a relatively easy maxim to remember.

The Oddsman's Bet

All the bets we have dealt with thus far at craps, each and every one of them, carry a long-term negative expectation for the player. Experts might quibble about the mathematics, or the best way to play, but no one denies that to win at craps you have to overcome a slight edge in favor of the casino. (I don't even consider the Crazy Crapper bets as a part of the craps landscape.)

However, there is one bet at craps that carries no vig or tax for the house, as we've seen, and that is the odds bet. Unfortunately, you can't take the odds without placing a Do bet on the layout and exposing yourself to the grinding effects of the casino's inexorable edge.

Or can you?

Well, once again, I have the Captain to thank for showing me that indeed you can place the odds into play without first putting up a Do bet—you can, that is, if you have class, charisma, and, more importantly, cajones!

You simply find a Pass Line bettor who has not taken the odds on his bet and politely ask him or her if you can proceed to do so. You will be surprised at how many people don't take the odds on a Pass Line bet, either because they can't afford to or just don't want to. So, you become the *Oddsman* and take the odds for them.

Of course, you will have to pick your players carefully. Some craps players will be suspicious of anyone wanting to place odds behind their bets—pass these people on by. However, if you have the verve and the nerve, the Oddsman's bet offers a very attractive opportunity for the guerrilla gambler— as you can hit with the odds and, let's hope, run with the win.

The Oddsman's bet, by it's very nature, is the ultimate guerrilla technique, and the Oddsmen and women of craps are the ultimate guerrilla craps players. In addition, with the explosion of Asian games in some casinos, and the Asian practices of piggybacking or backlining, the placing of oddsman's bets won't be such a strange event—eventually. Indeed, I have done it on occasion—without having anyone object (I pick my spots very, very carefully), and the lovely and charming AP does it with regularity.

Guerrilla Craps Techniques

I: Guerrilla Don'ting

We've covered everything you need to know to put into operation the guerrilla craps segment of your assault on the casino's bankroll. You have a number of attack options to choose from, each employing one or more of the Captain's betting techniques I've outlined.

The first guerrilla craps technique is called *Guerrilla Don'ting* because it requires you to bet the Don't part of the layout. Here you are looking to take advantage of one or more cold shooters.

As you scout out the craps area, look for a table where the majority of the players look glum and disaffected because this might indicate that the table has been cold. Since the majority of craps players are Do bettors it is a safe assumption that if the table is glum it's because the Do bettors are doing poorly. If you hear such comments as:

"Can't anyone here shoot those dice?"

"I'm getting killed!"

"This table is ice cold!"

"I'm getting blown away," you can be assured that the Do bettors are getting clobbered.

Now, glance at the bets. If a few players are playing the Don't portion and they seem reasonably contented, you are immediately going to place a Don't Come bet of one unit. Do not place a Don't Pass bet, even on the Come Out roll, because you don't want to get hit with a series of sevens and 11's by the same shooter. The tendency for Don't Pass bettors is to continue to throw out Don't Pass bets as a shooter hits a series of sevens and 11s on the Come Out. Sometimes the Don't Pass bettor even attempts a Martingale by doubling his previous bets. Don't do this. It's the surest way to dig a giant hole from which you will have trouble extricating yourself. So wait for the shooter to establish a point, then place a Don't Come bet.

One reason to see if there are several Don't bettors at a table has more to do with the psychology of the Don't player than anything else. Don't players don't stick around a table where they are getting clobbered. If you notice several Don't players at a table, it is a pretty good indication that they are doing well. If their presence is coupled with disgruntled Do players, then this table has been experiencing a cold streak. So look for satisfied Don't players.

If you go up on the number, then you can place another Don't Come bet. If you get up on two numbers, leave it at that. You do not want to suddenly find yourself facing a good roll with a lot of Don't bets out. Two are sufficient. If you lose those two, you are going to go to another table. Stay at the table for as long as you are winning. But once you have lost one bet on two shooters in a row or two bets back to back on the same shooter, leave.

However, if your shooter should roll a seven (thus, sevening out) when you place your Don't Come bet, you wait for the next shooter to finish his Come Out roll and then you place another Don't Come bet. If you lose that, you move on to another table or another game.

II: The Question of Streaks

Does the temperament of people at a table accurately predict what is going to happen in the near future? Does the fact that a table has been cold indicate that it will continue to be cold? Are past streaks indicative of future streaks? Is the fact that a shooter (who, we assume, can't control the outcome of the dice) has made nine points in a row indicative that he will make the next one? Of course not.

You could scout out a table where everyone betting Do has been getting clobbered, lay down your Don't Come bet, and suddenly experience the hottest shooter since the world began. But you need a criterion for judging which table to play at (even if that criterion is as cynical as "pick any table because who cares where you play?") and, since many seasoned gamblers have an unshakable faith in the power of streaks, why not use recent past performance as a criterion for a trend? Why not use what *has just happened* as a possible indicator of what will continue to happen? If it doesn't make any difference then it doesn't make any difference and you haven't hurt or helped your chances of winning. However, if there are such things as streaks, if tables have characteristics for somewhat extended periods of time, then you are in a good position to make some money. If it isn't so, so what? You aren't *increasing* the house's edge by using past performance as a guide to present conditions. It has no effect whatsoever.

I can't tell you that I think streaks are predictive. That is foolish. But I can tell you that streaks exist. I've experienced them (for good and ill) in all casino games. I've had hot streaks in blackjack where I couldn't lose a hand—when the decks favored the house! I've had cold streaks in blackjack jumping into games where the count was so high it had a fever—and lost hand after hand after hand. I've seen craps games where hours passed with no one making a point. I wish I could figure out a way to predict streaks—then I wouldn't have to write for a living. I'd just go to the casino, pick the streak of the day, and live happily and wealthily ever after.

Okay, so it isn't going to happen.

But I've had good players, solid, intelligent, successful players—from card counters in blackjack, to the Captain of craps himself—tell me that there are days when it just does or doesn't *feel* right. Should I deny the intuitions of seasoned pros? So I'm an agnostic when it comes to table selection, and streaks, trends, or whatever you want to call them. I take a middle course. I don't deny the existence of streaks, certainly, nor do I deny the *possibility* that a trend will continue. If you tell me that looking for hot or cold tables is irrelevant to my chances of winning or losing, then I'll look for hot or cold tables because it *can't* hurt me. (By the way, you could be really cynical and say that looking for hot or cold tables has to *help* you, since the time spent doing so decreases your playing time and, thus, decreases the inevitable drain on your bankroll from the casino's grinding edge at most games!) But I still say "God bless you" to someone who sneezes even though I know that the person isn't

---

on the verge of being inhabited by demons or of getting the plague. And I still like to play at a table that has been going in the direction that *I hope it will continue* to go in! It makes me feel better and what's so bad about that?

III: Guerrilla Doing—The 5-Count Pass and Come

Here you are going to make Pass Line and Come bets—after the shooter has successfully completed what the Captain calls the *5-Count*. This is of utmost importance because for Do betting you want to be reasonably assured that the shooter *is in the game*. An incredible number of shooters seven out quite soon after establishing their points. These shooters generally lose loads of money for themselves and everyone else at the table. If you are betting Don't, you love these shooters. If you are betting Do, you want to avoid them at all costs.

One way to avoid them is to set up criteria for deciding which shooters you will risk your money on. Almost anyone who has considered craps seriously realizes that if you bet every roll of every shooter you are inevitably doomed to be economically destroyed—sometimes in relatively short order. Thus, you have to pick what shooters you want to risk your money on. The picking of shooters falls into the same kind of category as streaks and hot and cold tables. Purists insist that any shooter is as good as any other shooter. I don't think this is so, nor does the Captain. There are good craps *shooters* and the problem is to figure out a way to find them. In *Beat the Craps out of the Casinos: How to Play Craps and Win!* I discuss the possibility of rhythmic rollers. These are individuals who, through practice or dumb luck, get into a non-seven groove. The problem is how to find them before all your money runs out. One way, of course, is not to bet on every shooter who comes along.

The Captain, through years of playing and observing craps games, literally stumbled upon his *5-Count* as I related in *Beat the Craps out of the Casinos: How to Play Craps and Win!* What the *5-Count* does is weed out the poor shooters in advance and position you to take advantage of *potentially* good shooters: those shooters who might be getting into a non-seven mode or rhythmic roll. For a fuller explanation, you'll have to refer to the above book but suffice it to say that the *5-Count* is the key to Do betting. Follow it religiously regardless of which guerrilla

Do betting program you select to implement.

In a nutshell the *5-Count* starts when a shooter first picks up the dice. If his first roll is a *point number*—four, five, six, eight, nine or 10—that is the 1-Count. If his roll is any other number, the count is still zero. The count only begins when the shooter rolls the first point number.

After the 1-Count, any number counts for the 2-Count, the 3-Count, and the 4-Count. However, to attain the *5-Count*, the next roll must be another *point number*. If the shooter should roll, say, an 11 after the 4-Count, then you are still on the 4-Count and *holding*. If the next roll is a two, then you are still on the 4-Count and holding. If the next roll is a four or any other point number, then you have achieved the *5-Count*.

Let's do a quick run to establish the dimensions of the *5-Count* solidly before moving on.

The shooter is on the Come Out roll.
Shooter rolls a three—no count
Shooter rolls a five—1-Count.
Shooter rolls an 11—2-Count.
Shooter rolls a six—3-Count.
Shooter rolls a 12—4-Count.
Shooter rolls a two—4-Count and holding.
Shooter rolls a nine—5-Count.

If the shooter sevens out before the *5-Count* (and you will be amazed at how many do and amazed at how much money you have saved and others have lost), then you must begin the process all over with another shooter.

However, during the *5-Count* process, if the shooter makes his point, you continue the count.

Let's go through that.
Shooter is on the Come Out roll.
Shooter rolls a six—1-Count.
Shooter rolls a six—2-Count (shooter made his point).
Shooter is on the Come Out.
Shooter rolls a seven—3-Count.
Shooter rolls a three—4-Count.
Shooter rolls a seven—4-Count and holding.
Shooter rolls an eight—5-Count.

The *5-Count* will protect you against ice-cold tables. Of course, it can't guarantee that you will win but it does position you to take advantage of hot rolls. Naturally, as in every system, there are flaws in the *5-Count*. Individuals can seven out on the 6-, 7- and 8-counts—when they have money at risk. But having played this way for a number of years now, I can tell you that the positive results of the *5-Count* easily outweigh the negative consequences of people sevening out just as you get up on some numbers. The *5-Count* is the best *cut* and *position* technique I have ever encountered for the game of craps. It *cuts* your losses due to cold shooters and *positions* you to take full advantage of hot shooters. Too many craps players are blown out by a series of shooters sevening-out within the first five rolls so that even a torrid shooter, if and when he comes along, can't get them out of the hole.

With all methods of play, however, your intelligence and free will enter the picture when it comes to proper application of *5-Count* betting. If you lose several times in a row after getting your money on the table, then quit craps for that session or at least move to another table. Do not be a fool and stay. If you find that you get blasted out after the *5-Count* several times running, then you better start running to a new venue.

Once the *5-Count* is completed, your betting begins. On the 6-Count, you place a Come bet or, if the shooter just made his previous point, a Pass Line bet for one unit. If a seven or 11 is thrown, you are a winner and up one unit. If a two, three or 12 is thrown, you have lost one unit.

You are looking for a win of 30 units for the session. After a win of 30 units you must determine if you want to take your win and leave or put 15 of it back and go for a larger win. This is up to you. However, don't allow yourself to lose more than 30 units on any given craps attack. Retreat and head for the hills.

(Note: If your unit of betting is $5 and you find yourself in a 10 times odds game, then bet $1 on the Pass Line or Come and put two units in odds when it goes up on the number. Your unit is still $5 but it is far better to have most of your money working in odds than on the Pass Line or Come.)

Once your Come or Pass Line bet is up on the number, you will take full odds. Now, place another Come bet. When this goes up on the number, again take full odds. Do this for a third number also.

Once up on three numbers, you will give the shooter four rolls in which to hit one of your numbers before taking them *off* for two rolls. This is called the *Law of Four*. You will place your numbers back *on* immediately when the shooter rolls a point number after the first *off* roll. Let's go through the procedure fully, taking into account the various kinds of scenarios that can occur. If you can follow the procedure, you should have no trouble being a guerrilla 5-Count Pass and Come Player.

Shooter's Come Out roll.

Shooter rolls a nine—1-Count.

Shooter rolls a three—2-Count.

Shooter rolls a five—3-Count.

Shooter rolls a five—4-Count.

Shooter rolls an 11—4-Count and holding.

Shooter rolls a two—4-Count and holding.

Shooter rolls a nine (making his point)—5-Count.

(*5-Count*—place a Come or Pass bet of one unit—in this case a Pass Line bet.)

Shooter rolls an 11—collect one unit win.

Shooter rolls a five—Pass bet with full odds.

(Place a Come bet of one unit on layout.)

Shooter rolls a six—Come bet goes up on six with full odds.

(Place a Come bet of one unit on layout.)

Shooter rolls a four—Come bet goes up on four with full odds.

(You now have the numbers four, five and six.)

Shooter rolls an 11—One-Roll with no decision.

Shooter rolls an eight—Two-Rolls with no decision.

Shooter rolls a two—Three-Rolls with no decision.

Shooter rolls a 10—Four-Rolls with no decision.

("My odds are off until I tell you.")

Shooter rolls a 10—One-Roll-Off.

Shooter rolls an 11—One-Roll-Off and holding.

(You are waiting for a point number to be rolled before going back on.)

Shooter rolls a nine—Two-Rolls-Off.

("My odds are working again.")

Shooter rolls a six—collect your bet and your win on six.

(Place a Come bet of one unit on the layout.)

Shooter rolls a five (making his point)—collect win on five.

(You are now up on two numbers: four and five.)

(Place a Pass Line bet of one unit.)

Shooter's Come Out roll.

Shooter rolls a seven—you win on the Pass Line and collect one unit.

You lose on the Come bets of four and five but your odds are returned because they are off during a Come Out Roll.

Shooter rolls a four—place full odds behind your Pass Line bet.

(Place a Come bet for one unit on the layout.)

Shooter rolls a 10—Come bet goes up on 10 with full odds.

Shooter rolls a 10—collect win on 10.

(You still have a Come bet on layout.)

Shooter rolls a 12—you lose your Come bet.

(Place a Come bet of one unit on the layout.)

Shooter rolls an eight—Come bet goes up on eight with full odds.

(You now have three numbers working—four, eight and 10.)

Shooter rolls an eight—collect original bet and win.

(Place a Come bet of one unit on the layout.)

Shooter rolls a six—Come bet goes up on six with full odds.

(You now have three numbers working: four, six, 10.)

Shooter rolls a nine—One-Roll with no decision.

Shooter rolls a three—Two-Rolls with no decision.

Shooter rolls an 11—Three-Rolls with no decision.

Shooter rolls a five—Four-Rolls with no decision.

("I'm off on my odds until I tell you.")

Shooter rolls a six—you win your Come bet but your odds are returned because they were off on this roll—One-Roll-Off.

Shooter rolls a two—One-Roll-Off and holding.

Shooter rolls a seven—sevening out.

You lose Pass Line and one Come bet but get back your odds.

Sometimes you will be up on two numbers and a shooter will roll a series of garbage numbers—twos, threes, 12s—while you're waiting patiently on the Come. If a shooter rolls four garbage numbers in a row, go off on your two bets until he rolls a point number to get you on a third Come bet. Then have your odds working on all three bets.

If you should really hit a hot shooter, you might want to spread to four or more numbers. You also might want to increase the size of your bets once you've made a hefty profit. If you are on four numbers, you will follow the *Law of Three* and go off for two rolls if none of your four numbers hits in the next three rolls.

In a double odds game, you can push the house to get a better bargain on the odds by betting $15 on the Pass and Come because many casinos will allow you to place $50 in odds behind the six and eight, $40 in odds behind the five and nine, and the regular double odds of $30 behind the four and 10. If you are a high roller and can afford a $30 Pass Line bet, you can take $100 in odds behind the six and eight, $80 behind the five and nine, and $60 behind the four and 10.

Of course, the bottom line with any betting is whether or not you can afford to make the wager. If a $15 Pass or Come bet makes you sweat, then don't make it. Getting better odds is not worth an anxiety attack.

IV: Guerrilla Place Betting for the high roller

If you are an action player (that is a polite way of saying that you are someone who is anxious to get into the action without waiting on the Come) and you can afford the amount of money necessary to utilize the Captain's Best Buys, then perhaps this next method of guerrilla wagering is for you.

You will still follow the *5-Count* procedure but you will get onto two or three numbers immediately upon the completion of the *5-Count*. This system of wagering is a follow-the-numbers type and it works like this: As soon as the *5-Count* is completed you Place and/or Best Buy the last two or three point numbers rolled.

Let's do a sample run
Shooter is on the Come Out.
Shooter rolls a seven—no count.
Shooter rolls a five—1-Count.
Shooter rolls a six—2-Count.
Shooter rolls a three—3-Count.
Shooter rolls a four— 4-Count.
Shooter rolls a nine—5-Count.

During this particular *5-Count*, the shooter rolled four point numbers—his initial point of five, followed by a six, a four and a nine. You will Place and/or Best Buy the last three numbers as follows:

Place the six for $42 (or $48, $54 or $60).
Buy the four for $39.
Buy the nine for $38.

At this point you follow the rule of four as stated in the previous Pass-Come section. If four rolls go by without the shooter making one of your numbers, you go *off* for two rolls.

I don't recommend going to four numbers initially because you are risking quite a bit of money. However, whenever you have four numbers working, be it initially or after a huge win, you will follow the *Law of Three* as do the guerrilla Pass and Come bettors: If three rolls go by without one of your numbers hitting, you will go off for two rolls.

Remember that many casinos have never seen the Captain's Best Buys so you might have to put up with a little attention from the pit when you make them. You might even hear a few snickers from veteran craps players when you buy the five or nine for $38. That's par for the course. The Captain has so revolutionized the game that you might feel somewhat uncomfortable being on the cutting edge. But don't let pit personnel perusal or player pokes prevent you from getting the best game for your money. You are not there to impress anyone, you are there to win money.

Of course, anyone who can afford to make the Best Buys should be accorded High Roller status by most casinos, so don't hesitate to ask for a full array of comps. And ask for them relatively early in your play because, if you hit a cold streak, you are going to leave the table fast.

And it's always a wise strategy to have your comp and beat it too!

V: Guerrilla Place Betting for the Low Roller

Not everyone can, should, or wants to be a high roller. Indeed, we in the gambling industry, no matter how wise, experienced or cynical; no matter which side of the table we are on, still imbue the words "high roller" with almost mystical connotations. Nothing could be further from the truth. A high roller just bets high, period. Yet when a man or woman is betting large sums, we automatically pause to watch. Some high rollers bet on one roll, or one turn of the cards, more money than some people make in a week or a month. Therein lies the fascination, I think: to see an amount of money equal or greater than we earn being wagered in a single instant. It takes the breath away.

Then to see these people lionized, fawned over, and patronized by the pit bosses, hosts, and hostesses makes the low roller feel—well, low. Big money in a casino usually means the big shot treatment. It's all phony, of course. The person getting the treatment is usually no 5th century Athenian philosopher-king, but just an average person who has a hell of an above-average income. And great money is no guarantee of great character. Some of the scummiest individuals I've ever met have been high rollers—yet these slime-turds are treated like gods, that is, they are treated like gods as long as they keep betting big.

When the casinos figure out some way to distinguish the high rollers with class from the high rollers who are merely crass, then maybe the high roller label will merit some moral distinction. Until then—unless the high roller has shown some high character, think of him or her as the human equivalent of a large bank where the casinos can make huge withdrawals. In truth, high rollers, while often treated with great dignity and affection, are looked upon by the casinos the way big, fat walruses are looked upon by killer whales—yummy meals to be devoured!

So for you low rollers, whether suffering from self-esteem problems or not, here's a good guerrilla Place betting procedure for you.

On the 5-Count, simply place the six and eight for $6, $12, $18, or $24 each. Allow the shooter five opportunities to hit one of them before calling them off for two rolls. If within five rolls the shooter makes one of them, start the count all over again. By placing the six and eight, you are only giving the house a 1.5 percent advantage. But you must use that 5-Count as the basis upon which to decide which shooters you will risk your money on. In the unlikely event that you hit a shooter who rolls sixes and eights until judgment day, you will press your bets one unit after you have made six hits on the combined numbers. If the dice gods are willing and you hit another six times, you press again and so forth until...well, until you win all the money the high rollers have lost!

Final Word and Recommended Reading

I enjoy playing craps. In fact, it's my favorite casino game. I've won more playing blackjack in my gambling career (I've also spent a hell of a lot more time at blackjack tables and for bigger stakes) but I have been quite successful at craps, too. Of course, this is not supposed to happen and I should be embarrassed as a self-respecting gambling writer to tell you that I am ahead at a game all experts know to be unbeatable. I should feel even more embarrassed to write about a man who is in his third decade of consistently beating the casinos at their own game.

I don't.

Not in the least.

In fact, I give full credit to the Captain who has taught me to keep my economic exposure small (I use the *5-Count* and the *Supersystem*) and my confidence large.

Except for the Oddsman's bet, there are no positive or neutral expectation bets in this game. Every bet has a house edge. I know this. You know this. The Captain knows this. Even if that edge is as small as two-tenths of a percent, as it is in some 10 times odds games on certain bets, if you were to theoretically play to infinity, that little edge would ultimately strip all the treasuries and banks of the world of their capital.

How is it then that individuals such as the Captain (Big Time) and myself (small time), among others following his principles, have long terms wins? I think it's because craps is not always what it appears to be. It is not always random. And its fluctuations can sometimes be ridden the way a surfer rides a wave. Some players have the ability to control the dice, consciously or unconsciously; there are such people as rhythmic rollers, and non-seven mode shooters. By following the Captain's *5-Count*, you limit your exposure to the horrendous shooters and that saves you money—a lot of money in the long run. Saving money is sometimes the key to winning money.

By going off shooters who aren't hitting your numbers, you also save a bundle. I can't tell you how many times I've called my bets off only to have the seven rear its ugly head. True, sometimes you call off your bets and they hit and, when you put them back on, the seven shows. But the former scenario, in my personal experience, far outweighs the latter.

If there are such things as rhythms in gambling, then craps is the most rhythmic game of all. The Captain firmly believes that the difference between winning and losing, when the house has a *slight edge*, is often not the house's edge but the edge to the player's personality. He believes that players have to impose their rhythms on the casinos, and not vice versa. The successful gambler, making the lowest house edge bets possible, can win in the long run if he can control himself. You can't get caught up in the casino's flow—then you drown.

That is why you must give yourself only so much money to play with and if you lose that—walk away. Even in games such as blackjack, where you can get a slight mathematical edge over the casino, you can hit a string of losses that can ruin you. Recognize the signs of your own internal casino and get away when that rhythm is not matching the rhythm of the casino game you are playing at the moment.

I know this is standard advice, but maybe there's a reason so many true professionals keep giving it—it happens to be true. So listen and follow it.

There are many books on craps, aside from my own, that I truly enjoyed reading. None of them are revolutionary, none of the authors or authorities have the insights into the game that the Captain has, but they are worth reading. I happen to enjoy reading interesting books by interesting people on games I find interesting. I'm sure you do, too. The following list is my recommended reading list of craps books *not* written by me. Read them for fun but if you are looking for the ultimate in insight and techniques—you must go with the Captain.

Casino Gambling for the Winner by Lyle Stuart. Lyle Stuart, Inc., Carol Publishing, 600 Madison Ave., New York, NY 10022. ($9.95) If you want to experience the game as a high roller; if you want to get inside the head of a big time gambler from the old school, then you'll enjoy this book. Although there is a section on baccarat, the book focuses on craps, Stuart's passion, and he delivers in his prose all the passion he feels about the game and how to play it. An enjoyable read.

The Dice Doctor (Revised & Expanded) by Sam Grafstein. GBC Press, 630 South 11th Street, Box 4115, Las Vegas, NV 89127. Sam Grafstein is an original—in every way. You will either love this book...or hate it...but it is like no other gambling book out today. I loved it. I've been a fan of Grafstein's for years and when I got an opportunity to meet him at the Gambler's Book Shop during an autograph session I was giving, I was as excited as a kid meeting one of his idols. I had heard that Grafstein could be cantankerous and sharp with other writers ("so-called experts") but he was gracious and we had a wonderful conversation. This book won't teach you how to play (Grafstein assumes you know what's up) but it will take you on a trip into the mind of a legendary craps player and how he sees the game. Grafstein has his own unique writing style and you will either love it or hate it. Try it. (During the writing of this book, Sam Grafstein passed away. Another great legend from the Depression and World War II era has left us. We'll never see their like again. So long, Sam!)

Loaded Dice: The True Story of a Casino Cheat by John Soares. Taylor Publishing Company, 1550 W. Mockingbird Lane, Dallas, TX 75235. ($9.95) This is a fun book by one of the great crossroaders (casino cheats) of all time. Although it covers cards and other scams, it focuses its greatest attention on how Soares and his band of renegades stole millions from casinos at the dice tables. Fascinating reading about a life on the edge. Wouldn't want to live it but sure as hell enjoyed reading about it. I think you will, too. There is something inherently fascinating about rogues.

Gambling Secrets of Nick the Greek by Ted Thackrey. Rand McNally & Company, New York, NY. ($5.95) I don't know if this book is still in print but it is a fascinating look at one of the legends of gambling. Has an interesting section on craps, although it covers many games. Nick the Greek's "secrets" are well-known and deal with streaks, money management, and understanding the odds. Before the Captain, there was Nick the Greek.

CHAPTER THIRTEEN

The Fundamentals of Poker

Poker is America's most popular card game and has been since the 1850s when card sharks roamed the bars, saloons, mining camps, and riverboats of the south and west. More poker games have been featured in movies than any single form of gambling and poker is the third most popular indoor pastime behind sex and television. Indeed, poker even invaded the sacrosanct precincts of the libido and a version of it called strip poker was all the rage in the 1950s and 1960s. In fact, more Americans have played poker than have played tennis, jogged, played softball or skied.

My guess is that *most* people have played poker at some time in their lives either with the family as little kids, or in school or college with their friends, or at work, or in "friendly" neighborhood games with acquaintances. Some of you have played for big stakes, some for nickels and dimes, some for match sticks.

Despite its raging popularity, however, very

few casual players really understand the basics of the game, and the overwhelming majority of these, perhaps 90 percent or better, are long term losers. Of course, if you are playing strip poker, losing can be fun; you might even say that losing can be winning. But when you are playing real poker in a casino against really skilled players—players who look at you the way the great white shark in *Jaws* looked at swimmers—then poker can strip you of your dignity and your dineros!

You might be a good player with your friends, you might think of yourself as a knowledgeable and apt observer of the playing foibles of your relatives. You might, in all objectivity, be a fairly competent player. So what often happens the first time a "good" neighborhood player walks into a casino poker room and plunks his money down? He's clobbered...but good!

He's clobbered especially if he plays in games with "regulars"—that is, with people who play a particular casino and/or game daily. He's clobbered if he spends too much time at a table chasing his losses. He's clobbered because the poker sharks see him for what he really is—human chum.

And don't be fooled by the size of the stakes. You will find many excellent poker players playing the low-stake games—waiting for "good" neighborhood players just like you, chum, to feast on. Casino poker is a cut-throat enterprise and should not be attempted unless you are thoroughly prepared—technically and psychologically. Despite the fact that poker can *theoretically* offer the expert player long range wins, very few poker players, expert or otherwise, actually make their livings from playing this game. Very few people can win at it. And, thus, it is not a game to enter lightly.

There are many different kinds of poker games. There are the traditional five card draw and five card stud games. These are no longer that popular and you won't see them as much in casinos, although you will see them in all those great old black and white movies about the wild, wild west. There are all the variations of poker that can be found in your local neighborhood games (*sixes and fives are wild except on a Thursday following a Wednesday where the temperature was below 40, then deuces and nines are wild except if the barometer reaches...*). However, by far the two most popular casino poker games are seven card stud and Texas hold'em. In fact, if you master the concepts of both these games you are in a good position to master most other casino poker games, since most are simply variations of them.

For the guerrilla gambler, you have a better shot at taking the poker pot in seven card stud and Texas hold'em than in any other poker game because you will be able to find these games more often. The guerrilla poker player is not like a "regular" poker player as I shall show you in the next chapter. The guerrilla poker player is like the feeder fish who feed right from the teeth of the sharks—without getting eaten.

However, a little review is in order.

Poker Overview

The object of poker is simply to win the pot. You can do this by either having the best hand or by convincing the other players that you have the best hand and force them to drop out. This latter technique is the classical *bluff* and it is greatly overused. (By the way, in some forms of poker the *best* hand is the *worst* hand!)

In neighborhood and higher stake games, it is customary for everyone to ante a certain small amount of money into the pot before the play of the hand. In many casino seven card stud games, usually for lower to moderate stakes, either the highest or lowest first up-card will have to make a predetermined minimum bet since there is no ante. Usually in Texas hold'em a blind is used. One, sometimes two, predesignated players, put up a small ante before the round begins. The blinds are usually rotated in a clockwise fashion around the table.

The goal of both seven card stud and Texas hold'em is to make the best five card hand.

The Ranking of Poker Hands

Royal Flush: 10, jack, queen, king and ace of the same suit.

Straight Flush: Any five cards of the same suit in sequence. If there are two or more straight flushes, the hand with the highest cards wins.

Four of a Kind: With four aces the highest ranking of this type and four twos the lowest ranking of this type.

Full House: Three of a kind and two of a kind. The highest ranking three of a kind wins. Thus, three kings and two twos beats three queens and two jacks.

Flush: Any five cards of the same suit. If two or more players hold a flush, the flush with the highest card(s) wins.

Straight: Five cards in sequence not of the same suit. If two or more players hold straights, the highest ranking straight wins.

Three of a Kind: Three cards of the same rank. Three aces is the highest of this type, three twos is the lowest of this type.

Two Pair: Two cards of one rank and two cards of another rank. If two players have two pair, the player with the higher ranking pair wins. If both players have the same higher ranking pair, then the player with the higher lower ranking pair wins. If in the unlikely event that both players have the same two pair, the player with the higher fifth card wins.

One Pair: Two cards of one rank. If two players have one pair, the highest ranking pair wins. If two players have the same one pair, the rank of the other cards determines the winner.

Highest Card: If no one has a pair, the player with the single highest card wins. If two or more players share the same highest ranking card, then the player with the second highest ranking card wins, and so on. Thus, an ace-king beats an ace-queen.

Poker Procedures

There is generally a set of procedures for the smooth running of a poker game. The dealer is in charge of seeing that these procedures are followed. Recently at the Biloxi Belle, a riverboat casino in Mississippi, I made a very embarrassing and amateurish blunder that cost me money and made the difference between having a winning poker day and a losing poker day. There were only two of us left in the pot. I had three of a kind, with two of the three hidden, and my opponent had a pair showing. I figured he had either a three of a kind of lower value or two pair, based upon his play.

He made his final bet. I was going to see it and raise it. But someone had just asked me for the ashtray near me, distracting me (never interrupt a player playing a hand) and I forgot to call out my raise. Instead, I had placed a bet equal to his bet in front of me and fumbled for a moment getting the raise out. Immediately the dealer pushed back my raise, scolded me for not at least calling it out, told me I would not be able to raise. Thus, I was forced to call. I won the hand. The other player did have two pair. But he said to me: "I'm glad you screwed up. I thought you only had a high pair because we were the only two in the pot. I would have reraised you!" And I would have reraised him. And I thought to myself, what a jerk I am—I would have won a nice little sum had he and I done our little raise and reraise dance, a sum that would have been the difference between being up about $100 that day in poker or down $10. But I had violated poker procedures and I was punished for it.

When you are betting, you must bet in a predetermined sequence depending on the rules of the game. In seven card stud, the person with the high hand will make a bet and then everyone around the table starting with the player to his left will get an opportunity to make a bet of equal size, or raise the bet, or fold. A player who acts out of turn can actually influence the play of the other players. In Texas hold'em, the first *live* player to the left of the *dealer* makes the initial wager after the first round blinds are over. A live player is one who hasn't dropped out of the game on a previous round. The "dealer" in hold'em is actually the player designated by the "button" which goes around the table in a clockwise fashion so that every player gets to be the "dealer" and act last on his hand. (Of course, the real dealer deals the cards.)

Another important thing to remember is never to throw your chips into the pot. Simply place them on the table near the pot so the dealer can see that you have either matched or raised the previous bets. If you are going to raise, do so at once and call it. Say: "Raise." Don't put a partial bet out and then return to your pile for more chips. Remember my idiotic play above and how it cost me? Also, be prepared to make a move when it is your turn. Do your thinking when the other players are making their moves. Don't be frimping and frumping when it is your turn to act.

Although you can raise your hole cards off the table, the casinos want you to keep the cards in front of you and over the table; this way there is no possibility of substituting cards from your sleeve, or wherever, into the game. A rule that might seem strange to some, but is strictly enforced, concerns the chips in front of you. If you are running out of chips but you still want to be in the pot at the end, you cannot take more money out of your pocket. You simply say, "I'm all in." If you should win the pot you will win all the money up to that moment—even though others may have bet more.

Two other traditions hold at casino poker tables, although not everyone follows them to the letter. Don't talk about your hand, whether discarded or active, and tip the dealer after you win a pot. Some annoying poker players, sometimes as part of their poker-player-persona or just because they're irritating idiots, will keep a running chatter about this and that, about what cards they have or haven't got, what you have or haven't got, and quite often the dealer and other players won't tell them to shut up. Technically they aren't doing anything but speculating out loud. In reality, if the player is a sharpie, he's looking for "tells"—a tell being your face or body language revealing what you have in your hand. As for tipping the dealer, that's protocol after a winning bet—if you find that the dealer is friendly and professional. However, if the dealer is an arrogant bore—as a small fraction of dealers can be—then the only tip he should receive is how to improve his personality.

Seven Card Stud Procedures

Seven card stud is one of the most detailed and complicated of all poker games because of the sheer number of hands that can be made from seven cards. In addition to its complexity, it can be a very expensive game, having five betting rounds, each involving potential raises and reraises. Because three cards are hidden, the other players' hands are difficult to compute. This adds to the game's volatility and the roller-coaster effects on your bankroll.

The game begins with each player being dealt two cards face down. These are called hole cards. A third card is dealt face up. In games with antes, the person with the highest face-up card gets to start off the betting. He can make a wager; he can check (indicate he won't make a wager but will remain to see if anyone else bets); or he can fold immediately. Sometimes if a player has a poor hand, say a two and a six of different suits in the hole with a 10 of a different suit exposed, he'll check to see if any other player wants to bet. If no one bets, he can get a fourth card for free and maybe begin making a hand.

All players will have an opportunity to match or raise the total bet as the play goes around the table. Or they can fold.

When the betting finishes, a second round is dealt face up. Now the best two card hand initiates the betting. Another round of raises, reraises and folds ensues.

A third round is dealt face up with the same procedures as before.

Now, a fourth round is dealt face up with the same procedures as before.

On the fifth round of play, the card is dealt face down. ("Down and dirty.") The final round of betting begins. All remaining players now have four cards face up and three cards in the hole.

Every casino has its own limits concerning how much can be bet on any given round, how many raises and reraises are allowed and so on. It's best to check the posted signs and ask questions if you aren't sure what the limits and betting procedures entail. You could easily find yourself in a game that looks affordable but is actually way over your head.

Texas Hold'em Procedures

Like seven card stud, Texas hold'em is a game where you have to make the best five card poker hand out of seven cards. However, the difference ends there because in hold'em all players share five face-up cards.

The round begins with one player designated as the "dealer" and the two players to his left putting up blinds of a predetermined amount. The cards will be dealt by the real dealer starting with the player to the immediate left of the "designated dealer." Now every player is given two cards face down. The player to the left of the blind now decides whether to see the blind, or raise, or fold. All players execute their judgments in order going clockwise around the table.

When the betting is over, the dealer will "flop" three cards face up in the center of the table. Now another betting round ensues. Next, the dealer will turn over a single card face up with another betting round following. Finally, the dealer will turn over a seventh card and the final round of betting takes place.

The "hows" of playing procedures for both seven card stud and Texas hold'em are a lot easier than "how" to play the hands. Unlike most casino games, your opponent is not just the odds of making a given hand, and knowledge of the odds is only partially helpful; your real opponents are the other players. Indeed, you have to know people as well as percentages to stand a chance of winning at either seven card stud or Texas Hold'em.

You especially have to know *yourself*.

CHAPTER FOURTEEN

Guerrilla Poker

I am an expert in poker because I know one secret about the game that no one else in the whole world knows (until this moment, that is): I know exactly how Frank Scoblete plays and feels and thinks. In fact, I know just how *bad* he is at the game. That is my big *advantage*.

That's right. I know my limitations. If I played poker every day for six or seven hours, going head to head with the same expert players day in, day out, year in and year out, I'd be begging quarters outside the Mirage instead of eating gourmet meals there.

Poker players of the traditional type are born, not made. I truly believe this. They have talent, tenacity, single-mindedness, and an almost suicidal stoicism about wins and losses. Money is simply how they keep score.

But talent is only one half of their winning equation. Coupled with that comes experience. It is rare to find a truly great poker player who hasn't been teethed on the game—just as it is rare to find a great basketball player, violinist, ballet dancer or writer who wasn't nurtured on his or her art. The greatest of the great have focused themselves so narrowly on their particular area of expertise that they can be supremely limited. Many great poker players I've encountered will not win humanitarian awards or be nominated for Nobel prizes. But they can beat the living daylights out of suckers who flock to the poker rooms of America to test their skill.

True poker players are killers. Fanatics.

They have been programmed by nature and experience to size up their prey (you) and pounce. That's it. That's the be-all and end-all of their existence. Want to talk about a great new novel? Want to discuss the philosophical implications of recent developments is biology? Want to share a great idea about the nature of the physical universe? Don't go to a poker player. Want to enjoy the delightful torment of a mouse being slowly shredded by a cat? See a poker player. Want to size up a political situation that could explode into violence? Talk to a poker player. Is it any wonder that some of our greatest foreign policy presidents were poker players? Truman dropped the atomic bomb—he wasn't bluffing and he called the Japanese on their hand!

I'm not like that. I actually don't enjoy playing poker with friends or even acquaintances. I feel funny if I win. Not funny ha! ha! but funny—sad. I love taking money from casinos. I rejoice in it. I just feel strange taking money from my fellow gamblers. It's a weakness with me. I want to see *people* win and corporations lose. That's why I love the games where you go head to head against the casino. So call me Don Quixote.

Even in Las Vegas, where I have done the bulk of my poker playing against total strangers, I have sometimes felt guilty about winning. I remember I was playing hold'em at the Maxim at a table filled with colorful characters. This particular hand boiled down to me against a woman of indeterminate age, but certainly her best days were behind her—if she had ever had any best days. She was dripping in gold (as many poker players are—they are like generals and gold is the indicator of their mettle) but she was leathery-skinned, constantly smoking and mostly toothless. Her lips were a little too wet and her skin a little too dry. She had a cackling voice and a terrible smoker's cough.

We were head to head.

She was a great player. I had seen her at the Maxim every day. I'm not a great player. She eyed me like a buzzard eyes decaying flesh. I raised her bet, she raised me, I raised her. She raised me. I called on the last round, going all in. In fact, she was down to her last few remaining chips too.

On the table (in the order in which they flopped) were a pair of fours, a 10, a queen, and a six. She called.

She turned over her cards—two queens! She had a full house: three queens and two fours. She had a smirk on her face and a little drool coming down the side of her chin. I turned over my hole cards—a pair of fours! I had four fours.

She coughed.

The other players at the table laughed.

One man, in a cowboy hat and dime-store cowboy regalia, himself dripping with gold, laughed loudly, then coughed phlegmily. Another man, grizzled, gnarled but gold plated nevertheless, cackled.

"He fixed your butt!" guffawed a big man with a big belly.

I collected my winnings—a tidy sum—and got up to go. The woman was eyeing me—her face a death mask.

"Hey," said the big man with the big belly, "you go in on one hand and now you leave?"

"I'm meeting friends for dinner at Da Vinci's," I said truthfully. Da Vinci's is the Maxim's gourmet restaurant. I am polite. I didn't like the big man with the big belly. I didn't particularly care for the guy in the cowboy suit when he laughed at the woman. If I hadn't been so well brought up as a child I might have made a caustic remark. But no, I was polite. Inside, however, I wished that it had been the big man with the big belly that I had beaten and not the woman. *That* is the sign of a bad poker player, by the way, wanting to beat someone because they irritate you or because you don't like them.

The woman lit up a cigarette. She still eyed me. I took my chips and went to the cage.

And that's why I'm a bad poker player. I take people personally. And poker is the most personal of games. One moment you are yucking it up at a table with people and the next you are severing their jugulars and drinking their blood and watching them twitch in torment as you delightedly rake in the pot.

The great poker players enjoy this. Treacherous by nature

and nurture, they would metaphorically bluff their own mothers out of the rent money if it meant winning a pot.

Yet I play poker. I play it frequently when I'm in Vegas or on the riverboats. But I am a guerrilla poker player. I play for a half an hour at most (that's a half hour *per* day), or until I've entered one or two hands. Then I leave, win, lose or draw. The next day, I play again, at a different casino against different players. If I'm in Vegas for a month or more, as I often am, I'll play almost every poker room in town. I don't return to a previous venue until another visit—and then I play whatever game I hadn't played on my last visit. So one visit is a seven card stud visit, the next is a Texas hold'em visit.

I try not even to talk to the other players, except to nod at the friendly ones who welcome me with comments as I sit down. I always play nervously, whether for big stakes or small stakes, because truthfully I am nervous. Why hide it? Poker is not my game.

I rarely bluff. I rarely go in on bad hands. I want to win just one pot and walk away. When I look at my poker stats, they read in general like this: two, three, and four days of small losses due to blinds or initial bets on promising hands that I discarded on the next round because I felt they weren't playable. One day of a nice pot, two days of small pots. Weekly win? Triple digits. Not bad for three and a half hours of work! On occasion, I've gone into pots where I thought I had the best hand only to get my butt "fixed" and those weeks might have shown a loss.

The longest I ever stayed at a poker table was 48 minutes. The shortest were the times that I won the very first hand. I left to the general grumblings and disdainful looks of the table.

The other players are irritated when you enter a game and leave. It doesn't give them a chance to size you up. If you only go in on a hand or two, they don't know when you go all in on the "shootout" (the last hand), just what kind of player you are. Are you bluffing? Is your face screwed up with tension because you are afraid of losing on a hand that you think can be beaten? Or is that your normal screwed-up face? The better poker players are masters of odds and personalities. They want to size *you* up as well as sizing up the pot. I don't give them the chance.

I wear my emotions as they come. I don't do poker faces. I look at my cards, look at the other players' cards (or the community cards), and I don't care if the other players see my eye-brows screw up as I try to figure out what others are working on and what my chances are of winning—and running.

I don't like the game—I like money—and I don't like some of the people who play the game. They aren't like me. We have different rhythms. I do enjoy beating certain loud mouths, certain "types" whom I've learned to despise in my years of play. Then it's fun to win and run and leave them glaring at you. But sometimes I enter a game with the nice guy from Cleveland who plays hands he shouldn't but, what the hell, he's in Vegas! Let it all hang out! Then I feel like a thief as I take him to the cleaners.

Here is a second secret I've learned. In the short run of cards, the greatest poker players in the world can be beaten. I can beat them. So can you. Once. Period. I don't give good poker players a couple of shots at me. If I did, I'd be foolish and I'd be broke.

So if you aren't a poker player by nature, despite your success at the neighborhood game, then guerrilla poker just might be for you.

Guerrilla Seven Card Stud

The most important decision you will make in seven card stud is whether to go in after receiving your first three cards. Poor players automatically go in figuring (hoping) that they'll make a hand as they proceed, that something will come up. This is the single biggest mistake in seven card stud and accounts for the majority of players being long term losers. Patience is the ultimate poker virtue.

You should only consider entering a pot if you have one of the following three card hands. These are the dirty dozen.

The Dirty Dozen

1. any three of a kind
2. any three cards to a straight flush
3. three high cards to a flush
4. a pair of aces or kings in the hole

5. a pair of aces or kings with one showing
6. a pair of queens or jacks in the hole
7. three cards to a flush
8. three high cards in sequence
9. a pair of queens or jacks with one showing
10. any pair in the hole
11. any pair with one showing *if no other player shows that card!*
12. any three cards in sequence

Now, although I say these are the dirty dozen, many of them are not absolutes. For example, if seven players are playing and you have three hearts and all six of the other players are showing hearts then your chances of getting a flush are almost non-existent—throw away the hand. Indeed, if only three players are showing hearts, your chances of making the hand are remote. So you must use common sense in applying the dirty dozen, especially after number seven. Look around the table, and when in doubt, drop out.

In fact, at any time in the contest between you and the other players, if you have failed to make your hand—quit. Even on the very last round, if you don't have the cards, gracefully bow out. Never think that just because you have come this far you might as well see it through. That's suicidal logic. Losing less, even on the last hand, means you will win more when the pot goes your way.

The average winning hand in seven card stud is three nines. With this in mind, as you assess your developing hand, realize that it should have the potential to beat three nines. If you are on the fifth round and you can't make a straight or a flush, and you don't have a high pair, fold, even if the other players aren't showing anything.

Know your opponents. How can you do this if you haven't played against them before and you are only sitting down for a half hour or so? Check out the players beforehand. When I know I'm going to be playing in a given casino that day, I make a point of going to the card room and casing it—at least two hours before I play. I look at the players faces. Then I'll go about my business for the next couple of hours. But I remember the faces, so that when I return, I take a quick look around and see if the same people are playing. If they are, I go over to the table of the game I wish to play that has the greatest number of familiar faces and I buy in.

Here is my belief: The people who have been playing for a few hours are getting the hang of each other; they're in the process of sizing each other up as players. In fact, some of them have known each other for years and years. The great thing about many poker players, for the purposes of guerrilla gambling, is that they love to talk and share with the world their insights into their opponents' foibles. So I keep my ears open and my mouth shut at a table.

After buying in, it is unusual that I'd be going all the way in on the first hand because the cards don't usually favor me so quickly. So I observe how the players talk to one another. When a player raises a certain other player is it because the other player is loose in his play? A loose player is one who goes in on poor hands. Certainly I'm not going to get a read on everyone at the table—but many of the people have a read on each other. It is easier to read someone *else's* read on another player than to build one up of your own in a short time.

"Say, Jim, you bluffing again?"

(Jim likes to bluff? He's been caught? Will he try to bluff me if we go head to head at the end?)

"Maybe you should quit, Sarah, you're getting killed today."

"Tell me," says Sarah as she loses a pot to a full house and she has a low pair. Is Sarah chasing? Is she making stupid plays to get her money back? Is she desperate enough to go after the new player (me) figuring that the nervous guy can't play?

Another thing I like to find out is how long the players have been playing that day. A tired player is a loose player. Fatigue makes poor players of us all. That's why I choose my playing time carefully. I like to play late afternoons or early evenings—at the tail end of the day-players' sessions but before the night crawlers come out to feast on players like me! I usually play my half hour somewhere between 5 pm and 6:30 pm.

One thing I have written on the tablets of my heart is to never, never, ever, try to bluff a loose player. Many players, especially those just in town for a day or two, are so happy to be playing that they almost don't seem to care that they are losing money. They'll go all in with you on hands that are awful. Try to bluff them and you will have lost a small fortune. And when you win because everyone has dropped out, never show your hand. Whether you had the cards or not is your business.

So now, you sit down and fifteen minutes into your guerrilla session, you get the cards and it looks as if a good hand is in the making. What do you do? Don't be afraid to bet them, and don't be overly concerned that you might be driving people out of the pot early. Good. It's better to take a small pot early than to loose a big pot to some idiot who hung in on a mediocre hand only to have Lady Luck bless him with several fabulous hits in the latter rounds. So as a general rule, don't try to be slick and lure players into staying in a pot—especially if your hand can be beaten by fortuitous hits.

If you start with three of a kind and several people stay in on the first round and, on the second round, you pair your up card—bet it, don't check. Otherwise, the good player will leave figuring you're trying to keep him in. If you bet it, the good player with a decent hand will figure you're strong but you're trying to eliminate everyone because you don't have the goods—as yet! So the good player will stay in.

What happens if you go all in and you lose? That's it for this session of guerrilla poker.

As a guerrilla poker player, you have a great psychological edge. No one knows how you play. You are an enigma. On a good hand many of the players will stay with you just to see if you are a bluffer or not. They don't know that you are there for a little while and that soon you'll be gone. They figure they have time to analyze you and your play. So some will stay in a hand just to get a read on you. Use that to your advantage.

Here are general guidelines for the playing of hands. The fewer players there are in the pot, the more likely a smaller valued hand will win. The more people in a pot, the greater the likelihood that a higher valued hand will win. If you have two aces on the first three cards, one exposed and one in the hole, and only two people stay in the hand—those two aces are a powerful hand against your two opponents. If no one folds, and there are several raises and reraises, those two aces are not going to win—unless you can get the third one and/or pair another card.

You have to be aware of those people who have a chance for a flush or a straight. Unlike blackjack, you are allowed to count the cards in poker. There are 13 cards of the same suit.

Your opponent has three hearts showing of his four up cards. You have a heart in the hole. There are six more hearts on the table. That's a total of 10 hearts. That means there are three hearts unaccounted for. Is it likely that two of his three hole cards are hearts? No. Especially not, if he wasn't betting big when the second heart came out as one of his up cards. *Most* especially not if he wasn't betting big *and* the other players didn't as yet have those hearts exposed.

I do believe that seven card stud can make a decent, but not great, player small profits if approached in the guerrilla fashion. It has for me. But if you intend to put in hours at the poker tables, you had better be better than decent, you had better be downright good, or you should enjoy losing money.

Guerrilla Hold'Em

Like seven card stud, Texas hold'em should only be played for a half hour at a clip. If you can't get a decent hand in that time, then leave and live to play another day. Again, there are certain hands that you should go in on and the rest you should throw in. Remember that in Texas hold'em you are dealt two cards face down. Then a betting round begins with the player to the immediate left of the blind. If you have any of the following two card hands, you will stay in to see the "flop" after the first round of betting.

The Top Twenty-Five Hands

There is some debate among the experts of the game as to the order of importance of some of the initial two card hands. But the general consensus would certainly support the list you are about to read. There might be quibbles as to whether one two card hand should be ranked higher than another two card hand but these 25 hands are the only ones you will risk money on in the initial betting round (with one exception: If you are the blind and no one raises, you stay in to see the flop on any hand since you are already in the pot!).

1. a pair of aces
2. a pair of kings

3. a pair of queens
4. an ace and a king of the same suit
5. an ace and a king of different suits
6. an ace and a queen of the same suit
7. an ace and a jack of the same suit
8. a king and a queen of the same suit
9. an ace and a queen of different suits
10. a pair of jacks
11. a king and a queen of different suits
12. an ace and 10 of the same suit
13. a king and a jack of the same suit
14. a queen and a jack of the same suit
15. a pair of 10s
16. a jack and a 10 of the same suit
17. an ace and a jack of different suits
18. a king and a 10 of the same suit
19. a king and a jack of different suits
20. a queen and a jack of different suits
21. a 10 and a nine of the same suit
22. a pair of nines
23. a queen and 10 of the same suit
24. a nine and eight of the same suit
25. an eight and seven of the same suit

Although the initial two card hand is important in hold'em, it is not as important as the initial three cards in seven card stud. For example, if you have the highest rated two card hand, a pair of aces, and the flop falls eight, nine, 10 of spades and there are several raises and reraises, you would be wise to fold your two aces because there are a multitude of ways you can be beaten on the next two rounds of play.

You have to be aware of the potential hands against you based upon the community cards. If you are working on a straight of a lower order, someone might just have that straight high. So be aware of the hands that can hurt you.

The best piece of advice I can give you, aside from playing the strongest hands, has to do with positioning. In seven card stud it is irrelevant where you sit at the table since the highest hand will initiate the betting. However, in hold'em there is a fixed position of betting based on who has the blind. When I sit down I try to get as close to the designated dealer's right as I can. That means I'm furthest away from the blind. This does two things. Initially, I will be last to act on my hand. After the flop, that is a very good position to be in. Of course, the longer I stay at the table, the worse my positioning becomes but my knowledge of the players is a little better.

Also, if I win an early pot and leave, I won't have to pay the blind since I'm history by the time the blind gets around to me! The more blinds you don't pay, the better. Of course, after the flop, if you don't have a good hand—fold. Those suited high cards were great—until the dealer flopped three cards of the same suit of a suit you don't have. But someone else might. Fold.

You will only go in on a potentially strong hand and you will only stay in on a potentially strong hand. I have found that I have a couple of sessions every week where I never get to the final round. Indeed, I have sessions where I never get to the flop! But that's the way it goes.

I don't have that stoic attitude about money. I don't mind playing and not getting into the action if the cards aren't coming. In short, I do not mind *not* losing. My poker future is all in the cards. Yours should be, too.

Recommended Reading

There are more books about poker than there are about blackjack or any other game. It is a field rich in research, history, lore, and baloney. The following books are the very best I've read on the subject, either for their playing strategies, insights, or colorful descriptions of life as a player. There are many more good books available as well. Beware, however. Some of the best poker players haven't read any of these books.

The poker world, be it small stakes play, large stakes play, or tournament play, and its literary offshoots, is a study in contrast. The most brilliant analysts and mathematicians and theorists are often beaten by illiterate and/or uncouth bores. The little pipsqueak often tames the loud-mouthed oilman in the final shootout. Geniuses in business, math, and science sit shoulder to shoulder with individuals who have never held a job. It's wonderful. It's the way of it. Most of the writers of poker books, unlike many of the pundits of craps and blackjack, actually *play* the game on a fairly continuous basis—as opposed to simply theorizing about it. They have a certain experience to go along with their computer work. As such, they have been burned in the fires of actual competition and are twice shy. I like this. It makes for good advice—sans pomposity. The following books are not the only books on the subject that should be read but they are the books that will give you everything you need to know to *start* entertaining some serious ideas about poker.

7 Card Stud: The Waiting Game by George Percy. Spiral Bound. GBC Press, 630 South 11th St., Box 4115, Las Vegas, NV 89127. ($8.95) Eighty pages loaded with excellent information for the beginning and intermediate seven card stud player. Percy knows the game and writes with precision. A must read if you are going into the card rooms for the first time.

Seven Card Stud for Advanced Players by David Sklansky, Mason Malmuth, and Ray Zee. GBC Press, 630 South 11th St., Box 4115, Las Vegas, NV 89127. ($29.95) This book is just what it says it is—for advanced and very serious players. You will have to read it slowly and more than once to digest all the excellent information. I like this book because it showed me how expert players *think*. If you are serious about risking money in extended seven card stud play, then this is the book for you.

Hold'Em Poker by David Sklansky. GBC Press, 630 South 11th St., Box 4115, Las Vegas, NV 89127. ($17.50) Sixty-four important pages of information for anyone who wants to learn this challenging game. Sklansky presents his ideas well.

Hold'Em Poker for the Advanced Player by David Sklansky and Mason Malmuth. GBC Press, 630 South 11th St., Box 4115, Las Vegas, NV 89127. ($29.95) The expert's guide to this game. Like their book on seven card stud, this will require several readings and an attentive attitude. The premier book on the subject.

Big Deal: A Year as a Professional Poker Player by Anthony Holden. Viking Penguin, 375 Hudson St., New York, NY 10014.

($19.95) Anthony Holden is that rare bird—an expert poker player and a fabulous, professional writer and translator. I think this is my favorite book about poker although it never teaches you how to play. It is Holden's story and it's a good one. You'll find it difficult to put it down.

The Education of a Poker Player by Herbert O. Yardley. Oldcastle Books, Ltd., 18 Coleswood Rd., Harpenden, Herts AL5 1EQ. ($9.95) One of the golden oldies of poker and a terrific read. It is the education of a poker player—for sure. You'll learn about a time in America that few people remember anymore.

The Biggest Game in Town by A. Alvarez. Houghton Mifflin Company, 2 Park Street, Boston, MA 02108. ($9.95) Another great writer, like Holden, and a friend of same. Alvarez takes you on a journey into the poker rooms of Vegas like no one has, before or since. A great read. He'll introduce you to all the famous and infamous characters who haunt the card rooms and you'll meet many of the living legends of the game.

Professional 7-Stud Report by Mike Caro. Self-published, Signal Hill, CA. ($19.95) A 32 pager packed with good information for the beginning and intermediate player. Analyzes ploys and strategies used by other players. This book is designed to fine tune your tactical and psychological game. Mike Caro is dubbed the "mad genius" of gambling. His advice is quite sane.

Caro's Fundamental Secrets of Poker by Mike Caro. Mad Genius Info., Las Vegas NV. ($12.95) Good book for beginners and somewhat experienced players. Has important sections on money management, seven card stud, Texas hold'em, and tells. Also contains good insights into psychology and how to play in tournaments. Some of Caro's best lecture material is included.

Professional Hold'Em Report by Mike Caro. Self-published, Signal Hill, CA. ($19.95) This is what it says it is—a book for advanced players. Offers valuable advice about starting hands and table tactics. Contains 20 excellent pages on the structure of the game, with strategy tables defining how to play a given hand based on the type of game being played—be it limit, pot limit or no limit.

The Theory of Poker by David Sklansky. Two Plus Two Press, Las Vegas, NV. ($29.95) Previously titled *Winning Poker*, this version has been revised and indexed. Considered one of the 10 best books of all time by many poker pros, it is for advanced players only. Packed with thoughtful analysis and good advice about seven card stud, Texas hold'em, draw and razz. Excellent discussions on bluffing, loose and tight play, implied odds, deception, slow playing and psychology.

High-Low-Split Poker for Advanced Players by Ray Zee. Two Plus Two Press, Las Vegas, NV. ($34.95) A big book full of great information by an astute theorist and advanced player. Two volumes comprise this set which should be read by beginners and advanced players alike interested in seven card stud split and Omaha eight or better players. Ray Zee is considered a class act in the cardroom and he is well respected for his playing and analysis of the game.

Poker Faces: The Life and Work of Professional Card Players by David Hayano. University of California Press, Berkeley, CA. ($13.00) Hayano analyzes individuals who enjoy the game and tries to explain people's fascination with poker throughout history and especially in the United States. Examines the role of luck, why people cheat, how the action of poker affects individuals and the world they live in.

Awesome Profits: From Kitchen Poker Table to Tournament Final Table by George "Profit" Elias. Ace-Hi Publishing, Las Vegas, NV. ($29.95) This big book has something for everyone—from the beginner to the professional. Covers most games, including seven card stud, Texas hold'em, seven stud hi-lo, Omaha, Omaha hi-lo, razz, lo-ball, tournament play, home games, money management and reading tells.

Winning Poker Systems by Norm Zadeh. Wilshire Book Co., Hollywood, CA. ($3.00) The price of this book is no joke. In a field where book prices are high (and sometimes value is low), Zadeh's book, although 20 years old, has excellent material on high and lowball draw, and good material on seven card stud. Has interesting statistics and probability tables. A good book.

Poker Essays by Mason Malmuth. Two Plus Two Press, Las Vegas, NV. ($24.95) This book is written for both Texas hold'em and seven card stud players. Divided into eight parts, it focuses on general concepts, technical ideas, structure of the games, strategy ideas, image, and tournament notes. Malmuth is an outspoken and original theorist.

Sklansky on Poker by David Sklansky. Self-published, Las Vegas, NV. ($29.95) A collection of Sklansky's articles. Contains many original ideas. Covers razz in depth but also has excellent material on Texas hold'em and tournaments. If you read Sklansky and become a fan, you'll want this book.

Omaha Hold'em Poker by Bob Ciaffone. Self-published, Las Vegas, NV. ($15.00) Solely devoted to Omaha hold'em poker. Ciaffone knows whereof he speaks—he finished third in Binion's world series of poker Omaha tournament. Can be read by beginners to experienced players.

Champion of Champions by Don Jenkins. Self-published, Odessa, TX. ($8.98) The biography of the great poker player, Johnny Moss, who is known as "The Grand Old Man of Poker." Moss, who is in his 80s, still plays poker professionally. Does not contain much playing advice, but does give you insight into the colorful life and times of a living legend. Read the book, then go to Binion's and see the man.

Bobby Baldwin's Winning Poker Secrets by Bobby Baldwin. B&G Publishing, Las Vegas, NV. ($9.95) One of the top players in world at no-limit and tournament games, Bobby Baldwin intersperses biographical and anecdotal material with his poker advice. Good book to get the flavor of high stakes poker.

Super/System by Doyle Brunson. B&G Publishing, Las Vegas, NV. ($50.00) The granddaddy of poker books. Many pundits believe that this book changed the face of poker in America by increasing the ability of average players. It is 605 pages and contains information by a coterie of writers including: Chip Reese, Mike Caro, David Sklansky, and Bobby Baldwin. Although some of the book is a little dated, it is well worth reading and the advice on no-limit hold'em and seven card stud is still top of the mark. Brunson is one of the most feared poker players of all time. Considered must reading by the poker pros. Earlier editions carried the subheading: *How I Made a Million Dollars Playing Poker.*

Magazines

The Card Player. Published every two weeks by B & F Enterprises, Inc., 1455 E. Tropicana Ave., Las Vegas, NV 89119. Runs approximately 80 pages in an 8½ × 11 format. Subscriptions: six months—$31; one year—$59; two years—$99. Single issue $2.75. Excellent journal for people interested in all aspects of poker. Has information on other table games such as blackjack but its main focus is on the various types of poker played in the casinos around the world. Considering its price, this magazine is loaded with information. You will find racks filled with *The Card Player* located in the poker rooms of almost every casino in Las Vegas. If you like poker, this is the magazine to subscribe to.

CHAPTER FIFTEEN

The Other Games People Play

C asinos have other games in addition to the big five (roulette, blackjack, baccarat, craps and poker) but these games are either so hideously tilted in favor of the house or they just don't have the widespread player interest. Usually it's a combination of both. I'll cover them all in this chapter. At the end of this chapter, I probably still will not have exhausted all the table games, as casinos invent new games continually in a never ending attempt not to give their suckers—ah, patrons—an even break. But I can state the following unequivocally: Few new games are introduced into a casino today unless they carry *at least* a 2.5 percent edge for the house. So beware. That charming game that has been introduced into your local casino has been introduced because it carries a nice edge for the house. I doubt if you will ever see a game introduced into a casino again that gives the player a chance at getting an edge such as blackjack. Or one that gives the player a close game—such as craps and baccarat. Only one of the new games, pai gow poker, opens itself to a guerrilla attack and this game I'll cover in a chapter of its own since it has begun to develop an increasingly large and enthusiastic following across casino country. Some of the more esoteric games associated with a single casino might not be there anymore...and in one case the casino associated with a particular game isn't there anymore either.

The Wheel of Fortune or The Big Six

This is essentially the old carnival wheel that spins and spins and where it stops nobody knows. One thing you should know, however, is how much of an edge the house has over the wheel of fortune player—anywhere from a *minimum* of 11.1 percent to a maximum of 24 percent! It's a wheel of fortune for the casinos but should be dubbed "the wheel of poverty" for the players.

The wheel itself is usually six feet in diameter and stands upright. It is divided into nine sections with each section containing sub-sections. The six sub-sections are the reason some casinos dub their wheels the big six. Thus, the wheel has 54 separate landing posts each designated by a given denomination of paper money; be it a one, two, five, 10 or 20 dollar bill. However, two posts on opposite sides of the wheel have special markings, sometimes a star, a joker, a casino logo, and so forth, and these are the highest payouts.

When you approach the wheel, you will notice a counter in front that has the same bills and symbols under glass that are on the wheel. You make your wager by placing your bet on the bill or symbol of your choice. Then the wheel is spun and where it stops—is usually in the casino's bank account. That's because you get paid based on the currency you are betting. So if you bet on the dollar, you are paid one dollar for every dollar you bet. Unfortunately, there are only 24 dollar posts—out of 54 total posts. You are getting paid one to one on a bet that should pay you five to four. You lose 30 bets but you win 24 bets which translates into five loses for every four wins and thus you should be paid five to four.

The following chart shows you the misfortune you face

when you play the wheel. The wheels throughout the country are not uniform, some pay more, some pay less; some have more of one denomination, some have more of another. Generally, however, you can divide the wheel of fortune into two types—the Las Vegas model and the Atlantic City model. Since more casinos use the Las Vegas model, this will be our standard with the Atlantic City (AC) model in parentheses.

Symbol	Total #	Payoff	Casino Edge
$1	24 (AC: 23)	1 to 1	11.1% (AC: 14.8%)
$2	15	2 to 1	16.6%
$5	7 (AC: 8)	5 to 1	22.2% (AC: 11.1%)
$10	4	10 to 1	18.5%
$20	2	20 to 1	22.2%
joker	1	40 to 1	24%
		(AC: 45 to 1)	14.8%
symbol	1	40 to 1	24%
		(AC: 45 to 1)	14.8%

With the wheel of fortune all the bets are bad. However, like any form of wagering, there are better bad bets and worse bad bets. If, for some unaccountable reason, you are *compelled* to place a wager on the wheel, and you are in Atlantic City, put your money on the $5. If you are in Las Vegas, go with the $1. If you are sane, go to another game.

Keno? or Yes?

There is one positive thing to be said about keno. And it is this: If you place the minimum wager (sometimes as low as 35 cents!), sit back in the relaxing chairs usually supplied by the keno rooms, open the newspaper, have a complementary drink or three, take a nap, and wait for each round of payoffs, you will probably lose less money than almost anyone in the casino for that period of time. That's because keno is a slow game with approximately six decisions an hour. It's an in-house lottery/bingo game—and your chances of winning the *big* payoff are remote and remoter—to be optimistic. In all my years of going to Vegas I have never been at a casino where someone won the big jackpot while I was there. I guess it happens but I haven't seen it, and I spend an enormous amount of time in casinoland.

I've been at casinos when Megabucks or other huge progressive slot jackpots were hit—but never when a poor keno player got to stand and shout: "Yes!" That's why it's called ke-no! (Okay, so that was a truly atrocious pun.)

The numbers on a keno ticket run from one to 80. Every 10 minutes or so, the casino caller will select 20 winning numbers. If you have any combination of these numbers as indicated on your ticket, you win an amount based on your wager and the odds stated by the casino. The amount, of course, is nowhere

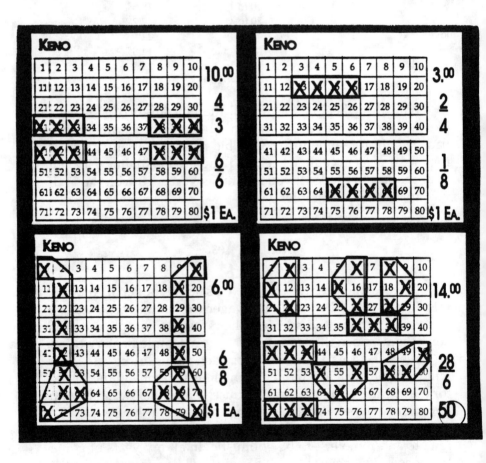

FIGURE 7
Keno Cards

near the true odds for a given number of numbers to hit but—what did you expect? Indeed, the casino edge can be safely said to be 25 percent to 40 percent—depending on how you bet.

I could spend an inordinate amount of time describing the various wagers but why bother? If you want to play keno, the casinos that offer it have booklets that show you how to play. It is really a very simple game—just select numbers and/or combinations of numbers, sit back, and hope. My advice when it comes to keno is to say: "Nope to hope!"

Sic Bo

This game is somewhat popular with the Asian gamblers, and the casinos in Las Vegas and Atlantic City have been more than happy to cater to their clientele who enjoy sic bo (which means "Dice Pairs") since it is another game with huge house edges. The table itself looks like a lighted highway map as different sections light up after each play.

The players make wagers by placing their chips in the appropriate spots on the incredibly elaborate layout corresponding to all the possible combinations that can be made with three dice. The game begins when the dealer shakes three dice in a shaker and then shows the result by lighting up those wagers on the board that have won.

Here are the bets that can be made at sic bo and the casino edge for all of them. Truthfully, you will be a sick bo' if you decide to play this game because, with one exception, the house edge ranges from the absurd to the obscene. It is a fast paced game and appeals to the heady gambler because every shake of the dice results in a decision. This is quite unlike craps, where you can ride out rolls with no-decision bets. Thankfully, you won't find sic bo in many places.

Dice Faces

The player wins if any one of the dice faces he bets on (ie., one, two, three, four, five or six) appears on the next shake. If one die has the face, he is paid off at even money. If two dice have it, he is paid at two to one. If three dice have it, he is paid

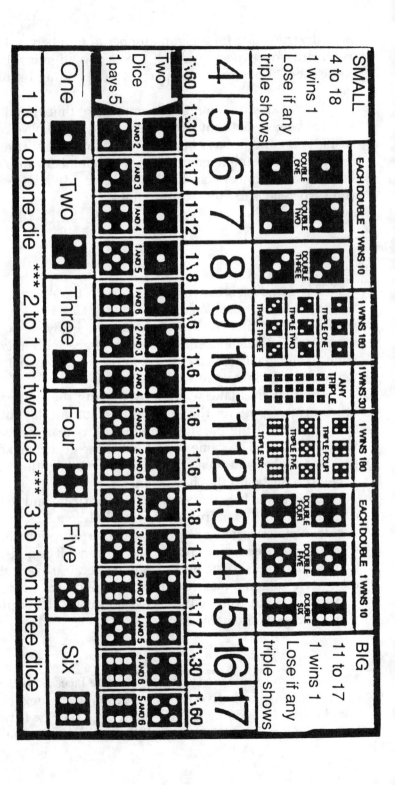

FIGURE 8
Sic Bo Layout

three to one. Yes, it is the old chuck-a-luck game! The house has a nifty 7.87 percent edge on this bet.

The Two Face Combination

A given two face combination will appear on the next shake, say, two-four. The wager is paid off at five to one which gives the house a tidy little 16.67 percent edge over the player.

The Three Face Combination

A given three face combination will appear. The casino pays this bet off at 150 to one. Not bad? Awful. The true odds are 215 to one. This gives the house a bloated 30 percent edge.

The Couplet

You are betting that a pair, say two twos, will appear on the next shake. The casino gives you eight to one if you win this wager. Sports. The edge they have is a brutal 33.3 percent.

The Triplet

If any three of the same face are shaken, you win 24 to one. The true odds on this bet are 35 to one. The house therefore has a mountainlike 30.5 percent edge.

The Totals Wager

This wager is on the total of the three dice. The house edge varies widely depending on which total of three dice you bet on. The following chart gives you the three dice totals, the pay-off and the attendant house edge. All of them are bad bets but three are pure thievery!

Total	Payoff	Casino Edge
4 or 17	60 to 1	29.1%
5 or 16	18 to 1	47.2%
6 or 15	14 to 1	30.5%
7 or 14	12 to 1	9.7%
8 or 13	8 to 1	12.5%
9 or 12	6 to 1	18.9%
10 or 11	6 to 1	12.5%

Small or Big

If you are betting *small*, you are wagering that the next shake of the dice will result in a three dice combination from four to ten. You lose on anything higher than 10 and on the three. If you are betting *big*, you are wagering that the next shake will result in a total of 11 through 17. You lose on any numbers below 11 and on the 18. If the casino allowed this wager to stay as is, it would be one of the best in the house as either *small* or *big* wins 107 times for the player and 109 times for the house (the house edge is on the three for *small* and the 18 for *big*) translating into a house edge of less than one percent. But the house isn't interested in giving their Asian patrons an excellent bet so they stipulate that if the dice come up triplets on either *small* or *big* bets—that is, 2-2-2, or 3-3-3 on *small* or 4-4-4 or 5-5-5 on *big*—the player loses. By imposing this rule, the house ups its edge to 2.8 percent—all things considered a bet within the realm of rationality but not as good as it should have been.

So if you like to watch a layout light up, then only play the *small-big* section and maybe you will be able to sing: *You Light Up My Life!*

Chuck-A-Luck

This game used to be known as "the bird cage" because it is played with a wired cage-like contraption that holds three dice. The bird cage resembles an hour glass. The game is quite simple. The dealer turns over the hour-glass and the three dice fall to the bottom cage. Whatever faces show on the three dice after they land are the winners. You bet which face will appear. Say you bet that the two will appear. If one two appears, you are paid off at even money; if two twos appear, you are paid at two to one; if all three of your twos appear, you are paid off at four to one. The casino has a nice 7.87 percent edge on this bet. Didn't I just say that about sic bo? Oh, well, as you will no doubt observe, the casinos wrap and rewrap old games to make them appear new and different. Most times, if it looks new, it is just something old that has had a face lift. You want to know why a caged bird sings? It was defeathered by games like this.

Hickok's Six Card

There's a new casino table game that is growing in popularity in Mississippi and a score of variations of it have surfaced at other casinos across the country. It's called Hickok's six card. It's a game that pays homage to one of the great American legends, Wild Bill Hickok. It is played with a single deck of 52 cards.

Legend has it that Wild Bill Hickok played his last poker hand in a saloon known as the *Number Ten* in Deadwood, South Dakota. Hickok got shot in the back of the head while holding a pair of black aces and a pair of black eights with the nine of diamonds as his fifth card. In poker circles, this rapidly became known as the "dead man's hand."

The Mississippi Hickok's six card is played as follows:

1. The dealer deals three cards face up to all the players.

2. Each player determines if he or she wishes to fold and surrender half his or her bet, or double the bet, or continue to play.

3. After all folded hands are collected, the dealer flops over two cards in the center of the table to be used by all players as community cards in order to complete their five card hand.

4. Players may stand and play their hands as is or they can "buy" a sixth card for one half their original bets. This sixth card will be used by *all* the players at the table to improve their hands.

5. All players are paid according to a set schedule of payoffs and only the highest ranking hand is paid off. Thus, if you have a full house you are not paid for having three of a kind and two of a kind.

Payoff Schedule

pair of aces, kings, queens or jacks	pays 1 to 1
two pair	pays 2 to 1

three of a kind	pays 3 to 1
five card straight	pays 4 to 1
five card flush	pays 5 to 1
full house	pays 6 to 1
four of a kind	pays 20 to 1
straight flush	pays 50 to 1
royal flush	pays 200 to 1

The Foxwoods Variation

The Foxwoods High Stakes Bingo and Casino in Connecticut has its own version of the Hickok's six card which is called Hickok's aces and eights. It is played as follows:

1. Three cards are dealt face up to the players. Dealer is dealt three cards face down.

2. Each player may fold and surrender half his or her wager, or continue to play.

3. Folded hands are collected. Dealer turns over his hand and flops two cards in the center of the table to be used as community cards for all players to complete their hands.

4. Hands higher than the dealer's are paid one to one.

5. Losing hands may buy a sixth card for half of their original bet. If they choose not to, the dealer will collect the losing bets.

6. After collecting the buy bet, the dealer flops over a sixth card to be used with the other two community cards already exposed. This card can be used by all the remaining players and the dealer to make the best five card hand.

7. If the player's hand beats the dealer's hand, the player is paid off at one to one.

8. If the player and dealer hands are identical, a push results.

9. The house takes a commission on all wagers.

Of course, while reminiscent of poker, the game lacks the competitiveness usually associated with head to head play against other players. In Foxwoods, it is much like blackjack because you are playing against the dealer. In Mississippi, it is much like video poker because you are playing for prearranged pots dependent on certain hands. In either case, the house has a clear advantage over the player because the hands are not paid off at true odds in Mississippi and all wagers are "taxed" in Foxwoods. The variations that are springing up across the country, even as I write this, preclude a detailed analysis.

Suffice it to say, that almost all new games carry a rather large house edge or the casinos wouldn't offer them. I estimate, based upon a preliminary study, that the Mississippi version of Hickok carries more than a seven percent edge in favor of the house.

The Foxwoods game is just as bad. Any game that requires you to put up extra money to receive another card—that can help the dealer as well as you!—is generally a ripoff. If you are going to play the Foxwoods Hickok, don't buy the extra card— you'll either beat the dealer or you won't. My advice is to pass these games by—or you'll be deader than Wild Bill.

Super Pan Nine

This is another very popular Asian game currently being played in the card rooms of California. It uses 12 decks of cards where all the jokers and sevens through 10s have been removed. It can be played by as many as eight players on a table that is reminiscent of a mini-baccarat table.

One of the players is always the *designated dealer* and all the other players will attempt to beat his hand. In the card rooms of California all the participants play against the designated dealer and not the casino. All players can choose to be the designated dealer in turn. Interestingly enough, the designated dealer has no limits on how much he can bet. However, a version where the casino books the bets is being considered for other venues outside of California.

The game begins when a shaker with three dice is pounded or slammed on the table by the designated dealer. Now all

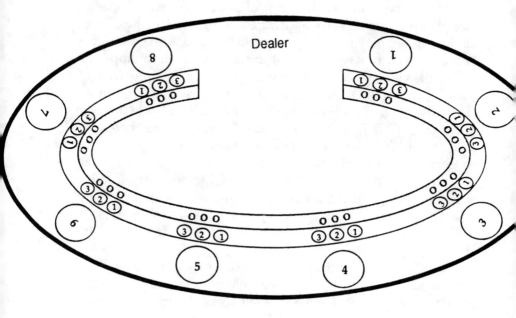

FIGURE 9
Super Pan Nine Layout

the players place a bet in the betting circle in front of them. The
caller (a casino employee) then reads the results of the dice
slam. The dice determine where the *button* is placed and this
individual is dealt to first and will be the first to be paid off or
lose his bet.

The casino dealer deals three cards face down to every
player starting with the player who has the button. The designated dealer's cards are now moved to the center of the table
and the *dealer button* is placed on them. All the players, except
the designated dealer, look at their cards. Picture cards are
worth zero but all the other cards are worth their face value
with the ace being worth one. The object now is to have a better
hand than the dealer but not to go over nine. Actually, you
can't go over nine since everything over 10 is automatically
reduced by 10. If your cards are 4, 4, 6, you don't have a 14, you
have a four. If you have three queens, you have zero. Yes, in

many ways this game is the Asian version of baccarat and perhaps this is why baccarat attracts so many high rolling Asian
players in Atlantic City and Las Vegas.

When the players have checked their cards they must each
decide whether to hit or stand. If the player hits, he receives one
card face down. He may not look at or touch this card until it is
his turn to flip it over. It is now the designated dealer's turn to
see his cards. However, this is a communal viewing as the casino dealer turns the three cards face up in the center of the table.
The designated dealer must now decide whether to hit or stand.
Once this decision is made, the casino dealer turns over the
other players' cards, beginning with the player who has the button. As the cards are turned over, those players who beat the
designated dealer are paid off from the designated dealer's
bank, those who have lost pay the designated dealer, and those
who have tied get a push—no money exchanging hands.

Super pan nine is very much like baccarat in scoring but it
also resembles blackjack and, to some extent, poker, because the
players have some free will in the matter of whether to take a hit
or stand. And the designated dealer, getting a read on his players, will often make decisions based on his assessment of his
opponents' play—just as many players do in poker. But this
assessment has a very narrow window of decision-making
opportunity because the designated dealer actually has
restraints on the playing of his hand—he must hit all hands that
are four or lower and stand on all hands that are seven or higher. So he only decides whether to hit or stand on five and six.

However, unlike blackjack and poker, the decisions that
you make at super pan nine are not based on elaborate playing
charts and odds decisions. If you are the player, you hit all
hands that are five or less and stand on all hands that are six or
more. That's it.

As far as the game among the players, assuming all of
them bank the bets in their turn, and none of them are psychot-
ically hitting three card eights and nines, it is an even proposition. So how does the casino make money? After all, that table
takes up space and the casinos must pay their dealers. The casino charges a tax on every hand played—win or lose! It is a
regressive tax because it is usually a flat amount—say, one dollar on any bet of $10 to $100. That's correct. The poorer player
is being taxed at a rate of 10 percent per hand! The richer player

is charged one percent. Since the game is taxed at different rates at different tables, you are much better off playing at a table that takes the least percentage from your bet. And remember this—a tie is actually a loss of a percentage of your bet. So here's the formula: when you lose, you lose your bet plus the tax; when you tie, you lose the tax; and when you win, you win less the tax. Long range prospects are not good.

I thought California passed a tax law a while ago? I guess it never filtered down into the cards rooms, huh?

Crapless Craps

Again, a new game is being introduced to take more money from the unwary customers. Currently, this game has only been seen at Vegas World in Las Vegas. Thankfully.

The rules of the game are somewhat similar to regular craps with several important exceptions. On the Come Out roll, a seven is still a winner but a two, three, and 12 are not losers. Instead, they become point numbers and you must hit them before you roll another seven. Unfortunately, the 11 is also no longer a Come Out winner. Should you roll an 11, it becomes your point. Because of this subtle difference, the casino now holds a 5.38 percent edge on the Pass Line bettor. And you cannot bet against a shooter on the come out because there is no Don't Pass bet. There are still all the other regulation craps options available and those crazy crapper bets with slightly better payoffs. But the game really isn't worth it; certainly not when you can go to another table and play real craps with 10 times odds!

Caribbean Stud

Despite the glamor of the "love boat" and the possibility of seeing exotic places or meeting Mr. or Ms. Right, cruises are a ripoff for gamblers because the ships have been notoriously stingy in the games they give their players. It's a "ship of fools" for real. This stinginess is only matched by some of the poor playing conditions in many a tropical paradise and port of call. I guess the local casinos on the islands (whatever islands they might be) figure that the sun has probably baked those tourists' brains so much that they can offer inferior quality blackjack and craps games. And for years they have been offering another sucker game called Caribbean stud, which should be called Caribbean dud.

The game is played on a blackjack-like table and, as in blackjack, all players play against the house. There are two betting places in front of each player—one labeled *ante*, one labeled *bet*. There is also a slot for the dropping of a dollar chip that makes you eligible for the grand jackpot. This is a side bet and is strictly optional. The grand jackpot is a progressive one and increases with each hand until someone hits it.

The game begins with the players putting a bet in the ante square and, if they wish, a dollar chip into the jackpot slot. Now the dealer deals five cards to each player. You are not allowed to show your cards to the other players. The dealer also deals himself five cards with the last one being dealt face up. The players check their cards. They have two choices. They can play out their hands, or they can surrender and give up their antes. If they decide to play out their hands, they must place a bet that is double the ante in the betting circle. Once the players have made their decisions, the dealer turns over his remaining four cards and makes them into the best possible poker hand.

However, the dealer must have at least an ace-king hand or better for the game to be fully decided. If he fails to have such a hand, he pays off the antes and pushes on the bets. If the dealer has a better hand that is ace-king or better, then all players' hands are judged against it. If the player loses, he loses both the ante and the bet. If the player beats the dealer, the ante is paid off at even money, and the bet is paid off at house odds. In addition, if the player had opted for a side bet for the jackpot, certain hands will win bonus awards, up to and including the entire jackpot. Although casinos can differ on their bonuses and payoffs, the following are relatively standard payoffs in the stud games in Las Vegas, on the cruise ships and islands. (Remember, you must beat the dealer's hand to get paid!)

Hand	Payoff	Bonus
one pair	2 to 1	none
two pair	2 to 1	none
three of a kind	3 to 1	none
straight	4 to 1	none
flush	5 to 1	$50
full house	7 to 1	$75
four of a kind	20 to 1	$100
straight flush	50 to 1	10% of jackpot
royal flush	100 to 1	jackpot

The strategy for Caribbean stud is rather straightforward.

    1. Do not put monies in any jackpot until the jackpot is $150,000 or more.
    2. You bet every pair or better.
    3. You bet A-K or better (if your hand contains the dealer's up-card).

This game is another tourist trap since even expert play, in which you make no mistakes in the above strategy, yields the house a 4.4 percent edge. However, most people playing Caribbean stud are making big strategy mistakes and are probably facing house edges of between eight to 12 percent. So if you find yourself on a tropical island, or a cruise ship, or even in hot old Las Vegas where Caribbean stud is offered, you are better off if you take out the deck chair, put on the number 32 suntan block and look for a soul mate or real Caribbean stud!

California Aces

California has a law that states that casinos can't bank games. That means that players must compete against each other, although the casino can charge players a tax for making rooms available for play. That's why traditional table games such as blackjack (also known as 21) and craps can't be found in the California casinos. But the California casinos are run by clever people, people who know a thing or 22 about getting around a law. People who also know that players love 21. So what to-to do? Make the game of 21 a game of 22 and call it California aces!

California aces can be played by upwards of eight people at a table. It is dealt from a standard deck of 52 cards with four jokers, known as California aces. The jokers and aces have a value of one or 11, the rest of the cards have their face value, with picture cards counting as 10. Yes, just like blackjack. Except that the goal is to get the best hand that is closest to 22. Since there are eight 11 value cards, there are potentially four *naturals* (two card 22s) in each deck. A natural is an automatic winner. The rest of the players are trying to get 22 or as close to 22 as they can—either over (23, 24, 25, etc.) or under (21, 20, 19). Should two players be tied, the hand closest to 22 but *under* it wins. Thus, 21 beats 23; 20 beats 24; 19 beats 25, and so forth.

However, unlike in blackjack, you are competing against everyone at the table because the best hand wins the pot! All real ties are pushes and no one wins. Once again, the players have an equal opportunity of winning the pot—depending on how they play their hands. Unfortunately, the casinos take a large tax from the pot and, unlike in poker, there are no raises and reraises and huge pots to allow the player to make up in expert play what the casino is making out in taxes. Like super pan nine, it's a losing long-range proposition, unless you can

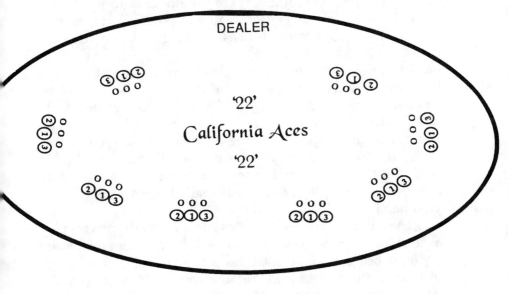

FIGURE 10
California Aces layout

win a greater proportion of the pots than is likely.

The California aces layout has three betting circles in front of you—labeled circle one, circle two, and circle three. To be involved in the hand, everyone must bet the minimum $5 bet in circle one. Now the players have the option of betting in the other two circles. In circle two, you can bet between $10 and $50; in circle three, you can place a wager of $25 to $250.

Now the dealer deals everyone two cards face down. You can draw to your two cards or stand pat. Again, the object is to get 22 or as close to 22 as you can—on either side. Once the cards are played, the circle three players turn over their hands. The bets are settled. Now the circle two players turn over their hands (the circle three players can also be in circle two, remember) and the pot is decided. Finally, the circle one players (including the circles two and three players) settle up.

Devising a strategy for California aces would be simple, if you could predict how the people at your table played—as you can predict how the dealers in blackjack will play because they must follow established rules. Unfortunately, the game is only played in certain California card rooms and most players are playing an idiosyncratic strategy. Indeed, version one of California aces is very much like a stud game—only a three card stud game. Of course, there are no head-to-head confrontations—raises or reraises as in real poker. However, you will greatly increase your chances of taking the pot if you realize that at least one or two of the eight players will have a final hand of between 19 and 25. It is this range which you wish to fall into when deciding whether or not to take the card. Thus, an elementary basic strategy for California aces would be: *to hit all hands that are 17 or less until you reach 18 or more.* The worst that can happen is getting a 10 value card on a 17 and going to 27. Remember that 27 is five points away from 22, as is 17, *but* the lower number wins in the event of a tie. Any other hit will marginally or substantially improve the value of your hand.

There is another version of this game where the players play against a designated dealer, with each player being given the option of being the designated dealer in turn. This is much more like the traditional blackjack because you only have to beat the designated dealer's hand. The designated dealer has a slight advantage because he gets to draw his cards last, thus seeing what the other players did. However, as in blackjack, the designated dealer has one of his initial two cards dealt face up. He also must hit to at least 18 and must stand on all 21s and 22s. Use the same strategy of hitting to 17 or less, standing on 18 or more.

Red Dog

If you play red dog you will be a dead dog in short order because the house has a significant edge on all the bets. This is probably why the game never got out of the kennel in Las Vegas, where it has taken up a mangy residence for years at some of the larger casinos. Now it has shambled across the country and taken up residence in Atlantic City. A dog is a dog,

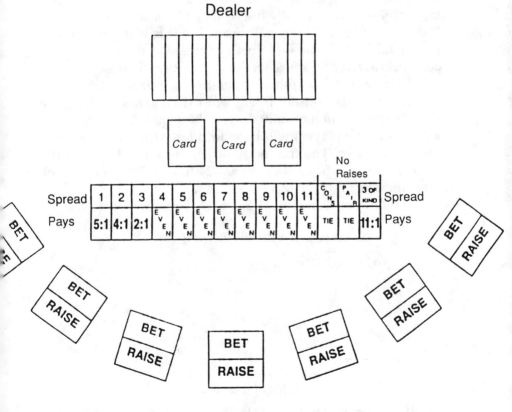

Figure 11
Red Dog Layout

and this mutt ought to be avoided or it will take a healthy bite out of your bankroll in no time at all.

Essentially, red dog is the old acey-deucy that some of you played as children. It is played at a blackjack-style table that can seat seven players. The players place a bet in the "bet" portion of the layout. The dealer begins the game by placing two cards face up in the center of the table in the boxes indicated. The player must now decide if he wants to place an optional "raise" at house odds—ranging from even money to 11 to one. The dealer then turns over a third card. If this card falls between his first two, the player wins his original bet at even money and any odds "raises" that he has made.

Thus, if the dealer has a hand of three and nine and turns over a four, five, six, seven or eight, the player is a winner. If the card turned over is equal to the end cards (in this case three and nine) or outside them (in this case two, 10, jack, queen, king, ace) the bet is lost. By the way, just because I call the extra "raise" an odds bet does not mean that it is being paid off at proper odds, as is the odds bet at craps. On the contrary, the odds bets at red dog are generally poor wagers at best.

There are several other things to recognize in red dog. If the dealer deals himself a pair hand (two cards of the same value), he will automatically draw a third card. If it is the same value card, the players will be paid off at 11 to one. If it isn't, the players lose. The true odds of getting a third card of the same value (in a 52 card deck) are 24 to one. In an eight-deck shoe, the true odds are 12.8 to one.

Hands in sequence (ie., 3-5; 7-8; Q-K, etc.) are pushes.

Card Values at Red Dog

two through 10 = face value

jack = 11

queens = 12

kings = 13

aces = 14

Spread and Odds

If the spread between cards fits one of these categories, it is paid off at the following house odds. Those categories that have a * are worth betting the "raise" because you have a better than 50 percent chance of making the spread.

Spread	Odds
one	five to one
two	four to one
three	two to one
four	one to one
five	one to one
six	one to one
seven*	one to one*
eight*	one to one*
nine*	one to one*
10*	one to one*
11*	one to one*

If you play perfect basic strategy at an eight-deck shoe (which is the usual game in Atlantic City), you can reduce the house edge to approximately four percent. However, the hold rates in Atlantic City (the actual amount being kept by the casinos) show that the casinos are keeping between 30 and 50 percent of all monies bet at red dog! Incredible.

Double Down Stud

This game comes in two versions—a table game and a video poker game. Therefore, without even explaining it, you know beforehand that there will be no way to beat it. Indeed, the house percentage has been estimated at between 12 to 21 percent, depending on how players play their hands.

Double down stud is played at a regulation blackjack table with two betting squares labeled "bet" and "double down." The dealer deals each round from a newly shuffled deck. Each player receives one card face up. Then the dealer deals one card face down and three cards face up in the center of the table. These cards will be community cards for all players. Now all the players are given an option of doubling their bets based on their first cards and the three community cards that are visible. Finally, the dealer turns over the fifth card and the players are paid off based on the following schedule:

Hand	Payoff
pair of sixes or better	push
pair of jacks or better	even money
two pair	two to one
three of a kind	three to one
straight	five to one
flush	eight to one
full house	11 to one
four of a kind	50 to one
straight flush	200 to one
royal flush	2,000 to one

Don't play this game but, again, if someone puts a gun to your head and demands that you risk money on double down stud—then never double down. You're giving away the ranch as it is—why give them the cattle as well?

Pokette

The ultimate hybrid, a combination of roulette and poker, pokette made its first appearance at Tropworld in Atlantic City in 1992. Played with 54 slots on a big wheel—52 standard cards plus two jokers are depicted—the object is to spin a three card poker hand. You can bet on either the final hand or each individual spin. There is no strategy, except to hope, and the house takes a hefty slice of all the action. The following chart shows you the bets and the house odds. To give you some idea of what you face when you play pokette, the *best* bets carry a house edge of 3.8 percent, and it gets worse from there. Another must miss game.

Bet	House Odds
one card or joker	51 to one
two cards or two jokers	25 to one
four cards	12 to one
one rank (four cards)	12 to one
red or black	one to one
two ranks (eight cards)	five to one
three ranks (13 cards)	three to one
full suit (13 cards)	three to one
Jacer: two jokers, two aces (4 cards)	12 to one

pair in two	11 to one
pair in three	five to one
three of a kind	11 to one
open straight	five to one
inside straight	11 to one
flush	three to one
open straight flush	24 to one
inside straight flush	49 to one

(*Note: I just returned from a visit to Tropworld and I didn't see pokette this time around. There was a lot of construction going on, so maybe they removed the game for a time. Or maybe it's gone. May it rest in pieces.)

Heads and Tails

From Australia, this is the dice equivalent of a double coin toss. The game made its debut as Caesars Palace in Las Vegas in 1992, but I didn't notice it on my last visit in 1993. Still, I wasn't exactly looking for it either. It is played at a blackjack table with a shaker containing two dice and two betting areas, one called the "fast lane" and one called the "slow lane." Each die contains three faces labeled H and three faces labeled T. The object of the game is to predict which faces will appear: two H's, two T's or an H and a T. In the slow lane, you can only bet on two H's or two T's and they pay even money. If an H-T rears its ugly face, it's a push. In the fast lane, you can bet on all outcomes. If an H-H or a T-T appears, you receive three to one (the true odds), if an H-T appears, you win even money. The casino charges a five percent commission on winning bets in the fast lane.

Two-Up

I don't think you'll find this Australian game in America anymore because the casino offering two-up, the Main Street Station in downtown Las Vegas, went belly up in the summer of 1992. Too bad, because Main Street Station was the classiest small casino I've ever been in. The stupidest thing the owner ever did was to let the town fathers of Las Vegas convince him to place this elegant venture on the edge of the downtown area. It was doomed from the beginning. It should have been erected on the Strip, across the street from the Sahara where it would have attracted the Pouilly Fuisse crowd interested in fine dining and fine accommodations, instead of the beer drinkers and barfers for whom it had to compete with the other downtown joints. (I exclude the Golden Nugget. It's an anomaly—a Strip joint amidst the downtown strip joints!)

Two-up is a literal two coin toss. The game has 21 players who stand at a circular table that surrounds the tossing pit. A scoreboard hangs overhead to record the tosses. Three banks of colored lights represent the three possible outcomes of a toss: One red light represents tails; three green lights represent heads; and five yellow lights represent odd tosses—that is, a head and a tail.

There are two basic bets. The player who is selected to toss the coins (called the spinner) must bet that he will toss three pairs of heads before any pair of tails or five odds in a row occur. If the spinner succeeds, he is paid off at 7.5 to one. The spinner is not allowed to touch the coins with his hands. Instead, he is given a paddle upon which the two coins rest, one heads up and one tails up. Now he tosses the coins at least three feet above his head. They land on the carpeted area of the pit and a decision is rendered. The other players are betting even money on one event of their own choice—either heads or tails. All players lose if those five odds in a row occur. The players cannot bet with the spinner and all bets are placed at the opening of a round. Thus, the player's bets are decided in one to five tosses. For example, if I bet heads and the very first toss is two heads, I win. If it is two tails, I lose. If it is odds, I wait for the next toss and so on. The house has an edge of 1.56 percent on the players and approximately one percent on the spinners. All in all, not a bad game.

But as far as I know, it is not around anymore, except perhaps "down under," nor is the beautiful place that offered it. A shame.

Fast Action Hold'em

This game is dealt from a six-deck shoe. Each player receives four cards, face down. If you receive four of a kind on the very first four cards, that's a natural and you are paid off at five to one. However, if you don't receive a natural, you must select which of your two cards you will continue to play and which of your two cards you will discard. You are given an option of using all four of your cards as two separate hands for an additional bet. This is very much like splitting cards in blackjack. Now the dealer will create his two card hand from his four cards.

Next, the dealer will flop four cards in the center of the table to be used as community cards. Each player's hand is the best five card hand using the two down cards and the five community cards. To win, you have to beat the dealer's hand and all winning bets are paid off at even money. The casino makes its money by charging a five percent commission on all winning bets, including a natural. By doing this the casino is giving itself a 2.5 percent edge. (Remember, the five percent commission is only being taken from *winning* bets—arguably 50 percent of the action.)

Since there are six decks involved in play, the ranking of poker hands is somewhat more dramatic than what you encounter in normal versions of hold'em.

1. flush with five of a kind
2. royal flush
3. flush with four of a kind
4. straight flush
5. flush with a full house
6. five of a kind
7. flush with three of a kind
8. flush with two pair
9. flush with one pair
10. four of a kind

11. full house
12. flush
13. straight
14. three of a kind
15. two pair
16. pair
17. highest card

This is an interesting table game variation for players, although even the most adroit setting of hands probably can't overcome the casino's 2.5 percent commission edge.

Pai Gow

You will most likely find this game in the card rooms of California, although a couple of Las Vegas casinos have been experimenting with it for their Asian customers. Pai gow is played with 32 dominoes and the name is often translated as "heavenly dominoes" or "make nine." (The different translations come from different Chinese dialects.) In its poker version (see next chapter), the game has gained a tremendous following in casinos across America.

Pai gow is played at a blackjack-like table that seats up to eight players. The players bet against each other and each player has the option of being the "bank." The dealer begins the game by mixing the dominoes face down. The mixed dominoes are placed in eight stacks of four each. Now the players may put up a bet.

The banker shakes a brass bowl containing three dice and slams it down on the table. The numbers on the dice decide which player shall receive the "button" and the first stack of dominoes. Each player now receives four dominoes which he separates into a high hand ("front hand") and a low hand ("back hand"). Many skilled players don't even look at the dominoes but read them with their fingers (like braille). To win, a player must beat *both* the high hand and the low hand of the banker. If the player wins on one but loses on the other—it is a push. However, when the banker and player have the exact ranking on both hands or either hand, the banker wins. Thus, an equal high hand and a winning banker's low hand is a win

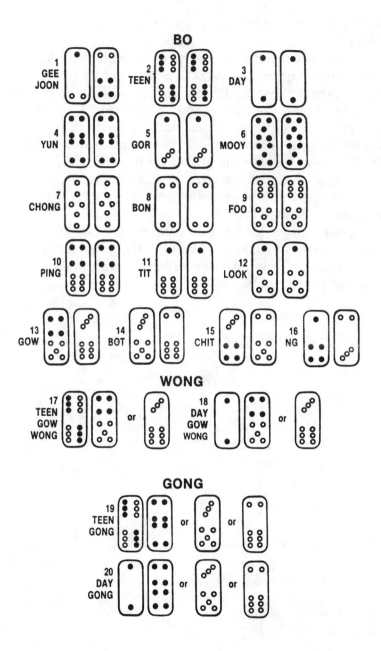

FIGURE 12
Ranked Hands in Pai Gow

for the banker. The banker therefore has a natural edge over the player.

The banker can only lose as much as he bets. Thus, if the banker has wagered, say, $1,000 on his hand and the first player (that is, the player with the button) has wagered $1,200, should the player win the banker only pays off $1,000. Should the player lose, the player would only lose $1,000. If the banker should run out of money before paying off any other players at the table—well, that's the luck of the draw or, rather, the shake of the dice which determined the order of play.

The chart on the preceding page shows the list of ranked hands from high to low.

Although pai gow has an enthusiastic Asian following, its Asian-American cousin has become the new table game rage and may someday rank right up there with blackjack, craps, roulette, poker and baccarat.

CHAPTER SIXTEEN

The Fundamentals of Pai Gow Poker

I don't think it is an exaggeration to say that pai gow poker (pronounced *pie gow*) is the fastest growing table game in casinos across America. That's because it offers the players many opportunities for decision making and, indeed, good play can result in *theoretical* long-term wins. An expert pai gow player can get a slight edge over the casinos, just as an expert blackjack player can.

However, unlike in blackjack, much of the player's edge must come from assuming the role of *dealer* or *banker* and playing against players who are not as expert at setting their hands. Thus, there are quite a few variables in the play of pai gow that are not found in blackjack, including the fact that the casinos take a five percent tax out of winning hands! Even with this rake, the game is beatable—but only marginally at best. However, compared to most casino games, pai gow poker does give you a chance. If you learn some basic strategy decisions, you can reduce the house edge to less than two percent. And if you become truly an expert pai gow poker player, you might even have a half percent in your favor. Is it any wonder, then, that the game is growing? Casino players want a chance and this game seemingly gives it to you. Is it any wonder that games such as red dog and sic bo flounder and a game such as pai gow grows? No, no wonder at all.

How the Game is Played

The game begins when one player is designated as the *dealer/banker*. He must bank the bets of the other players. If no one wishes to assume the role of dealer/banker, then the casino dealer will bank the bets. It is played with the standard deck of 52 cards, with one joker added that can be used as an ace. It can also be used to complete a straight, a flush, or a straight flush. In some casinos, in pai gow poker a "low" straight (that is, ace-two-three-four-five) is the second highest straight behind ace-king-queen-jack-10. In other casinos, the regular poker order prevails.

Before the actual deal, three dice are shaken and displayed to determine the order of the deal. Each player is then dealt seven cards with which he must make two hands based on poker rankings—a back hand of five cards and a two-card front hand. The five-card back hand must have a higher value than the two-card front hand. If the player accidentally sets a stronger two-card hand, he automatically loses his bet. However, if the dealer/banker should make this mistake, the casino dealer will reset the hand based on casino policy.

To win, both your five-card back hand and your two-card front hand must beat the dealer/banker's respective hands; otherwise it is a push. However, if the player and dealer/banker have exact hands, either back or front, the decision goes to the dealer/banker. Such a happening is called a *copy*. All copies go to the dealer/banker. Thus, if the dealer/banker and the player have exactly the same five-card and two-card hands, the dealer/banker wins. (Don't hold your breath, a double copy happens rarely.) The fact that the dealer/banker wins all copies gives him a natural edge in the game and this edge is why, as dealer/banker, you want to play as many hands as you

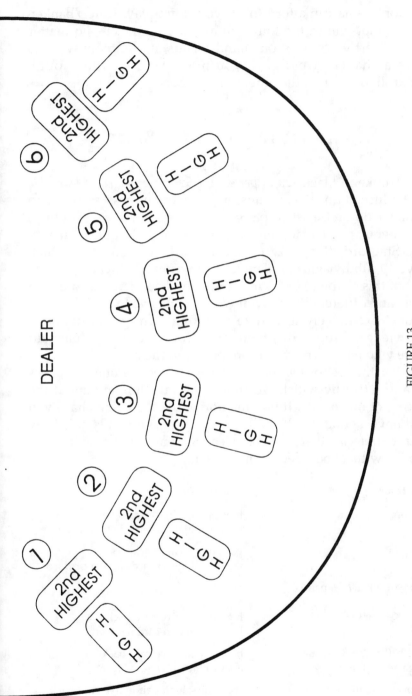

FIGURE 13
Pai Gow Poker Layout

can (or as you can afford to). If you don't play dealer/banker, you cannot win in the long run at pai gow poker—no matter how expertly you set your hands. Thus, if you truly want to have a chance at pai gow, you must have a large enough bankroll to cover all the other players' bets.

A Basic Strategy for Pai Gow Poker

Unlike in blackjack, a *perfect* basic strategy *that is learnable* in the lifespan of the average, non-driven, unpossessed casino gambler doesn't exist in pai gow. It exists in *theory*, of course, and if you are the mad-genius type you might be able to memorize Stanford Wong's 27 categories of hands, some of which have 40 subdivisions of play! (See recommended reading at the end of this chapter.) Of course, once you had memorized over a thousand different hands, you would still have to be the banker almost exclusively to realize any long term gain from such knowledge. Supposedly, there are a couple of individuals out there who have done this. More power to them.

For the rest of us, the best basic strategy is one that gives us a *direction* by which we should set our thinking about the setting of our hands. If you memorize the following chart, you will have a good handle on how to make your hands. It is truly a *basic strategy*—that is, it is the least you need to know in order to play with a good degree of efficiency.

You Have	You Should
no pair	highest card in five-card back next two highest cards in two-card front
one pair	pair in five-card back next two highest cards in two-card front
two pair when *high* pair is:	
A-A; K-K; or Q-Q	high pair in five-card back low pair in two-card front
J-J; 10-10; 9-9; 8-8; 7-7; 6-6 (with ace or king)	both pairs in five-card back ace or king in two-card front
(above without ace or king)	split pairs: high pair in five-card back low pair in two-card front

5-5; 4-4; 3-3 (with ace, king or queen)	both pairs in five-card back ace, king or queen in two-card front
(above without ace, king or queen)	split pairs: high pair in five-card back low pair in two-card front
three pair	second and third highest pair in five-card back highest pair in two-card front

three of a kind:

A-A-A	two aces in five-card back one ace and next highest card in two-card front
all others	three of a kind in five-card back two highest cards in two-card front
two threes of a kind	lower three of a kind in five-card back two higher in two-card front

straight or flush or straight flush with:

no pair	lowest complete hand in five-card back two highest cards in two-card front
one or two pair	lowest complete hand in five-card back two highest cards (pair or not) in two-card front
three of a kind	complete hand in five-card back pair in two-card front
full house	three of a kind in five-card back two of a kind in two-card front
two threes of a kind	lower three in five-card back highest two in two-card front

four of a kind composed of:

aces, kings and queens	always split between hands
jacks, 10s, 9s (with ace or king)	four of a kind in five-card back ace or king in two-card front
(above without ace or king)	split
eights, sevens, sixes (with ace, king, queen)	four of a kind in five-card back put ace, king, queen in two-card front
fives, fours, threes, twos	four of a kind in five-card back highest cards in two-card front
five aces	three aces in five-card back two aces in two-card front

Guerrilla Pai Gow Poker

Pai gow poker lends itself to a brilliant guerrilla strategy, something like the classical *wonging* in blackjack. You play only the dealer/banker hand, since this has an edge over the players. Remember that all players must be given a turn as dealer/banker but some players refuse it because they can't book the bets and don't want to be embarrassed by being caught short. (You can always offer to share the bank with these individuals if the casino will let you and/or if you can set the hands.) Some casinos will allow the same player to bank two hands in a row, some two of every three hands. (Some will not let you be dealer/banker more than once every seven hands, some once in even more!) So you go from table to table and play dealer/banker. You try to play in casinos that allow you to be dealer/banker as often as possible. You move around, hit and move some more.

Now, when you get to a table that has a favorable dealer/banker rule (say, one of every two hands, or two of every three hands), you let everyone know that you have been quite unlucky that day so you are trying to get it all back by being the dealer. Tell them you are chasing your losses but, what the hell, it's all or nothing and it's only money! You are doing this little routine to encourage people to bet heavily against you, much more heavily than they normally would and certainly much more heavily than when you are playing against a dealer/banker. Indeed, when you are playing against a dealer/banker, bet the minimum! Your edge as dealer in one of every two hands or two of every three hands will not give you an overall edge in the game unless the players bet big against you. That's why I made a point of stressing in the opening of this chapter that your edge in this game is purely *theoretical* because so many factors enter into the game—one of the most important of which is how often and for how much you can be the bank.

But as a guerrilla strategy, hitting pai gow poker is not without its rewards and dangers. On the plus side, you can get a good run of cards and wipe up easily and quickly in a hand or two. On the other hand, you must have a large bankroll and steel nerves to weather the wild fluctuations that will occur in your bankroll when you hit a losing streak. Imagine losing to every player on the table? Whew!

Recommended Reading

As with any game gaining in popularity, more and more information is coming out about pai gow poker. Some of it is quite good. Some of it is idiosyncratic. Some of it is geared to the California game exclusively, some to the traditional Las Vegas and Atlantic City casinos.

Optimal Strategy for Pai Gow Poker by Stanford Wong. Pi Yee Press, 7910 Ivanhoe Ave. #34, La Jolla, CA 92037. ($19.95) Best book on the game. Chapter 3 could be the most daunting chapter ever written in a gambling book as it gives you the *almost* complete basic strategy to pai gow poker as figured by Wong on his computer. Exhausting reading. Try memorizing it? It would probably be easier to walk on water. But Wong also gives a simplified version that is much easier to learn and execute. The rest of the book is, as is usual with Wong's books, thorough and right to the point. This book is the premier source of information on the game and I recommend it highly if you really want to delve into the game in a somewhat more detailed way.

CHAPTER SEVENTEEN

Deus Ex Machina!

Here's the typical slot machine opening to an article or a chapter in a book. If it's not the opening, you will find it somewhere in the book or article. If you don't find it, you are probably reading a pamphlet that is strictly concerned with playing strategy for video poker (see next chapter).

So here's my slightly jaundiced, but nevertheless evocative, slot machine chapter opening:

Bertha Bottlebottom had come home from a hard day of sitting on a park bench, made herself a bologna sandwich with lard and mayonnaise on white bread, washed it down with a container of half and half, and then decided to try her hand at the local casino. She had put in only two dollars' worth of quarters when the bells started ringing and people started slapping her on the back. She had won $400,000! "I knew this would be my lucky day!" the publicity brochures of the casino quoted her as saying.

There was a picture of Bertha smiling with her new teeth that sparkled. She was holding an oversized check that was about six feet by three feet and next to her, all smiles, were two well-dressed casino executives.

Mary Mammon was at Augustus's Pleasure Dome, fully comped as usual, playing Megabucks. She had put $300 in the machine when the incredible happened. She won! How much? $5,000,000! Mary laughed and jumped up and down. Her husband, Mortimer, came over and shouted with joy: "Honey, we're retiring! Right now." That quote was used on a big sign in the Augustus's display ads showing the smiling winner with her now retired husband. They were on either side of another giant, oversized check, and there were two smiling, well-dressed casino executives with them in the picture.

Donald Downtrodden was facing eviction for failure to pay his rent. Also because he had 16 cats living with him. He decided to take his last $50 and get on a charter bus to Atlantic City that stopped at the local diner. As Donald walked into the lobby of the casino and saw the giant blowup pictures of lucky winners holding oversized checks, he "just knew it was gonna be my day!" It was. On the very first pull of the handle, the machine exploded for a jackpot of $250,000! Donald was quoted in the casino in-house paper as saying:"Now my little pussies will eat well!" There was a fuzzy picture of Donald, who had still not bothered to shave, holding a cat, a cashier's check and a cigarette, and with him were two smiling, well-dressed casino executives.

You get the picture. The slots offer a dream ending to many people's nightmares. They offer the hope of the big score with *no effort, no knowledge, and no sweat*—the true American Dream! Just pull the handle (actually, today, you can just as easily press a button), watch those symbols go round and round, and maybe, just maybe, you will be up on a wall with a big smile, an ever bigger check, and two smiling, well-dressed casino executives.

The reason casinos advertise their slot winners is to hold out that big kill to the gullible. Unfortunately, for most slot players, it's the big chill, not the big kill, as they lose coin after coin, year after year, till death doth machine and player part. Seriously, do you really believe that the same casino executives who ban card counters are gushing and gushing over mega-slot winners because they like giving away all the money? They must know something, some secret, about the difference between certain table game players and slot players. The same executives who will photograph a suspected card counter from the eye-in-the-sky and then distribute those pictures to other casinos alerting them to the fact that this person could win a few (measly) thousand dollars from them if they're not careful; these same unctuous, well-dressed slimeballs wriggle their way into every blown up photograph of every guffawing jackpot winner. So, do they know something about the difference between certain table game players and slot players?

They do.

And you do too.

The slots can't be beaten by the average slots player— unless that person has a sledge hammer and a dream—or a devilishly clever way of rigging the machine, or has inserted his own computer chip into the mechanism. Sans cheating, the slots are unassailable in the long run.

The slots make more money for the casinos than any other form of gambling. It's guaranteed money because the machines are programmed to pay back only a certain percentage of the total monies put in them. If the casinos had their way, no one would want to play table games (where in some cases, you have a chance to win), everyone would play slots. And really, those of you who have witnessed the slots explosion in this country, and the decline of table game activity, can readily see the future— row upon endless row of monster machines, jingling, jangling, clanging, flashing—with mesmerized humans pumping an infinite amount of coin into the machines' voracious gullets, themselves being nourished on a hope and a dream.

The Percentages of Slots

You may have seen the signs in Las Vegas: "Our slots return 99%!" or something to that effect. Almost every Las Vegas casino proclaims the looseness of its slots as well as the happiness of its winners. How truthful is this?

When Pontius Pilate asked Jesus, "What is truth?", Jesus, unfortunately, remained silent. But most slot experts are not silent and most agree that when a casino lauds the paybacks of its machines, it is actually lauding only a select few that are paying the advertised high percentage back. The rest are paying back whatever the casino, or the casino control commission in that particular state, wants. For example, in New Jersey, the machines must pay back no fewer than 83 cents on the dollar. That is the law. That is the same as saying that the machines must return 83 percent.

As a general rule that you can take to the bank (for a withdrawal to play the slots): The machines in casinos throughout America will return anywhere from 80 percent to 98 percent of the money put into them. In Las Vegas, where there is greater competition, the machines on *average* return between 94 and 98 percent. In Atlantic City, with its high overhead and low competition, the machines return on *average* between 88 and 92 percent. On the Mississippi and other riverboats, the machines are paying back *on average* between 90 and 93 percent.

As a general rule, the machines in gas stations, airports, laundromats, diners, restrooms, candy stores, mom and pop stores, local bistros and bars, bus and train stations will pay back much less. I've heard estimates as low as 40 cents on the dollar! The most generous estimates I've heard for small operations is 75 percent. The reason for this is simple. The casinos are looking for return business. The local gas station operator knows you are only pumping some coins in the machine as a diversion while he pumps your gas. You aren't going to come back day after day (not if you have to fly in!) to tank up your car and pump that handle.

And so it goes.

However, let us pretend that *every* slot machine in a given casino actually is programmed to return, say 99 percent. What does that mean? Well, the casinos know that most slot players think that if they bring $100 to the casino, they will theoretically leave with $99 after seeing such a sign. But the casinos also know that the average player doesn't just play through the money *once*, but keeps pumping that hundred into the metal monster over and over and over in the course of his or her play.

A return of 99 percent means that for every dollar you put into the machine, you will theoretically receive 99 cents in return. Now, you put your hundred dollars in the machine and it returns $99, now you put your $99 in the machine and it returns 99 percent of that or $98.01. Now watch: The left hand column will show you the progression, rather, the digression of $100 bet on a mostly mythical machine that returns 99 percent; the right column will show you the return on a more realistic 93 percent, which is somewhere between the Las Vegas low and the Atlantic City high, and in line with the riverboats.

Machine with 99% Return		Machine with 93% Return	
Input	*Return**	*Input*	*Return**
$100	$99.00	$100	$93
$99.00	$98.01	$93.00	$86.49
$98.01	$97.03	$86.49	$80.44
$97.03	$96.06	$80.44	$74.81
$96.06	$95.10	$74.81	$69.57
$95.10	$94.15	$69.57	$64.70
$94.15	$93.21	$64.70	$60.73
$93.21	$92.27	$60.73	$55.96
$92.27	$91.35	$55.96	$52.04
$91.35	$90.44	$52.04	$48.40
$90.44	$89.53	$48.40	$45.01
$89.53	$88.64	$45.01	$41.86
$88.64	$87.75	$41.86	$38.93
$87.75	$86.87	$38.93	$36.20
$86.87	$86.00	$36.20	$33.67
$86.00	$85.15	$33.67	$31.31
$85.15	$84.29	$31.31	$29.12
$84.29	$83.45	$29.12	$27.08
$83.45	$82.62	$27.08	$25.19
$82.62	$81.79	$25.19	$23.42
$81.79	$80.97	$23.42	$21.78
$80.97	$80.16	$21.78	$20.26
$80.16	$79.36	$20.26	$18.84
$79.36	$78.57	$18.84	$17.52
$78.57	$77.78	$17.52	$16.30
$77.78	$77.00	$16.30	$15.16
$77.00	$76.23	$15.16	$14.09
$76.23	$75.47	$14.09	$13.11
$75.47	$74.71	$13.11	$12.19
$74.71	$73.97	$12.19	$11.34
$73.97	$73.23	$11.34	$10.54
$73.23	$72.50	$10.54	$ 9.81
$72.50	$71.77	$ 9.81	$ 9.12
$71.77	$71.06	$ 9.12	$ 8.48

$71.06	$70.34	$ 8.48	$ 7.88
$70.34	$69.64	$ 7.88	$ 7.33
$69.64	$68.94	$ 7.33	$ 6.82
$68.94	$68.26	$ 6.82	$ 6.34
$68.26	$67.57	$ 6.34	$ 5.90
$67.57	$66.90	$ 5.90	$ 5.49
$66.90	$66.23	$ 5.49	$ 5.10
$66.23	$65.57	$ 5.10	$ 4.75
$65.57	$64.91	$ 4.75	$ 4.41
$64.91	$64.26	$ 4.41	$ 4.10
$64.26	$63.62	$ 4.10	$ 3.82
$63.62	$62.98	$ 3.82	$ 3.55
$62.98	$62.35	$ 3.55	$ 3.30
$62.35	$61.73	$ 3.30	$ 3.07
$61.73	$61.11	$ 3.07	$ 2.86
$61.11	$60.50	$ 2.86	$ 2.66
$60.50	$59.90	$ 2.66	$ 2.47
$59.90	$59.30	$ 2.47	$ 2.30
$59.30	$58.71	$ 2.30	$ 2.14
$58.71	$58.12	$ 2.14	$ 1.99
$58.12	$57.54	$ 1.99	$ 1.85
$57.54	$56.96	$ 1.85	$ 1.72
$56.96	$56.39	$ 1.72	$ 1.60
$56.39	$55.83	$ 1.60	$ 1.49
$55.83	$55.27	$ 1.49	$ 1.39
$55.27	$54.72	$ 1.39	$ 1.29
$54.72	$54.17	$ 1.29	$ 1.20
$54.17	$53.63	$ 1.20	$ 1.11
$53.63	$53.09	$ 1.11	$ 1.04
$53.09	$52.56	$ 1.04	$ .96
$52.56	$52.03	$ .96	$ .89

*figures have been rounded up (so should the people who make and distribute these machines)

What you have no doubt noticed immediately about these figures is the incredible difference six percentage points makes in the rate of loss. The player at the machine returning 93 percent lost almost all his money, while the player at the 99 percent return machine lost approximately half his money in the same number of trials.

Now, the above scenario is unlikely to occur when a person plays the slots because in the short run anything can happen. The payouts are discontinuous. Sometimes a machine will hit over and over. At other times, it will gobble up every penny a person has in no time flat. But all around the casino's slot area will be bells ringing and lights flashing. There's a palpable sense of excitement in the air; a palpable sense of anticipation. That's what the casinos are banking on—players feeling lucky, players seeing the pictures of happy winners, players figuring their moment has come.

However, over the long life of one machine or averaged among all the machines in a given casino in one month, you will see that the win percentage of the machines reflects their programming. What's more, the return percentages are sometimes deceiving. I talked to one slot expert who works for a very famous casino on the Strip in Las Vegas. This is what he had to say about casino practices:

> "The players have to beware when a casino advertises that it pays back a large percentage on its slots. You have to find out if the slots being referred to are progressives, with a big jackpot and whether that jackpot's theoretical hitting is calculated into the win percentages. If it is, a machine that is advertised as returning 97 percent may actually be returning much less because the jackpot is figured into the return. Sure, on average, because of the huge jackpot, the machines in this grouping are returning 97 percent, but the jackpot is skewing the figures. In reality, people are losing a lot more and only one person at a time and over an extended period of time will hit the jackpot. Before that jackpot is hit, we can still advertise that the payout is 97 percent. However, everyday we'll be taking much, much more and getting interest on it so that when we pay out the jackpot, we're not even losing the total jackpot monies. Of course, we'll put the winner's picture on the wall and that will encourage even more people to put money in those particular machines."

Pretty snappy, no?

But still, more people do play slots than ever before in history. And to accommodate them, the casinos have given over more and more floor space to these machines. Indeed, today's slot machines are a marvel of scientific and computer wizardry. The old "one armed bandits" are mostly gone—as are the bandits of the old West. In their places we have sparkling machines of every description, linked progressives, in-house progressives, single machine progressives; two, three and four line payoff machines and with these, we have those smiling executives in perfectly fitted suits. Those old time bandits and the newer models have a common goal in mind—to separate you from your money. The only difference is that today they can do it faster thanks to science, the advance of civilization, and a new god known as *microchip*.

Those Newfangled Machines

The old machines, lovingly called one-armed bandits, were mechanical devices with reels and levers. They could be beaten by certain individuals who could finesse the machine—or break it. Then came the electronic machines. These, too, were open to various methods of cheating. Some of them are still around. Now, however, most machines, even if they have reels, are computer-generated programs and are run by a single microchip that determines lights, camera, action—and payout percentages. They cannot be beaten by finesse—but that sledgehammer can still get them to give up some coins before you're carted off by the security guards.

The microprocessor machines (that's the fancy name for a machine controlled by computer chips) are now the most common machines in the casinos. Built into the memory chip is a program that generates a series of random numbers. This is called a *random number generator* (how creative!) and it is constantly selecting numbers...at random. These numbers translate into symbols when a player plays the machine. Some symbols correspond to many numbers, and these symbols will come up more often. Some symbols, on the other hand, correspond to very few numbers, and thus they will not come up frequently. Obviously, the more opportunities for a symbol's appearance, the less the payout will be. The random number generator is the *god in the machine* and (let's anthropomorphize this, shall we?) it is *his* choices that determine the slot player's fate.

The interesting point about the *deus ex machina* microprocessor is this: The symbols (or rather the random numbers corresponding to the symbols) are constantly being selected—

even when the machine isn't being played! The tree is falling in the forest and it *is making a sound* whether or not a person is there to hear it—in other words. The player putting in a coin is merely activating the *display* portion of the program. When you put your coins in, you are finding out what the will of the god in the machine is, but your placing the coin had nothing to do with which number came up. Had you placed the coin a split second earlier or later, the god of the machine would have had a different set of random numbers generated and thus a different set of symbols would have been displayed. In short, the slot player, unlike the table player, has no free will in the matter of what will happen when he plays.

The table game player can make at least some accurate predictions. For example: "I will not throw the dice at that obnoxious drunk on the other side of the table." And even though I can't control the outcome, it is *my* rolling that generates the result on a crap throw. I can determine whether or not I get another card at blackjack. But on the new slot machines, the results are already there one moment, the next moment, and the moment after that. Your playing just lets you know what the result is.

And, naturally, the god in the machine, having an almost infinite amount of time in which to make decisions, determines the long-range payout most favorable to itself. In the short run, anything can happen as millions, no, billions, of decisions are being made. But everything works out in the end, just as the god in the machine randomly determined. We poor mortals just didn't see the grand design as we sacrificed our coin to the god in the machine. Slot playing is, in short, an ungodly trinity of microchip, machine and human greed—all contributing to the bottom line of the casino—profits!

Types of Machines

In the good old days of the one-armed bandits, you played one coin and most machines had one line, and you either won or lost. Those single line, single coin machines are dinosaurs. Clumsy and dead.

The new machines are all multiple line, multiple coin machines. Some of them pay a better percentage back when you play more coins. For example, if you play one coin the machine pays, say, 100 coins back on its maximum payout. But if you play two coins, you get back, oh, 250, and if you play three coins, you get back 600. (I've exaggerated the payouts for demonstration purposes.) These machines generally have a single line for payouts.

Some multiple machines pay off on more than one line. However, to play the better payout line requires more than one coin; to play the best payout line requires maximum coins. Other machines require more coins to get certain payoffs at all. For example, with one coin in the machine, two vampire bats won't pay off, but if you have two coins in the machine, two vampire bats will pay off something.

Still other machines are progressive, some of which are *linked* with similar machines in the *carousel* (a carousel is a nice way of saying a bunch of machines of the same type in the same place), or with other machines of their type in the casino, or in an entire city. These latter machines are the ones with the monster jackpots.

10 Tips on Slot Playing

1. Always know what the payouts are. Are you benefiting by putting the maximum number of coins in? If so, do so. If not, don't.

2. In general, today's machines should be played with maximum coins. You don't necessarily increase your *chances* of winning but you do increase the actual and proportional win. This cuts down the casino's hold on you. If playing a machine for maximum coins returns 96 percent of the money played because of bigger payouts, rather than 90 percent for fewer coins, you are better off playing the maximum. Remember that chart comparing 93 percent and 99 percent?

3. Always make sure that after you place the number of coins into the machine that you wish to play, the machine's line reflects that. Sometimes machines are slow to light up your line of play and then suddenly you hit—but you get paid off at a lower rate than you deserved to be. By the way, don't

look for sympathy from well-dressed, smiling casino executives. Most machines come with a warning to wait for your line to light up before pulling the handle or hitting the button.

4. When playing progressive machines of any type, choose the ones where the jackpot is at or past the amount of its payouts in the past. Some jackpots are reputed to be payable only after reaching a certain total—that's when the god in the machine kicks in and starts including the jackpot in his calculations. Before that, the jackpot is just a pretty sign flashing meaningless numbers. (I haven't been able to verify this particular advice, but even a quick perusal of in-house progressive machines shows that there seems to be a floor below which no jackpot is won. You have nothing to lose by following this advice—except your coins. But then again, that's what you'd lose if you didn't follow it. I have a belief: I follow the advice of people with experience as long as I know that advice can't hurt me. I received this advice from an old slot "pro". So if you play a progressive machine that is over its floor, you can't be hurt, you can only be helped by that.)

5. Always play the machine nearest the door. No, not because it's programmed to pay out more but because you'll have a faster exit when you lose all your money. Also, if you don't smoke, you can always get some fresh air. Usually there's more leg room too. This old adage used to be true. At least, every major gambling writer of the 1950s 60s and early 70s gave it. Casinos were supposed to put their loosest slots by the doors, the entrances to showrooms, the restaurants, etc., in an attempt to lure people into playing them. But if you look around a modern casino, you don't have to lure anybody into playing the slots. You have to lure them away. *(Come on, Jim, little Timmy is all grown up since you started playing that machine and he's graduating from medical school tonight!)* Indeed, one casino executive in Atlantic City laughingly told me: "We put our *tightest* machines at the doors now because so many people believe the doorway machines are loose!" Everyone has read the same books on slots or received this advice from their Aunt Kathryn. These doorway machines get a tremendous amount of play and there's no need to make them loose. But, I'd still advise playing them because— who knows?

6. Always keep records of your losses. If you are an inveterate slot player, you might just hit the big one one day (see,

even I am giving you hope!), or one worth more than $1,200, and then guess what? That's right. The taxman cometh! So you want to be able to show how much you've lost in the past to write against your wins. The tax people are interested in any slot winnings that are worth $1,200 or more. For table game players, any win of $10,000 or more in one 24 hour period will come under scrutiny. The casino has these forms it fills out and sends to the IRS. Although you can't write off gambling losses against salaries or business profits, you can write them off against gambling wins—up to the amount of your win! So keep some kind of running record—even if it depresses you knowing how much you're donating to the gods in the machines.

7. Avoid the little places, like gas stations, and small slot parlors because their payouts reflect their floor space.

8. Avoid slot promotions that sound too good to be true. They probably are. "Try a free spin every hour on our jumbo jackpot!" To do this you have to hang around the slot parlor for an hour. In that hour, the slot promoters know you'll play and play and play at inferior games. Sometimes the big, jumbo jackpot is for more free spins in another hour!

9. Never play more machines than you can comfortably watch. I have no idea why someone would want to play more than one machine but if you do, be aware of the fact that there are slot cheats just waiting to claim your payouts by dipping their hands into your trays when you aren't watching. These are the only people who win consistently in the slot areas of the casinos!

10. Only play *through* your money *once*. This is probably the best advice I can give you. However much money you bring to a casino for however long you intend to stay, you should divide it up into session stakes of equal proportions—depending on how many sessions you want to play. At each session, play that money through the machine—once. *Do not play any of the coins that you win.* Put those aside, or leave them, untouched, in the tray. When you have played through your session stake, that is, when you quit, win or lose. By playing this way, you limit your exposure to the grinding effects of the god in the machine's programmed payback scheme. If is far better to bring more money with you, knowing that this is all you can possibly lose if you don't hit one payout, than to bring less, hit several good streaks, only to

give it all back. In reality, this latter scenario will cost you more than bringing more money with you to play. Think about it and consider a single play-through as your modus operandi from now on. It gives you a better chance to come home a winner.

The key to coming home a winner on any given sojourn into the world of slots is not to get caught up in the mania. In fact, one of the best books on slots is actually called *Slot Machine Mania* (see recommended reading), and these authors are not kidding when they dub the behavior in the slot areas manic. The slots are mesmerizing to many people. It is almost as if they were at worship. Constantly plugging, pressing, hoping, cursing, plugging, pressing, hoping, praying. Personally, except for the rare coins here and there, I don't play slots as a regular feature of my gaming activities. They give me a headache and I don't like that maze-like atmosphere of the slot areas. There also seems to be more smoke.

Why people play them is beyond me. Perhaps it's the privacy. Perhaps it's the fear of being embarrassed at the table games where you have to have some knowledge of how to play in order to increase your chances for success. Maybe it is religion. You and the god in the machine in a one-on-one relationship. You are like a prophet and although your god can be cruel, he offers great rewards to the faithful in the afterlife. (The *afterlife* here defined as: your life *after* you hit the big one as opposed to after you bite the big one!)

Blessed be the slot players, for theirs is the hope of a better day dawning.

Recommended Reading

Slot Machine Mania by Dwight and Louise Crevelt. Gollehon Press. Grand Rapids, MI. ($5.95) Great book on the slots and the only one I consider worth reading. The authors are respectively an engineer-programmer of slot machines and an English teacher. So the book contains great information and is quite well-written. If you are into slots, this book is a must read. However, no one can help you beat the slots—except your local hammer supply store!

CHAPTER EIGHTEEN

Video Poker

M achine worshipers distinguish between the lowly slots of the last chapter and video poker machines. The slots offer no expectation of the long term wins because the god in the machine precludes them. Not so with video poker, the enthusiasts contend. Video poker can *theoretically* be beaten by expert play at *certain* machines. Like some table games, the players' decisions can actually affect the outcomes. There is choice involved. The god in the machine merely (metaphorically) shuffles the cards, deals them, and you play them. (Assuming, of course, that the god in the machine isn't slightly altering the probabilities of certain hands being made.)

There is no question that expert play at video poker is better than non-expert play. According to one casino slot executive I spoke to: "Most of the video poker machines we have are supposed to return approximately 97.5 percent of all monies played, but in actual casino operations they have been returning somewhere in the vicinity of 92 percent and sometimes lower. Even the so-called full-pay machines that we have are returning in the 94 percent range. We're making as much or almost as much from our video poker machines as we are from our regular slot machines."

However, whether expert play can actually gain an edge is highly debatable. To do so you have to meet the following conditions:

1. Only play on full payback machines—that is, machines where expert play will theoretically return 100% or more of monies played. You have to know which machines are full payback and which aren't. This isn't always easy as machines that often look alike, and are standing right next to each other, often don't *pay* alike.

2. Have a large bankroll to sustain you through incredibly long losing streaks because even when you are playing at full payback machines, the house has an edge of three percent or more until...

3. You (must) hit the royal flush once every 40,000 hands, on average, to see your theoretical edge materialize in the real world. The odds on getting the royal flush are 40,000 to one. These odds are not cumulative: They represent independent trials. Even if you have played 39,999 hands without a royal, the very next hand is still 40,000 to one against getting it!

The problem with video poker is that while theoretically you can get an edge, in the practical experience of every single video poker enthusiast I've interviewed for this chapter, that theoretical edge has not "as yet" materialized in the real world (see Chapter 21, "A Day in the Life of the Guerrilla Gambler", for more information). That's because most of them are not getting their theoretical share of royal flushes, without which video poker is a losing proposition.

Very few casual video poker players have the time, bankroll, or temperament to play the awesome number of hands needed to have a shot at breaking even or getting a slight edge in the long run. Stanford Wong, in his excellent book *Professional Video Poker* (see recommended books), estimates that a good video poker player can play 500 hands per hour! He states that "professional" players can play even more, upwards of 700 hands an hour. Just what is 500 hands per hour? That's playing a complete hand every seven seconds! Coins in, results shown, cards discarded, new cards shown, payouts if any, new coins in and so-forth. A person would have to be an Olympic athlete to play at this rate. But evidently some people can do it.

Naturally, the people who want to do this high-speed play are those who wish to get into the long run. If they know that a royal flush is the only hope of getting an even or better-than-even game against the casino, then the more hands they play, the better their overall chance is of hitting that royal flush.

Many of the video poker machines are progressive as well. They have an ever-increasing progressive jackpot which, at a certain point, allows the expert player to have a slight theoretical edge (should he hit that royal flush!). In Vegas, these banks of machines will be packed with "pros" attempting to get the royal jackpot, and all their losses back, when the progressive meter indicates it is at the proper level. But only one royal will take that jackpot, if and when it comes, and only one "pro" will get to walk away actually realizing in practice his theoretical edge. Of course, there are teams working the casinos, tying up banks of machines at the proper time. That's why many casinos have recently reduced the size of their progressive jackpots to discourage the professional teams from getting an edge and, more importantly, from upsetting the other players who can't get to their favorite machines.

Is it worth being a professional video poker player? Is expert play a gold mine? Should you quit work and head for the casinos? Well, does $12.50 an hour sound like a good living? Because $12.50 an hour is the most you can theoretically expect to make by playing full-pay machines until Armageddon. That's assuming you can find them; get in 500 or more hands an hour; hit your theoretical compliment of royal flushes; have a bankroll to sustain you through *long* losing streaks; tolerate the casino slot environment day in and day out; have lungs of iron to handle the smoke and don't die from some rare video-display terminal disease! Now, take out your taxes from the $12.50 an hour; buy your own health insurance and...being a video-poker pro doesn't sound so good does it?

But does that mean you shouldn't learn expert strategy? Of course not. If you enjoy video poker then you should play the best possible strategies. The casinos give themselves enough of

an edge without us helping them with foolish playing procedures. So by all means, if you are a video poker player, please
learn the strategies in this chapter because they will help keep
the house edge at bay and, maybe, just maybe, you will get
your share of royal flushes and be one of the rare ones who can
walk out of the bowels of the machine world a winner—having
plucked the golden tooth from the god in the machine.

Full-Pay Machines and Their Strategies

I hate to say this but...full-pay machines are not always
easy to find. For example, Atlantic City has comparatively few
of them; Las Vegas comparatively more; the riverboats somewhere in between. No matter where you play, however, quite
often you will have to hunt for full-pay machines as the casinos
aren't in the business of making it easy for their patrons. In
addition, you must play the maximum number of coins or the
machine will not be theoretically returning 100 percent. (For the
purposes of this chapter, I considered any machine a full-pay-
back machine if it returned more than 99.75 percent of monies
played based on the strategies recommended.)

I: Jacks or Better

The full-pay jacks-or-better machine has a nine for one
payout for a full house and a six for one payout for a flush. This
is sometimes called a 619 or a 6-9 machine. There's a handy
way to quickly eliminate other machines. If you walk by a
machine and don't see a nine for one payout for a full house
and a six to one payout for a flush—pass it by. However, if you
see that these payouts are in place, look for the following complete schedule. The payouts are based per coin played, but you
must be betting the maximum number of coins allowed. Thus,
a 50 for one payout will pay 250 coins for a maximum five coin
machine.

Hand	Payout
royal flush	940*
straight flush	50
four of a kind	25
full house	9

flush	6
straight	4
three of a kind	3
two pair	2
pair of jacks or better	1

*Note the following: most full-pay machines won't offer 940 on their royal flush line. Instead, they will offer 800. This makes these machines approximately 99.5 percent payback machines. Also note that unlike regular poker, video poker doesn't distinguish between types of hands in the same categories. Thus, four twos is the equal of four aces. Only on the pair line is a distinction made. You must have jacks or better to get a coin back.

Hand	Decision
1. mixed low cards	draw five cards
2. one high card (A,K,Q, or J)	draw four cards
3. any two high cards	draw three cards
4. any three high cards	draw two cards
5. break any three high cards for two suited	draw three cards
6. three to straight flush	draw two cards
7. four to a straight	draw one card
8. four to a flush	draw one card (break low pair)
9. four to straight and flush	draw one card to flush (break low pair)
10. break A-K-Q-J if K-Q;K-J; Q-J are suited	draw three cards
11. break A-K-Q-J if three are suited	draw two cards
12. 10-high card suited	draw three cards*
13. two high cards suited	draw three cards*

(*do not break a high pair or three of a kind.)

14. three cards to a royal	draw two cards (break low pair)
15. four cards to a royal	draw one card (break anything but straight flush)
16. four cards to straight flush	draw one card (break high pair)
17. two pair	draw one
18. three of a kind	draw two

(All pat hands—four of a kind, full house, straight, flush, straight flush—stand.)

II: Deuces Wild

Here the four deuces can be used to complete anything but a *natural royal flush*. Even if the full-pay machine you are playing offers a special bonus for a natural royal flush—DO NOT DISCARD A DEUCE! Here's your quick rule of thumb for bypassing non-full-pay machines. Bypass any machine that is not offering five for one for four of a kind. If you see a machine offering five for one, compare the payouts against the following chart.

Hand	Payout
royal flush (natural)	800
four deuces	200
royal flush (w/deuces)	25
five of a kind	15
straight flush	9
four of a kind	5
full house	3
flush	2
straight	2
three of a kind	1

Hand	Decision
any pat hand	stand (discard low nine in straight flush with no deuces showing and go for the royal flush)
four to a straight flush	draw one card
four to a royal flush	draw one card
three to a royal flush	draw two cards
two pair	discard one pair and draw three cards
four to a flush	draw one card
four to a straight	draw one card
any three to a straight flush	draw two cards
Q-J;Q-10;J-10 suited	draw three cards (draw five cards if one of other three is of the same suit)
any four-card straight	draw one card (except on A-3-4-5, then draw five cards)
6-7 (or better) suited with one deuce	draw two cards
three-card royal flush with one deuce	draw one card
any four-card straight flush including one deuce	draw one card
any pat hand with one deuce	stand (break flush, straight or three of a kind for any four-card royal straight flush or four-card straight flush)

6-7 (or better) suited
with two deuces   draw one card

four-card royal flush with
two deuces   draw one card

four of a kind with two deuces   draw one card

five 10s (or better)
with three deuces   stand

royal flush with three deuces   stand
five of a kind with four deuces   stand

(All other hands—discard everything but deuces.)

III: Joker Wild

You will find fewer full-pay joker wild poker machines than you will either deuces wild or jacks-or-better machines. A quick appraisal can tell you which machines to avoid. When you are passing a joker wild machine, check the payout on the four of a kind. If it isn't 20 for one, it is probably not a full-pay machine. The following chart is the full payback machine that you are looking for.

Hand	Payout
royal flush (natural)	800
five of a kind	200
royal flush with joker	100
straight flush	50
four of a kind	20
full house	7
flush	5
straight	3
three of a kind	2
two pair	1
kings or better	1

Hand	Decision
two pair	draw one card
flush	stand (break for four-card royal flush)
straight	stand (break for four-card straight or royal flush)
A-A or K-K	draw three cards (break for three- or four-card straight flush or royal flush)

low pair	draw three cards (break for four-card flush or three-card straight flush)
three cards to a straight flush	draw two cards
four cards to a straight	draw one card
K-Q, K-J or K-10 suited	draw three cards
Q-J, Q-10, or J-10 suited	draw three cards
ace or king	draw four cards
ace-king	draw three cards
full house with joker	stand
flush with joker	stand (break for a four-card royal flush or a four card open straight)
three of a kind with joker	draw two cards (break for four-card straight flush)
high pair with joker	draw three cards (break for three- or four-card straight flush)
four cards to a flush with joker	draw one card
four cards to a straight with joker	draw one card
three cards to a straight flush with joker	draw two cards
All other hands with a joker	draw four cards to the joker

Progressive Jackpots

Progressive jackpots offer the video poker player an opportunity to fully capitalize on potential royal flushes. Unfortunately, as I previously stated, only one player wins the jackpot at any given time (excluding teams) and the banks of machines are fairly loaded with players when the jackpot reaches the necessary level. To have a jackpot, most casinos will lower the payouts on their full-pay machines from 9-6 to 8-5 for the full house and flush respectively. This means that the player will be facing a much greater house percentage against him until he hits the progressive royal flush. Stanford Wong, Dan Paymar and other video poker analysts (see recommended reading) have categorized the levels the progressives must be at in order to make an otherwise inferior payout machine worth your play. Here are Wong's estimates for jacks-or-better machines. Unless the jacks-or-better machines are paying the following jackpots, they are not worth playing.

Machine	Jackpot
quarter (five for maximum payout)	$2190 or more
fifty-cent (five for maximum payout)	$4380 or more
dollar (five for maximum payout)	$8760 or more
dollar (three for maximum payout)	$5256 or more
five dollars (five for maximum payout)	$43,800 or more

To play these machines properly when they are at and above the progressive floor requires some changes in strategy. These Wong fully explores in his book, *Professional Video Poker*.

Dan Paymar has indices for all the progressives (including less than full payback machines) one is likely to encounter. These indices can be found in his excellent booklet, *Video Poker for Precision Play*. Here is a sampling of full payback progressives.

Type of Machine	Jackpot
quarter joker wild (five for maximum payout)	$765 or more
quarter deuces wild (five for maximum payout)	$890 or more

The strategies I have given you for the three most popular video poker games are basic strategies and can be used even on machines that are not full payback. If a given casino is only paying back 97.5 percent for expert play—you want to get your 97.5 percent payback. Why would anyone want less? So, memorize or bring a copy of the basic strategies with you when you next pull up to the video poker terminals. There are, of course, a myriad of video poker machines. You will find strategies for most of them in the recommended reading list that follows.

Recommended Reading

The video generation has arrived. My guess is that many of the under-50 baby boomers have played some kind of video game either at the arcades or at home on their computers. The phenomenal rise of video poker in the casinos leads me to conclude that, in short order, the traditional slots will be diminishing rapidly as the older slot patrons leave for that giant slot machine in the sky. The growth in gaming books about video poker has been no less dramatic.

Video Poker Mania by Dwight and Louise Crevelt. Gollehon Press, Inc., Grand Rapids, MI ($4.95) This is an excellent introduction to the world of video poker. It does, however, repeat much of the authors' information from their previous book, *Slot Machine Mania*. If you know nothing about video poker this should be the first book you read.

Professional Video Poker by Stanford Wong. Pi Yee Press, 7910 Ivanhoe Ave., La Jolla, CA 92037. ($19.95) This is a great book about jacks-or-better video poker and thoroughly explains what it really means to get an edge over the casinos in this game. Wong is a thorough theoretician. Although Wong claims there are video poker pros, I don't think any rational person would want to enlist in their company. A must read for video poker enthusiasts.

Video Poker Precision Play by Dan Paymar. Enhanceware, 2413 Eastern Ave., Suite 121, Las Vegas, NV 89104. ($12.95) This booklet is an excellent reference work and covers most of the better known games. Paymar offers excellent and easy to learn strategies for many of the more popular games. In addition, he has an exhaustive list of casinos where full-pay machines can be found. This is invaluable information. More importantly, he is constantly updating this booklet as new information comes in. He is not pedantic in his approach. He has the gift of being able to simplify the most arcane and difficult ideas and strategies. This is a must read for video poker buffs.

Expert Video Poker for Las Vegas by Lenny Frome. Spiral Bound. Compu-Flyers, LF-425, 5025 S. Eastern Ave (16), Las Vegas, NV 89119 ($9.95) Lenny Frome is a cottage industry and this is one of the many booklets he has produced on all aspects of video poker and other machine games. All his booklets are highly recommended but, beware, at times Lenny is so detailed that you can lose the thread of his analysis in a wealth of information. Still, I recommend his booklets. Write him at the above address and he'll send you a catalog of all his worthwhile publications.

CHAPTER NINETEEN

Take 'Em for All They're Worth

N ow you know what the casinos do to get an edge on the players. You know which games are suicidal and which games give you an opportunity to come home with some of the casino's money safely snuggled in your pocket or purse. You have strategies for almost every game, even those which I wouldn't recommend playing. To me the following 12 games give you, the guerrilla gambler, a shooting chance. I'm listing them in the order of most favorable on down.

I have not based the order strictly on mathematics—for, as you will see, I have placed video poker at the bottom of the list even though *theoretically* you can get an edge in this game. I think *practically* most video poker players, and I mean *expert players*, are just spinning their wheels. I have no evidence that the casinos or the manufacturers are mucking about with the random-number programming of the micro-chip but it just seems to me that having to rely on a 40,000 to one shot to attain a theoretical edge is just asking too much from Lady Luck. I think you have a much better chance of finding a biased wheel by using the Big Number strategy in roulette than you do of hitting the jackpot in video poker.

I think you have a better chance of making money at craps, even though it is a negative expectancy game, than you do at pai gow poker. That's because you can reduce the casino's edge to a mere fraction of a percent whereas in pai gow poker, your theoretical edge (on the order of .3 percent) depends on being the banker, having people bet heavily against you and so forth. The real world of gambling does not always neatly conform to the theoretical world. In the next chapter, I shall delineate what I consider to be a good money management program for the playing of all these games, either singly or in tandem.

The Top 12 Recommended Games

1. Blackjack—card counting, single deck

The best game offered in the casinos is the single-deck blackjack game with good rules. It is also the most difficult for card counters to play without being banned. Scan techniques work beautifully to give you an edge without walking on the precarious ledge as most card counters do. Also, learn how to act like a gambler so you can blend in with the crowds. If you sit for a regular session, try to leave after 45 minutes. If you feel the least bit of heat, even if you think it's your imagination, get up and go. Take a tip from the beautiful AP: "There's no such thing as paranoia in blackjack!"

2. Blackjack—card counting, double deck (multiple decks)

The double-deck game is volatile and will give the card counter plenty of opportunities for increasing bets in positive situations. Scan techniques work well here too. Four and six decks with good shuffle points (80 percent or more) are right behind. Eight-deck games with good shuffle points should be approached after the first two decks have been played and in positive counts only.

3. Craps—the Oddsman's bet

If you can use the 5-*Count* and then get money behind the Pass Line, all well and good. Even if you can't employ the 5-*Count*, this is still a great bet as the house has no edge on you whatsoever. You may be able to get odds on Come bets if the person is a friend, otherwise it could get awkward (see Chapter 21).

4. Craps—10 times odds

You can use either the Captain's *Supersystem* (see *Beat the Craps Out of the Casinos: How to Play Craps and Win!*) or the 5-*count* Pass and Come. This latter bet gives the house a mere .18 percent edge (that's less than two-tenths of one percent!). My opinion is to skip the Don't side taking of odds, so the 10 times odds games are not important for the Don't bettor.

5. Craps—Five times odds (other odds)

This is a good game also for the *Supersystem* and the 5-*Count* Pass and Come. However, you want to be able to get more behind the five and nine than the odds stated. For example, if you have $5 on the Pass Line with nine as the point, you want to put $28 (or at least $26) behind it in odds. The casinos can't pay off a $25 odds bet because five and nine pay three to two. Thus, you need an even amount of money. Try to push the house to $28. Try not to let the casino push you down to $24. If you are at a casino where you can play a dollar on the Pass and Come, try to place $6 behind the five and nine. A *true* five times odds game can give the house less than .32 percent edge against you.

Next best bet is to find a casino that gives *true* triple odds: three times odds behind the four and 10, four times odds behind the five and nine, and five times odds behind the six and eight. This game gives the house less than a .47 percent edge. Even if you have to play the usual double odds game, the Captain's methods of craps play will give you a great shot at the casino bankroll.

6. Baccarat (mini-baccarat)—Four percent commission on bank or streaking

You can do nothing to get an edge in baccarat. However, the house takes so little as its cut that a short session can turn into a winning (and longer) session. Always look for games that take a four percent commission on the bank bet and *only* go with bank bets in these games. Or look to exploit possible streaks in the usual five percent commission games. Give yourself only "X" amount of money to find a streak and then quit and go to one of the other games if nothing positive occurs.

7. Pai Gow Poker—banker only

This will be difficult to pull off *but if* you learn the proper strategies for making hands *and* get to be banker, say, two-thirds of the time *and* get the other players to really bet against you heavily *and* have a large bankroll, you can approach this game with a certain amount of cautionary hope. That's quite a few *ands* and an *if* and a *but*—however, it is at least theoretically possible to bring home the bacon in this game.

8. Poker

At first I hesitated to list poker as a possible winning game because of the level of competition you might face in the casinos. However, I've changed my mind. If you are a disciplined poker player and use the strategies that I outlined for which hands to play, there is no reason why you can't have a good shot at winning. Short-term play is the key. Hit and run and don't let anyone nip at your heels.

9. Craps—Don't betting

Take it easy here. Don't chase and only go up on two Don't Come numbers. Don't lay any odds. The math is misleading on the Don't side of craps. Once up on the numbers you don't want to water down your edge.

10. Roulette—Big Number and Clocking wheels

Although I didn't go into detail about clocking wheels, the books I recommended will give you good formulas for deciding which wheels are actually biased. These will take time to find and analyze. Naturally most players aren't interested in this kind of long term analysis. For you, the Big Number strategy is probably the best. However, like baccarat above, give yourself "X" amount of money for a quick hit against Big Number(s) but don't stay too long. If you don't make money in 38 spins, move on to another game. The casino has a large edge on an unbiased wheel so you don't want to get suckered in.

11. Craps—the Captain's Best Buys

This is strictly for high rollers because you must be able to afford the high buys of the four and 10, five and nine. Use the 5-Count religiously and call off your bets at the appropriate times. Your level of comps playing this way should be high—this should offset somewhat the two percent you're approximately giving the casinos by placing the six and eight and buying the other numbers.

12. Video Poker—full-pay machines only

Maybe it's because I never played computer games or cared much for arcades, but I am leery of all machines programmed by an establishment that has a vested interest in taking my money. You might have a theoretical edge in full-pay machines but I still trust a player rolling the dice more than I do a machine. I am probably wrong here but I just can't help feeling that the joker in video poker is on us. I don't know anyone who is ahead in this area who has played for several years. I can't say this for most of the other games.

The 12 Worst Bets in the Casino

Sometimes knowing what not to play is almost as important as knowing what to play. Here are the 12 worst bets in the casino. Avoid them.

1. Sic Bo

This might be the single worst game in the casino. Avoid all bets at this game. If someone puts a gun to your head and says you must play sic bo, then bet the small and big.

2. The Wheel of Fortune

Watch it on television. Better yet, watch the news. Better yet, read a book. Still better yet, read a book written by me.

3. Proposition Bets at Craps

These are all Crazy Crapper bets. Players make them because they either don't know any better or because they get so caught up in the excitement of the moment that they forget to protect themselves. Famous last words, no?

4. Caribbean Stud

At its best it is a poor game. If you decide to bet that extra side bet for the jackpot, it is an even poorer game.

5. Red Dog

Kill it before it bites your bankroll.

6. Super Pan Nine

You're better off playing baccarat, which this game resembles not a little. The tax on your bets is just too much for any serious hope of gain.

7. Place Bets of four, five, nine and 10; Big Six and Eight; Field bets at craps, crapless craps

Pass these on by.

8. Slots

Unless you are absolutely guaranteed a 98 or 99 percent payback (which you aren't) why give the casinos your money? The top 12 games are not hard to learn and they offer some bangs for your gambling bucks. I guess I'm a Luddite at heart when it comes to machines. Look at how many dealers these things have put out of work. Get those hammers ready, men!

9. Blackjack—"I have my own strategy!"

And this strategy is guaranteed to make you lose. The unskilled blackjack player, or the blackjack player who has been playing for years "my way" is a loser from the word go. He probably gives the house upwards of 20 percent on him. Blackjack, the game, is as dangerous as blackjack, the weapon, if you don't know how to play.

10. Keno

The keno area of a casino is great for taking a nap in. Leave it at that.

11. Video Poker—non full-pay machines and poor strategy

The flip side to the mathematics of beating video poker is the fact that most machines are not full-pay machines. Even with the best strategy, the casino will have four percent or more on you. With inferior strategy, you might as well mail a check to the casino and stay home. Better yet, mail the check to my publisher and tell him to forward it to me. I mean, if you're feeling generous...

12. Hickok's Six Card and most new games

The casinos are bringing in new games to make money, not to give you a shot at their bankrolls. Any game that requires side bets or extra money for extra cards is generally a sucker trap. In California aces, you can't overcome the house tax on your win or on your seat! As a general rule—avoid all new games, no matter how attractive they look.

Other ways to Beat the Casinos at Their Own Games

American gamblers have gone comp crazy. Players will lose thousands to win a comp worth a hundred dollars. The casinos know that many players want to get "free" food and lodging, or, for lower rollers, substantial discounts on the same. The casinos have set their comp policies with one thing in mind—making you play at a certain level for a certain period of time to lose a certain average amount of money to get a comp worth maybe one percent or less of your total action. (Total action is the total amount of money you bet during your session or stay at a casino.)

I recently heard the story of a great high rolling Australian billionaire with a love for blackjack. It is typical of Las Vegas high roller stories and you can substitute Japanese, Chinese, Texan, movie star, baseball team owner or whoever for the Australian lead character. This man likes to bet $50,000 a hand—and play all seven hands at a table. That's $350,000 in action per round! He prefers shoe games. The casino of his choice flies him and his party in first class, puts him and his party up in the most luxurious of suites, lavishes him and his party with gifts and gourmet meals. Nothing is too good for Mr. High Roller. A casino host told me in private that the hotel spends $30,000 a visit on this individual.

Sound like a lot?

The last visit Mr. High Roller lost—$9,000,000! That's nine million. NINE MILLION DOLLARS!

The casino made $9,000,000 for an investment of a lousy $30,000! Mr. High Roller could buy a lion's share of the hotel for $9,000,000. Sadly, in their desire to be treated like kings, many high rollers will bet their kingdoms.

To a lesser extent this is what the casinos try to do to everyone. Even the lowliest of low rollers wants a comp. To get it, the casinos demand action. They demand you bet high enough and for long enough to justify "giving" you a freebie. For low rollers this comp often comes at the expense of their dignity for, unlike the high roller who gets everything "up-front," the low roller must literally beg for every comp. While the high roller is fawned over in a sickening manner, the low roller must grovel to get a few crumbs. I can't tell you how often I have heard the following conversation:

> *Low Roller:* You think I could have a comp for lunch?
> *Pit Person:* (*pretending to look a little surprised but quickly pretending to cover his astonishment that such a plebeian would dare to ask for a comp*) I'll have to see about that. (*pause for effect*) One?
> *Low Roller:* (*embarrassed by his lowly stature in the eyes of the*

casino world, stammers) Two. Me and the wife. (*seeing the pit person's eyes narrow in horror*) For sandwiches, you know.
(*Low roller feels that if he specifies sandwiches, the pit person might take pity on him*)
Pit Person: (*frowning ever so slightly*) I'll have to check your action. (*Subtle hint that the man might not have played sufficiently long enough to merit a sandwich.*) I'll be right back.
Low Roller: Thank you. (*Low roller continues to play.*)

Now the pit person writes something on a piece of paper. If the casino where this little charade is taking place is computerized, the slip of paper goes to a rather bored man or woman who types some information into the computer. While this is happening, the pit person goes to the farthest end of the pit and busies him or herself with something or other. (If the casino is not computerized, the pit person takes the slip of paper to the farthest end of the pit and busies him or herself with something or other.) Ten, 15 or 20 minutes later, the low roller asks the dealer what happened to the pit person. The dealer will shrug or say something to the effect that he'll be right back. A little while later, another pit person walks by and the low roller calls out to him or her to come over.

> **Low Roller:** I asked for a comp about 20 minutes ago and the guy disappeared.
> **Pit Person:** (*looking suspicious*) Who did you ask it of?
> **Low Roller:** The guy at the end of the pit, all the way down there. (*Pit person eyes the low roller. Low roller, feeling awkward, blurts out...*) It was just for sandwiches.
> **Pit Person:** I'll see what I can do.

Now the new pit person walks down the pit, stopping to chat with the dealers, talk to high rollers, breathe in the smoke-filled air. In five minutes he gets to the other pit person and a long conversation ensues. The low roller looks anxiously down the pit. He thinks they are making a big decision about his comp. In fact, they are talking about the barbecue held by one of the dealers the previous week. At the end of a discussion of how drunk so and so got, the new pit person says to the previous pit person, "Oh, player A at table B seat two wants a comp." Of course, the decision had been made earlier by the original pit person. Sure the guy was going to get a comp—if they could keep him playing another 20 minutes to half hour! The little charade of giving it to the computer person and walking down to the end of the pit was to get the low roller to play more.

Now the original pit person comes back and either hands the comp to the low roller or takes a comp from the computer person and hands it to the low roller.

> *Pit Person:* Sorry this took a little while. I had to get this authorized (*which means that the low roller's action was so low that only one of the casino gods could authorize a comp for a sandwich*) and the boss wasn't here. I can't authorize comps at your level of play. (*By saying "your level of play" the pit person shoots home the message that next time there won't be a comp and maybe Mr. Low Roller should consider betting more heavily.*)
> *Low Roller:* (*feeling grateful as he takes the comp from the pit person*) Oh, thanks.
> *Pit Person:* (*magnanimously*) You're welcome. (*pause*) Enjoy your meal.
> *Low Roller:* (*grateful*) Thanks, really, thank you so much.

The low roller takes off for the cafeteria with his $15 comp. The pit person whispers to the dealer, "How much did he rebuy for?" The dealer whispers back, "Another hundred." The pit person marks the following on a piece of paper: *Mr. Low Roller cashed in originally for $100. Played a half hour, asked for comp. Cashed in for another $100. Half hour later. Cashed out for $50. Loss $150. Comp $15.*

Scenes like this occur quite frequently in casinos. The pit crew's job is to get you to play as much as possible. When you ask for a comp, if you are a low roller, they will delay, hem and haw, to get you to play overtime. Don't do it.

In fact, the guerrilla gambler attempts to play less and get more. The guerrilla gambler wants to extend his body time at the table but not his at-risk time. The casinos generally rate players on two criteria—*how long* you play and for *how much*. They multiply *how long* by *how much* and come up with a bettor's profile. Once they have a profile, they can determine how much in comps this particular individual's play deserves. Thus, your goal as a guerrilla gambler is to distort the profile so that you appear to be a much bigger player than you actually are.

This can be accomplished in any number of ways—

depending upon the game you are playing. In craps, the 5-
Count automatically extends your body time but not your "at-
risk" time. Let us say that as a low roller, you place the six and
eight for six dollars apiece after the *5-Count*. If you can stay at a
table for two hours but only risk your money for one hour *and*
have the casino rate you as a two hour player, you will get
more comps. More reward for less risk!

The following are techniques that extend your body time
but not your at-risk time. Included will be some methods
designed to deceive the casinos into thinking you bet more
heavily than you actually do. I have used many of these methods with varying degrees of success. Some of the methods I
have not used but acquaintances have. I can't state unequivocally that all these methods will reap in the comps for you but
you have nothing to lose by trying them.

If you feel that the more devious methods of getting
comped are "cheating" and "immoral" then don't use them. I
used to think that all of these techniques bordered on the shady
until one time at the Taj Mahal in Atlantic City showed me the
error of my thinking. There was some poor, pathetic blackjack
player, obviously drunk and stupid (a lethal combination) who
had just signaled for a hit on an 18 against a dealer's six. He
had a one hundred dollar bet up. The dealer hesitated and said,
"Are you sure you want to hit that?" The drunk nodded. The
dealer still hesitated.

The pit person came over and nudged the dealer. The dealer gave the drunk a card. Obviously, the drunk busted. The pit
person whispered to the dealer, "You're not here to help the
players." For the next half hour that poor, pathetic drunk hit all
manner of absurd hands—and lost thousands of dollars. The
pit person hovered near the table at all times and the dealer
kept his peace. Finally, the drunk staggered off and the pit person very matter-of-factly wrote down the drunk's losses.

I turned to AP, my beautiful and quite moral partner, and
said, "I guess all is fair in love, war *and* gambling." She agreed.
And I thought to myself, *How many times have you seen players
do suicidal things and the casino honchos just snicker into their rating pads? Answer: too many. How many times have you seen low-
rolling players who have taken substantial losses—for them—of $50,
$100, $150 and when they asked for a comp the pit crew let them stew
and wait and wait and wait? Answer: too many.* Well, I say, to hell

with playing by the casinos' rules. As long as you don't steal chips, mark cards, substitute dice, hit slot machines with sledgehammers, or do anything *illegal*, I'll leave morality to the saints.

I think of these tricks the same way a poker player thinks of a bluff. If I can make the casinos think they have a better edge over me than they really do and their misconception leads them into giving me more than what they would otherwise think I deserve—so what? Casinos do the same things to the players with their psychological warfare departments—better known as public relations and advertising departments. Casinos attempt to get you to bet over your head and bust out. That's why more gamblers have gone belly-up than have casinos. So bring on the comps!

Getting Your "Fair" Share

1. Always join as many players' clubs as the casinos offer. If you are a slot player, join the slot clubs of as many casinos as you enjoy playing in. Casinos compete for players and you will find that, with little or no action, you will be offered discounts on many things during promotional periods.

2. If you are a table game player, you should never begin playing until you have either asked to be rated *and* given your name in, or handed in your player's comp card. Some casinos, especially in Atlantic City, have pit crews that watch a player cash in and play for several minutes *before* ambling over and picking up the player's card. The player then has missed part of his rating. So when you sit at a table, cash in but don't place a bet until your rating begins! You want every second you've earned!

If you are a card counter, sometimes you don't want to draw attention to yourself. One of the best ways *not* to draw attention to yourself is—*to draw attention to yourself!* A regular gambler wants a comp and wants to be rated. The pits know this. They also know that many card counters are somewhat timid and withdrawn in the face of pit scrutiny. The pit people are going to notice how you bet—whether you give your name in or not. So give them your name first. "Hey, Mollie, can I get a rating?" "Hey, Joe, don't forget to take my card!" "My name is Jimmy Jackson, can I get rated?" Of course, if you are playing for serious money and you are a brilliant card counter, you might not want to give in your real name. But don't hesitate to give in a name. Let the pit crews think you are just one of the sheep wanting a comp for your shearing.

3. Try to have three or four players' comp cards in your name. An acquaintance of mine puts cards in machines of players who are not getting rated. This gives her their time. She thinks of this little maneuver as the equivalent of donating blood. The player is donating his or her time. She sees nothing wrong with doing this—after all, she reasons, the machines are being played, time is building up, comp units are being earned. Why not have someone get them?

4. At the craps tables, always use the *5-Count*. No matter what system you are playing, the *5-Count* will extend your time at the table without extending your risk. Pit crews at craps tables know that many players don't bet on every roll. So you will fit right in.

5. In blackjack, during low counts, or when you have to go, make sure you head for the bathroom in *mid-shoe*. Don't wait for a shoe to finish to go to the bathroom (especially if you are counting cards and the count is in the basement). Your rating points will still be accumulating but your risk will be nil. A visit once an hour in a low count can really reduce the casino's edge and increase your comp value. This is true of baccarat, too. If you aren't in the midst of a torrid streak and winning bundles of money, make your pit stop mid-shoe.

6. Put up a larger than usual bet when the pit person comes over at the beginning of a shoe. If your normal bet is $20, then make the first bet $40 and the next two $10 each. Your risk will still be $60 (albeit skewed on that first hand) but your rating will be double. (In a single-deck game, you are even with the casino off the top so in the long run that first bet is an even proposition.) In a shoe game, the pit person does not observe every hand. He moves around. If you want, whenever he

comes to you, up your bet. If you are counting and the count is low, don't up your bet—up your body and go to the bathroom. First, however, start pushing out a hundred dollar bet and at the last minute indicate that your bladder is about to burst and head for the restroom. You might even get that hundred dollar bet down in the ratings.

7. In baccarat, the streak method of betting will help you to avoid playing every hand. Like craps, not all players bet every hand in baccarat. You should be able to get your rating.

8. Once you have asked for a comp, *stop playing*. Either that or ask for the comp 10 minutes before you intend to finish. Never play one second longer than you want just to be comped. If they make you wait, *sit* and wait. You might even want to call out loudly every few minutes: "Hey! How's my comp coming?" The reason you want to sit is to speed up the process. If they know you aren't going to play any more hands, they will get the comp to you sooner to free up a chair.

9. Don't be afraid to grovel. Oh, yes, the beggar who grovels the most is sometimes the beggar who gets the most. Think of asking for a comp as an act, that's all. It doesn't reflect on your dignity. And be effusive in your praise of the pit person who gives you the comp. And always use that first name as if the two of you are best buddies. "Oh, *Billy*, thanks for the comp. Really, *Billy*, thanks so much. Billy...Billy, Billy, *Billy*."

10. If groveling is not your style, then ask for the comp in such a way that the pit person knows that not only do you *expect* a comp but you have *gotten* a comp before, perhaps even from him, for this level of play: "Comp for two for lunch, Willie." Oh, yes, always talk to the casino pit people as if they are your buddies. They will do that to you, so you do that to them. Sometimes it's hard to turn down a buddy.

11. Put up a large bet at the time a casino pit person is observing, but take it down *before* actual play. I once put up a $300 inside bet in roulette in an Atlantic City casino that I rarely frequent. It was an accident. I had reached for the wrong pile of chips. The only reason I had a pile of black chips at the roulette

table was that I had played a Big Number that had hit several times in slightly more than several spins. The dealer yelled out: "Blacks in action." I looked over at the layout and thought to myself, *what idiot would put a $300 inside bet at roulette?* and lo and behold those were *my* black chips sitting on number four! The ball was not as yet being spun, so I just left the bet there. The pit person asked the dealer who had placed it and the dealer nodded towards me. He wrote something on the pad and turned away. I took the bet down the moment the dealer began to spin the ball and replaced it with three blue chips (roulette chips worth $15 total)—a far cry from the three black chips! Several weeks later I received an invitation to *fly to the casino at the casino's expense!* Okay, it wasn't an invitation to fly to Vegas, but still, the casino was willing to put me on a plane at their expense and fly me from New York to Atlantic City. And I believe this was all the result of one inadvertent bet.

12. Always look for coupon books and play the coupons that give you a better game. For example, in Las Vegas many casinos have coupons that will pay three to two or two to one on even money bets such as the Pass Line in craps, the red and black in roulette, player or banker in baccarat, etc., if you bet a ceratin amount (but no more). This amount is usually five dollars. Now, if you have a friend or partner, you take one coupon and place it on the Don't Pass; your partner takes one coupon and places it on the Pass Line. The two bets will cancel each other out but the coupon returns double for the winner. Thus, you win no matter what. The only number that can hurt you is the 12 on the come out roll—a once in 36 occurrence.

When the lovely AP and I are in Las Vegas for extended periods, as we often are, we do a daily run of casinos offering this option. Some casinos are most ungracious when you do this, however. The Tropicana used to offer this coupon and when the lovely AP and I did our Do and Don't bet, one of the dealers became somewhat inflamed.

"That's almost like cheating," he said.

"In what way?" said the delightful AP.

"It just is," he said.

"You offer this coupon, I'm playing this coupon," I said.

The dealer grumbled. I wondered if he actually owned the Tropicana. After all, what did he care if we won five bucks?

When last I looked the Tropicana and the company that owns it were still around. AP and I hadn't busted it.

However, most casinos don't even notice and wouldn't care if you played the coupons as I suggested. After all, the majority of the customers are willing donators. If you are guaranteed $20 to $30 a day with almost no risk—go for it! Think of your coupon trips as breakfast money (see Chapter 21).

13. Don't be afraid to sell a comp to someone else. The Frontier in Las Vegas has been offering an incredible deal during its rancorous strike with the culinary workers union. If you play blackjack for a minimum of five dollars or more, every time you receive a blackjack, you get a special silver coin. Collect a certain number of silver coins (originally 10, then 11, and by the time you are reading this—who knows?), you get a free room! You have to collect a few more for a free room on a weekend. Well, several of my Las Vegas buddies who play the Frontier game have found a way to add to their advantage. They sell the silver coins! For two dollars or more, they will give you their coins for a free room! This deal appeals to low rollers who could truly benefit by a "free" room. Some Las Vegans have quite a business going selling "free" rooms. They hope the strike never ends.

Say you are playing at one casino and your friend is playing at another. Both of you get a comp for two for lunch. One of you sells the comp for half price! There's no end to the ingenuity with which you can approach resale in America! If two of you are playing at different tables but at the same casino—then both of you ask for comps for *two*. Then sell one comp. You can usually sell the comp as you wait in the line to the restaurant. If the casino has a rule about selling comps, and they stick it to you as you are peddling your comp—give it away! Make a donation to the poorest slob you can find. He deserves a gourmet meal, too, no?

14. Some casinos offer free shirts, jackets, vases, picture frames, bookends, mugs, wine glasses or what-have you to regular players. Even if you have more of the aforementioned items than you could ever want—collect them. The casinos record the fact that you are interested in receiving their merchandise and thus they will tend to keep offering it. I have a

wardrobe full of jackets and shirts with casino logos. Wearing them in a casino makes the casino pits look at you as just another dopey gambler.

15. If you are *not* a card counter, always cash in for *much, much* more than you intend to play with. At craps I always cash in for four times what I'm actually willing to lose in a session. This makes it appear as if I'm a higher roller than I actually am because the pit person always writes down your initial buy-in. The figuring goes that what a person cashes in for is what that person is willing to lose. What you are willing to lose sometimes helps the casinos decide what they are willing to give you. Especially after you have a winning session, the pit will want to get a handle on what you would have been willing to lose had you been clobbered. That would be your buy-in.

Card counters should be wary of doing this as astute pit crews know that card counters like to have enough backing them so they can withstand the inevitable swings of luck—those "fluctuations in probability" the mathematicians are always writing about. So if you count cards, cash in for much, much *less* than you expect to play with!

16. Always collect whatever coin vouchers are offered by the casinos. In Atlantic City, for example, the players comp clubs are always mailing players coupons for coins. I know some members of the Captain's Crew who used to ignore these generous coin offers. After all what do mega-rollers need with some coins? Then one day, the Captain himself added up what he collects *weekly* from Atlantic City casinos in coin vouchers— a staggering $120! That is truly free money. So always collect your coin vouchers and redeem them. I always set aside a part of any trip to tour the casinos where I have coin vouchers waiting.

17. Never be afraid to ask for a comp. When I first started my war against the casinos, I was embarrassed to ask for something for free. It was my upbringing, I guess. Now, I ask for comps even if I play for 15 minutes in a casino. I don't consider a comp a freebie, I consider it a part of my game. The worst the pit people can do is say no. Big deal. One caution, however, for high rollers. Don't make a pig of yourself when you are fully

comped. If you can't eat it, don't order it. Some high rollers are such oinkers that many casinos have tightened their comp requirements for their gourmet restaurants. This hurts medium rollers who like a gourmet meal.

I'm sure there are other ingenious ways of getting more for less that you will come up with in your own personal attack on the casinos. If you do, send them along to my publisher and he'll forward them to me. In the next edition of this book, I'll include them. Hey, we have to help one another against the enemy!

CHAPTER TWENTY

Money Management: Sacred Cow or Silly Goose?

Some gamblers claim that the most important aspect of their game is money management. Others, mostly mathematicians or gaming writers steeped in math and secure in jobs outside of the gambling arena, claim that money management is an illusion since most gamblers are essentially playing negative expectancy games— that is, games where the casinos have the long term advantage. No matter how you manage your money, you are destined to go broke— sooner or later. It's just a matter of time.

I agree with the gamblers.

I agree with the gamblers because I know that the mathematicians are correct. In most negative expectancy games, sooner or later you will go broke. However, the longer you can hang in there, especially in games such as craps where more is going on than just random fluctuations in probability, the better chance you have of hitting hot streaks. So you need economic endurance.

This is the reverse of the mathematicians' argument that the best way to play a negative expectation game is to take all the money that you intend to bet and bet it on one spin of roulette (on an "even" money bet) or one hand of baccarat. Go for the big one right away and, if you win, never play again. If you lose, walk away with your head held high, secure in the knowledge that you did the mathematically correct thing.

Yeah, right.

Mathematicians are quite practical and have a *true* grasp of human nature.

Wrong.

The one guy who played like that—all or nothing on one decision at a negative expectation game—was the infamous "suitcase" player who bet almost a million dollars on the Don't Pass line at Binions in downtown Las Vegas. He had carried the money into the casino in a tattered suitcase. He put it all on the Don't Pass line. For one decision only. The first year he did this, he won. He walked out of the casino, his head held high, indicating he would never return. But, being human, he did return—the following year. Again with his tattered suitcase. Again, he bet the Don't Pass line for one decision. This time the seven was rolled on the come out and the gentleman lost his almost-million dollars. Once again, he walked out of the casino, his head held high, vowing to never return. This time he kept his vow. He blew that high-held head of his off its shoulders with a shotgun when he got back to the hotel room. He didn't even leave a tip for the maid.

Unfortunately, real life and real gamblers are not mathematical formulas.

Life itself is a negative expectation game because, sooner or later, you are going to go broke—that is, die. So why not just take the gun out and put a bullet in your head, right now, today? Because most of us feel that it is better that the end come later rather than sooner. The more you live, and the more healthily you live, the more you can experience what life has to offer—for the good.

And that is my theory of money management.

You want to be able to hang in there for as long as possible, losing as little as possible, with as healthy a bankroll as possible, so that when luck comes your way, you have the opportunity to take advantage of it and get ahead. To do this, you must have enough money to weather all the inevitable cold streaks. This applies to *positive* expectation games like blackjack, pai gow poker (dealer only), regular poker, video poker (full payback only); this applies to *even* expectation games like the Captain's Oddsman's bet in craps; and it applies to *slightly negative* expectation games like the Captain's 5-*Count* Pass and Come, and his *Supersystem*.

Money management is also *character* management. You have to know when to quit—when ahead *or* behind. The best example I can give of this just happened to me yesterday.

I decided to take a short breather before starting this chapter. So the lovely AP and I headed for Atlantic City for three days—Monday, Tuesday, and Wednesday. Today is Wednesday. I am not in Atlantic City. I'm home. Because I lost all my money and had to hurry home? No. I'm home because I had a single extraordinary night at the craps tables at Showboat on Tuesday; a night that saw me have my greatest roll—a 35 minute monster where I made nine points and constantly hit my numbers. It was a dream evening. (AP estimated I hit close to 30 of my numbers, including my points, all totalled!)

On Wednesday morning (that is, this morning), the lovely AP looked over at me as we were eating our breakfast. I was gazing out of the window of our room—at the beautiful view of the ocean. The towering Taj Mahal was on our right. I could see the people, like ants, walking on the boardwalk, even though it was only 9 AM. In an hour or so, I would be on that boardwalk, going from casino to casino, looking for opportunities to hit and run during positive counts at blackjack, place oddsman's bets at craps, or attempt to find a biased wheel in roulette with the Big Number strategy.

"Let's pull a Captain," said AP.

"What?"

"Let's pull a Captain," repeated AP.

I realized what AP was referring to. Yesterday, the Captain and one of his Crew, Jimmy P., had been playing at Resorts where they offer five times odds at their $25 minimum tables. If you can afford it, you can take $125 in odds behind your Pass and Come bets ($150 on the five and nine). This is chump change to these two. The Captain and Jimmy were both playing the *Supersystem*. The first two rollers had good rolls. The Captain and Jimmy were up what *for me* would be a small fortune.

Jimmy turned to the Captain, who was already placing his chips on the table to be colored up, and said: "Let's go home." Then they both colored up.

The four of us, the Captain, Jimmy, AP and I, had dinner at Capriccio, a wonderful gourmet restaurant at Resorts, and then the Captain and Jimmy headed home. They had driven one hour and 45 minutes to play for 25 minutes! They ate and went home. Of course, the Captain would be coming back in a day or two, since he plays several times a week.

"If I win early and significantly, I leave," said the Captain. "I don't give the casinos an opportunity to get their money back—on the same day! Of course, you could always say that *if* I stayed I *might* have won more. I don't buy that. I'd rather have a bird in the hand than two in the bush."

So at breakfast, the eagle-eyed AP was looking at me. She knew what I was thinking.

"You wanted to take a break from writing and you know that the second you enter the house, you'll be up in the office pecking away at the word processor. You're a little boy and you don't want to leave the game. But you are a little boy who has made a lot of money."

"You're right," I said.

"Let's savor the win."

She was right, of course. Savoring a win is like savoring a fine wine.

"Let's pull a Captain," I said.

We checked out right after breakfast and even as my fingers are typing this, I'm still savoring the win! It's a delicious sensation.

There was a time in my gambling career when I would not have been able to cancel a day of a casino trip because I enjoyed playing as much as I enjoyed winning. Today, I enjoy *winning* and playing is what I have to do to win! I believe that my character has improved with my skills over the years.

Bankroll Requirements

Essentially what I have just said is: "Don't play with scared money. Have enough money to back you. Know when to quit."

I wanted to put this standard advice into somewhat more human terms.

How much money do you really need to play the games *worth* playing?

There's no easy formula for deciding such a question because we are all different. I prefer to have a lot of money backing me because I'm essentially a chicken. The thought of losing my whole stake is so unnerving to me that I have built up my stake over the years to the point where I'd have to suddenly go berserk in order to put a big dent into it, much less lose it.

Some players are far more adventurous and daring. If you are the devil-may-care-to-hell-with-money (and-the-rent) type, you can probably reduce by 50 percent the bankroll requirements for playing the various games that I recommend. This reduction will mean that your chances of going broke are much greater. However, your chances of doubling your bankroll are also much greater since you are betting more in proportion to your bankroll. Your temperament must be the key to your money management decisions. You must play within your bankroll and within yourself.

For the following games, I will once again use units of betting as opposed to dollar amounts. What money those units translates into is up to you.

Blackjack—Card Counting

For *single-deck* games, you want to start with multiple-unit bets off the top and either increase in positive counts or decrease in negative counts. You are looking for an effective spread of one to six. So, start with a three-unit bet, go to four units on a +1 and six units in any positive count of +2 or more. On minus counts, go to two units on -1; one unit on -2 or less. To back one single-deck session, you will need between 100 and 120 units. You will need a total bankroll for single-deck blackjack of 1,500 units.

For *double-deck* games, you want an effective spread of one to eight units. Start off the top with a two-unit bet; increase one unit for every *running* count over +2, but never more than double the size of your previous bet. Go to one unit on any negative count. For one session you will need 160 units. You will need a total bankroll of 2,000 units for double-deck games.

For *four or more* decks, you want an effective spread of one to 12 units. Start with a one-unit bet and increase one unit for every *true* count over +3. Stay with a one-unit bet in all negative counts. However, if you are winning in negative counts, place an extra chip on top and do a small progression—as long as you are winning, you can increase your bets. This makes you appear to be a gambler and will also help you to take advantage of high card clumping. For a single session you will need 200 units. You will need a total bankroll of 2,500 units.

For all card counters, you are looking to get away with a win of any kind. When fatigue sets in—quit. Don't chase losses. If you blow the entire session stake, take a nap. As a counter you stand to lose your session stake more often than a flat bettor since you will be experiencing explosive swings of fortune with big money out in high counts. A few losses in high counts can seriously cripple you. Then again, a few wins can have you singing, "The hills are alive with the sound of *money!*" I have found that many sessions boil down to one or two high count hands. They either make you or break you. In the long run, they make you.

Blackjack—Basic Strategy only

For single- and double-deck games, you will play two units off the top. If no aces appear on the first round, you will go to three units. Otherwise, you stick with basic strategy and two unit bets. If you are winning consistently and have made a 50 percent profit, you might want to increase to three units and do a small progression. If your profit slips below the 50 percent mark, go back to two-unit bets. Try to get away with at least 25 percent in winnings. If you should double your stake, put 50 percent aside and play with the other 50 percent and so on. Have a session stake of 80 units and a total stake of 800 units.

On the losing end, if you are losing consistently at one table, get up and move to another. Reduce your betting to one-unit bets until you win back at least half of what you lost at the previous table. If you get clobbered at your new table, take a break. Remember, the fact that you give yourself a certain amount of money to play with doesn't mean you *must* play until you lose it.

In multiple-deck games, start with one unit. If you win 50 percent of your session stake, increase to two units. If you are winning consistently look to do a small progression of 1-2-3-2-1. If you double your session stake, put 50 percent of your win aside and play with the other 50 percent. Keep doing this until you lose the last 50 percent, then quit for the session. You'll need 40 units for a session and 400 units for a bankroll.

Craps—the Oddsman's bet

You are playing a mathematically even game with the house. You might even decide to be a little daring here, using a Martingale—a mini-Martingale, however. Let us say that you are at the typical double odds game and the point is four (or 10). A player has a Pass Line bet of $5 up but he is not taking the odds. Put $5 (one unit) behind his Pass Line bet in odds. Now, if the shooter makes his point, great. However, should he fail to make his point, put $6 behind (then $7, then $10) the next shooter who has a four (or 10). You are risking a total $28 on four rolls. If any one of those four rolls is a winner, you come away with a win. If the first roll is a winner, you win $10; if the second roll is a win, you win $7 ($12 win minus previous $5 loss = $7); if the third roll is a win, you win $3; if the fourth roll wins, you win $2. It's an interesting way to play the Oddsman's system.

Whatever Martingale you use must be for a particular set of numbers. Don't increase your bet when you lose on a four if the next point you are placing odds behind is a six, for example. You might have to keep a record and do separate mini-Martingales for four and 10, five and nine, six and eight. Of course, remember that as you progress in a Martingale, you are betting more to win less. So make four steps your maximum. Also, remember that these Oddsman's Martingales are not double-up types. You increase the next bet by the number of units necessary to be ahead if you win the next roll. I'm not a big Martingale fan but for a fair game, in the long run, no matter what you do, you will break even with the house. Do not, I repeat, *do not* use this type of Martingale if you are playing the Pass Line or Come yourself. This is strictly for the Oddsman's style of play. You should have a total bankroll of 500 units.

Craps—Pass and Come with full odds

It's tough to decide what kind of bankroll you require for a prolonged assault on the craps tables. Rather than give exact figures for every conceivable odds bet, let us just talk about total risk. If you have 12 units in total risk, you are better off having it as two units on the Pass Line with 10 units in odds (assuming a five times odds game). Thus, you want to get as much money up in odds as possible. Now, decide how much you wish to risk on any one roll and divide that by the three. (I always assume that players should be on three numbers. It's not a law, it's a predilection of mine.) So if you are willing to risk, say, $45, you can do it by placing a combination of three Pass/Come bets of $5 with $10 odds on each in a double odds game and so forth. If $5 is your basic unit, then you are risking nine units. (Of course, you would want $12 bets if the numbers were five and nine. Remember, you always want to push the house!)

Obviously, the numbers are imprecise and you would be better off giving yourself a range of risk—say, $45 to $65 depending on the odds involved—or nine to 13 units. So for craps play, of any kind, you need at least 1,000 to 2,000 total units. Divide these into 10 session stakes.

Do not increase your bets when you are losing. In fact, reduce your risk by either betting smaller or by betting only two numbers. When you are winning don't be in a rush to increase the number of units you are betting. Wait until you have at least tripled the money you have at risk during a given roll before pressing to the next level. Thus, if you have nine units at risk, do not increase your bets until you have won 27 units. And always be quick to leave a table if you've lost a third of your session stake.

Baccarat

You aren't going to spend an inordinate amount of time at baccarat if you aren't hitting a streak. Thus, your session stakes will be relatively small—one-unit bets, with 20 units backing you. Remember that regular baccarat is usually $20 to $25 minimum, so a session needs a minimum of $400 to $500. Your total baccarat stake should be 250 units. Mini-baccarat takes substantially less money to play.

Pai Gow Poker—banker only

You will probably have to be a real banker, a real wealthy banker, to play this game. Check out the table *maximums*. Do you have enough money to cover this if every player bets the max—which is theoretically what you want? What about two hours of every player betting the maximum? What about…you get the picture. Pai gow is one of these theoretically good bets—if you are wealthy enough to afford it. How many units would you need? Multiply the maximum by—oh, a hundred?

Poker—guerrilla style only

One hundred times the table minimum per session. Enough in reserve to go 12 sessions without a win.

Craps—Don't betting

You will only go up on two Don't Come numbers. One unit each. Thus, you will be risking two units maximum per shooter. Have 50 units per session. Six hundred units as a total bankroll.

Roulette— Big Number

A session for big number roulette is no more than 38 spins, unless you are winning relatively handily—at least, 50 percent of your starting session stake. Maximum of three or four Big Numbers working at any one time. Remember you can divide a table minimum or your unit of betting among four numbers in most cases. Approximately, 76 to 114 units for a full roulette session. Twelve hundred units for a total bankroll. Be careful, the purpose of playing the big number is to find a biased wheel. Maybe, in 10 sessions, you'll find one and really rack up! That's the idea. Otherwise, roulette would be on the 12 worst list! Caution is the buzzword for roulette.

The Captain's Best Buys

Only high rollers can play this way. Remember, you are putting out $40 on the four and/or 10 ($39 + $1 commission) and $39 on the five and/or nine ($38 + $1 commission). At this level, you would want to place the six and/or eight for $42 or

more. I think you would need $20,000 in reserve to play this
way. Divide that into 10 session stakes of $2,000 each. You must
use that *5-Count* perfectly because despite the fact that you
have reduced the house edge tremendously on these outside
bets, the casino still has a potent 2.5 and 2.6 percent edge on the
four and 10, five and nine respectively. The casino edge on the
six and eight is still 1.5.

Video Poker—full pay machines only

Figure you are going to lose and lose and lose *until* you hit
the royal flush. That might be a long time coming. You will need
$12,000 (minimum) to see you through the video poker electro-
magnetic storms. What happens if you don't hit that 40,000 to
one shot? Just don't take Mr. "suitcase" man's way out.

The Guerrilla Bankroll

If, like me, you intend to play more than one casino game
in the guerrilla fashion, hopping from one to another, hitting
and hopefully running with the money, you have to have some
economic proportion between or among the games you intend
to play. For example, you would never bet the same per spin of
roulette as you would in a high positive count in blackjack, or
on a single roll at craps. That could prove quite costly since you
are bucking odds of 37 to one but only getting a payout of 35 to
one on the double zero wheel. So you want to keep your guerrilla bankroll heavily weighted towards the games with positive expectations.

Here is my formula.

For every 1,000 units, I risk them in approximately the following way, depending on the venue. I have divided this latter
into Las Vegas and Atlantic City, the places where I have done
the bulk of my gambling these past years.

Game	Las Vegas	Atlantic City
Blackjack	800 units (single/double decks)*	700 units (six/four decks)*
Craps	130 units (10X odds only)*	260 units (2X, 3X, 5X odds)*
Roulette	10 units	20 units (Big Number only)
Baccarat	10 units	20 units

Poker	40 units	0 units***
Pai gow	0 units**	0 units**
Video poker	1 unit	0 units
Sports betting	9 units	0 units***

*You'll notice that I risk more units at the craps tables in Atlantic City than I do in Las Vegas. This isn't because the craps games in Atlantic City are superior. On the contrary, certain craps games in Las Vegas are much better. If you play exclusively at the Las Vegas casinos that offer 10 times odds, you have an almost even game. The reason I risk twice as much at craps in Atlantic City is two-fold.

1. The blackjack games in Atlantic City are essentially ripoffs, so I avoid them more. Also, the blackjack games are more expensive, so I play less, risking more per hand but playing substantially fewer hours and only during high counts. I *wong* much more in Atlantic City. I play much longer in Las Vegas at both blackjack and craps than I do in Atlantic City—I just bet less at craps. So I spend more time at the tables with fewer units at risk. This explains part of the disparity.

2. The other part has to do with the Captain, the greatest craps player in history. Since he does most of his playing these days in Atlantic City, I make a point of playing with him as often as I can. Hey, how many opportunities do you get to play with the craps equivalent of a Babe Ruth, a Muhammed Ali, a Wayne Gretsky? So I take advantage of the opportunity afforded me to be with *the man* himself.

**I won't play pai gow poker because I don't have the bankroll to do it properly. I figure you need close to $12,000 per session with at least 15 times that in reserve. No way am I risking that much on one game where I have only a .3 percent theoretical edge—that is, *if* I can be the bank at *all* times. There are too many *ifs* and *buts* for me to tackle pai gow as other than just an interested spectator.

***As I write this, Atlantic City is considering poker. Indeed, as you are reading this, there will be a good chance that poker is being played there. If so, I'll be doing my guerrilla attack on it. As for sports betting, that seems to be a dead issue for the moment in Atlantic City. But who knows? Maybe, as the competition gets fiercer from the riverboats and the Indian reservations, the New Jersey legislature will reconsider sports betting.

As I stated, when I'm in Las Vegas I play much more—easily four hours a day at blackjack, maybe two hours at craps, and another hour or so divided among the other games. It doesn't feel like work. It's fun. It's profitable. My typical playing time in Atlantic City is probably half as much in total—with about two-thirds the amount of time at the craps tables, but drastically reduced time at the blackjack games. I walk the boardwalk a lot.

Many of my gambling pals won't even bother going to Atlantic City. Those from the East coast prefer getting on a plane and flying to Las Vegas. To them Atlantic City just doesn't offer decent games, which are defined as games where you have a decent chance to win.

Even I spend almost twice as much time in Las Vegas as I do in Atlantic City. I spent 78 days in Las Vegas last year, 40 in Atlantic City. I also toured many of the smaller venues, the Indian reservations, the riverboats. These will probably cut into my Atlantic City time in the future, too.

Although I am a New Yorker, born and bred (with that New Yawwk accent that the linguistically pure AP has been trying to rid me of for years), I consider Las Vegas to be my second home. My days there are of a dreamlike and fantastic character. Let me share one with you now—the good, the bad, and the revelatory—this is the *inside* story of guerrilla gambling, the internal milieu.

CHAPTER TWENTY-ONE

A Day in the Life of a Guerrilla Gambler

The telephone rang at 5:30 in the morning. I pushed my arm out from the covers and mumbled: "Umm."

"Good morning," said the cheerful voice. "This is your wake up call."

"Thanks," I mumbled. I turned over and began to go back to sleep.

"Don't fall back asleep," I heard AP say from the bathroom.

I put my head under the covers and began to drift.

The covers were yanked from my head.

"Up," said AP.

"I don't feel like walking today," I said, grabbing a pillow and putting it over my head.

"Up," said AP, taking the pillow. "Every day you don't feel like walking until we're halfway through and then you say, 'I'm glad you made me walk today.' "

"That was a great imitation of me," I said, getting out of bed. AP had been an actress, a ter-

248   GUERRILLA GAMBLING

rific actress, and she had a knack for mimicry. Indeed, as the fates would have it, we had met and fallen in love when we were both playing the lead characters in a play called *The Only Game in Town*. It was the story of a gambler and a chorus girl in Las Vegas. The gods are certainly ironic. That was some years ago—before I had ever placed a single bet!

"Today's the big day," she said.

"Don't remind me," I said.

AP was referring to the fact that today, or rather tonight, somewhere in Virginia, I had a new play opening. I wasn't going to be attending opening night. I hadn't gone to any of the rehearsals. I had told the director and producer that they were free to make any changes they wanted in the script. My typical quote is: "If they can change the words of Shakespeare, they can change the words of Scoblete!" Spell my name correctly in the programs and send me the royalty checks promptly. The only interest I had in the play was that the audience would like it. The theatre was sending me a tape of the opening night, so I would be able to see it when I got around to it.

AP was on the floor doing abdominal exercises. I've never met a woman like her. She wakes up bubbly and energetic every day—every damn day! Me? Well, I mumble and moan for my first half hour. My morning aerobic exercise is to complain. I looked at AP doing those abdominals on the floor. Then I looked at my own protruding gut in the wall mirror and walked into the bathroom.

"I think I drank too much last night," I said from the bathroom.

"You drank your usual," said AP in the middle of crunches.

"Well, my usual is too much. I'm becoming a big fat tub," I said from the bathroom. "I used to be the leading man and I'm slowly becoming the fat friend."

"So don't drink a whole bottle of Pouilly Fuisse," said the unsympathetic AP.

By six o'clock, we had gone through our morning ritual of me not wanting to get up, of me complaining about getting fat, of AP scolding me that if I just reduced my caloric intake I'd be fine, of me saying sincerely: "Yeah, yeah, yeah, you're right," and of both of us knowing full well that that night, like every other night when I'm in Vegas (or any gambling venue), I'd be sitting with a bottle of my favorite wine, dining at a fine restaurant with my good friends and having the time of my life. And then the next morning the ritual would be repeated again.

This particular week we were staying at the Sahara. It was summer. At 5:30 in the morning it was *only* 83 degrees.

When I'm in Las Vegas, I like to stay a week at a time at whichever hotels will give me the best deal. I don't look to get comped rooms because I don't want to be under any obligation to play where I stay. Indeed, most times I prefer to stay where I don't play! I don't want to be tempted to play should I wake up early (unlikely) or return in the evening early (quite likely). In Las Vegas I only play the best games—single- and double-deck blackjack with the best rules, poker, and craps with 10 times odds. The Sahara's games, with the single exception of the occasional four percent commission on the bank bet in baccarat, have been uniformly awful for the past few years. Yet it is a good hotel, especially the newer towers and the refurbished rooms. It's also relatively inexpensive. The staff is friendly and pleasant and that's always a plus.

Usually my trips to Las Vegas are in two to four week stretches. I just can't see flying across the country from New York to Nevada (four-plus hours) in order to spend a few days there. I feel that I can't get on track, that I can't establish my rhythm in a short stay.

I don't even like to play my first day in town. I want to have absolute control over myself when I go into a casino and usually after a long plane ride, I'm groggy and not at my best. So I wait. That's why I like a minimum of two weeks, but I really *prefer* four week stays—something that is hard to do considering my writing schedule. I believe that the casinos are banking on people to be tired and simultaneously anxious to get in playing time. I think that's a part of the casinos' winning formula. On the few occasions when I've been in Vegas for short stays—a week or less—I have felt the pull of the tables quite strongly and I'm much more anxious to get into the action than on longer trips.

I don't do it, though.

If I arrive in Vegas at night, I won't play until the following late afternoon. If I arrive in the afternoon, I won't play until the following morning. I want *me* to be in control of *me*. So on a short stay, it can be tough to discipline my gambling heart! (But I do it.)

AP and I like staying at the Sahara because it gives us easy access both to Las Vegas Boulevard (known as "the Strip") and to Paradise Road which runs roughly parallel to the Strip. Our daily six mile walk takes us south along Paradise Road to Flamingo Road and west to the Strip, then north along the Strip, passing all the famous hotels, and back to the Sahara. It takes us slightly under two hours to complete (we're not power walkers) and by 8:30 AM we are showered and meditating peacefully in a darkened room.

After a 20 minute meditation, we each have some fruit and head for our first game of the day. On this particular morning, that meant the Frontier, which had been offering the best single-deck blackjack game in town. We drove down Paradise Road and entered the Desert Inn's parking lot from the back road, the Desert Inn Road, appropriately enough. I parked at The Desert Inn because I was nervous about parking at the Frontier. For a couple of years a very nasty strike had been going on and I didn't feel safe parking my car in the Frontier's lot. I'd heard stories of rental cars becoming caught in the cross-fire of thrown bottles.

AP and I crossed the street and entered the Frontier. Two of its front windows had been smashed in the night. They would be fixed in a day or two. We entered at the side entrance and none of the early morning strikers seemed interested in insulting us. There were days, however, when entering the Frontier had been a lesson in labor-management dialogue—with labor brow-beating, castigating, and cursing those of us who crossed their picket lines to play.

One night the previous week when we were entering the Frontier, one of the strikers got into our faces and called us names that no publisher would see fit to print. In true Zen fashion, we ignored him, looked right through him.

Inside the Frontier, AP said, "I wish I could tell that idiot how much money we've won from this place."

"Forget it," I said. "We know the only reason we play here is that they're offering a superior game."

And that was true. As a serious blackjack player, I go where the games are, even if it means crossing a picket line. After all, I'm not there to give the casino my money. I'm there to take the casino's money. But try to explain that to someone who has lost his job. I think I would cross the Lake of Hell itself if there were a good blackjack or craps game on the other side. But I won't eat at the Frontier anymore or stay there anymore (even for free). Maybe when the strike is over...

However, the strike against the now not-so-new owners of the Frontier had done much more than make entering the place unpleasant. The place *itself* had become unpleasant. It was a moldy skeleton of its former self, a run-down dive where once it had been an elegant and exciting place that used to cater to high rollers. Now the pit bosses sweated five dollar players who seemed to be winning. Many of the players were so uncouth that they didn't even tip the poor cocktail waitresses. If something wasn't done soon, the Las Vegas Frontier would go the way of the American frontier—it would close.

But for this day, for this trip, and for however long they offered them, the Frontier had the best single-deck blackjack game in town and one of the three best craps games with its 10 times odds.

AP and I played blackjack for 40 minutes and then cashed in. We were up $350. Not a bad morning's play.

At 10 o'clock we were meeting two of our good friends, KF and Alan Tinker, at the Rio for a breakfast buffet and an 11 o'clock blackjack tournament.

The Rio is one of the nicest small casinos in all of Las Vegas. It is somewhat off the beaten track, west of the Strip on Flamingo Road. Every Tuesday and Thursday at 11 AM, the Rio holds a small blackjack tournament. This particular day would be my first blackjack tournament.

We left the car with valet parking and went inside. The Rio has a tropical theme and the dealers and cocktail waitresses all look like they are preparing for a luau. We headed across the casino to the buffet.

Alan Tinker was waiting outside the cafe. It was 10 AM on the nose. KF wasn't there and they were supposed to come together.

"KF's in the bathroom," said Alan.

"Oh, I thought he was on a hot streak," I said.

We have a rule. You must be prompt for all engagements— gambling sessions, meals, shows, boxing matches—that you've agreed to attend. EXCEPT—if you are somewhere WINNING. So when AP and I had initially seen that KF wasn't standing with Alan Tinker, we naturally assumed that he must be somewhere playing and winning. Had he been, the three of us would have waited for 10 or 15 minutes and then proceeded to eat without him. This rule is very important for gambling friends because nothing is worse than having to leave a session when you're winning in order to meet people who are waiting impatiently at some restaurant or show.

Alan Tinker, KF, AP and I all have the same basic approach to money management during gambling sessions. At a certain point we take a percentage of our winnings and only play with that. If we lose it, we leave. But if we continue to win, we stay. No dinner. No show. No anything interferes with a good session.

KF came into view.

"I'm sore," he said.

"Why?" I asked.

"I ran a little more than I should have this morning, seven miles," he said. "I saw you guys walking down Paradise. I was too tired to yell."

KF looks like Robert Redford. He's in his early 50s but could easily pass for 35. He's a man heavily invested in real estate and he raises and rides horses as a hobby. He runs most mornings. He is lean but solidly built.

Alan Tinker had been KF's childhood friend. They went to the same summer camp as kids. Then they went their separate ways. In 1988, at a blackjack table in the Maxim, KF heard a familiar voice. Just then Alan Tinker whispered in his ear, "It's not fair that you haven't aged in 35 years. Do you have a painting somewhere in your home of a shriveled old man?"

That was the great reunion. The friends had had a lot in common as kids and now they both discovered that they had something in common as adults—a love of Las Vegas and blackjack. It was that same summer that AP and I met both of them.

Alan Tinker and KF have radically different temperaments. Alan is an exuberant player. He wins with aplomb and loses with aplomb. He plays with joy and a certain abandonment. I have never seen him upset. On the other hand, KF is a deadly serious and introspective player. He analyzes his play after every session. He is constantly seeking information on his game of choice—blackjack—and he will not settle for anything less than perfection.

Alan Tinker doesn't just play blackjack. He is an avid craps player and a video poker nut. KF will only play blackjack and, on occasion, place the odd sports bet or two. KF, however, has the ultimate sense of the absurd and a sharp and ready wit which he puts to good use. When the four of us play at the same table, within minutes we are laughing so hard it's hard to keep track of the cards.

My temperament is somewhere in between KF's and Alan Tinker's. However, all three of us are fueled by a desire to beat the casinos at their own games. And thus far we have. And what of my beautiful AP? Where does she fit on the gambling temperament index? She is a stoic. She plays because she enjoys it. She actually enjoys the process of attacking a casino game, whereas I enjoy the results the most. She has as much fun playing blackjack in practice, for no money, as she does playing for real. And she enjoys everything about our travels. If it weren't for her I would probably not go to a show. I would probably be more prone to going on tilt. Whenever I'm weak and about to make a stupid move, she says the right thing to get me back on track. She is not as obsessed with the games as we three men. "You're all like little boys," she says, "you take your games so seriously. None of you makes your living gambling, yet you all act like this is the only thing that matters. It's as if a dollar won at a game is worth more than a dollar earned somewhere else."

She's right. It is.

And she was also right about none of us making our primary living from gambling. I had my writing, KF had his real estate holdings in the east and horses in the midwest, and Alan had his very successful law practice in the east.

That morning at breakfast, the conversation turned to just that subject—making a living at gambling.

"I couldn't do it," said KF. "I couldn't take the swings of luck, the fluctuations. I like doing what I do now. Regular trips to Vegas and then something else. I couldn't take a steady diet of the anxiety."

"I couldn't do it because I think I could easily be lured into degeneracy. I like it too much," said Alan Tinker. "I'm the kind of guy who could wind up broke."

"I'd be bored," said AP. "The games are fun now because they represent an adventure, a challenge. But to make a living? Forget it."

"Not me," I agreed. "I'd have an ulcer if I had to depend on gambling for my sole income. I like traveling from place to place, meeting the people, playing and analyzing the games, writing about my experiences and ideas. But to depend on gambling as my sole income? Forget it. Even if this town or any gambling town allowed you to count cards and play for whatever stakes you wanted, even the best card counter in the world isn't guaranteed a winning day."

"Or a winning year," said KF.

"You can be great and still lose," I said. "When I first learned to count cards I thought I was on my way to being a millionaire. The very first trip I took to Atlantic City in the early 80's, I played for a week straight and won every day. I won just about every session. Since I was disenchanted by what I was doing at the time—producing, directing, acting and writing shows that toured—I was looking for something else. I thought I had found it, too. I was ready to chuck everything and just play blackjack. Then two weeks later, on my second trip, I lost every penny I had won previously and then some. Then I realized that blackjack would not be my new career. I think I lost 10 pounds from sweating at the tables that week. I lost hand after hand. It never dawned on me when I had been reading all those books that you could be a great player and still lose."

"You have to have other ways of making money," said Alan Tinker.

"I also think that gambling professionally is a narrowing experience," said AP. "I mean there is only so much you should think about a game. You have to have other intellectual outlets and pursuits."

"I haven't met many professional gamblers who are all that well-rounded," agreed Alan Tinker.

"In this new book," KF said to me, "you should really give your readers a sense about how it *feels* to play. Get in some of that emotional side to playing—win or lose."

"Yes," said Alan, "you have to walk the fine line of letting people see that they *can* win with proper play against certain games but that there are no guarantees. You really have to watch your money and not get lured into bad judgements."

"You don't think people know that?" I asked.

"I didn't," said KF. "And you didn't either when you first

started. Even people who read gaming books, perhaps especially people who read gaming books, are prone to overlook the good advice and the modifying statements and allow their hope to take control of their heads."

"Your next book is on every game?" asked Alan Tinker.

"Just about," I said.

"Don't make it dry," said Alan Tinker. "Give people not only strategies but a sense of what it is you do. How you actually play. What it is actually like to be a casino gambler—and I mean an expert gambler. Let them know the truth about the games, which can be beaten, which are close calls, but most especially about how you feel when you play."

"Most games aren't worth playing," said AP. "We've traveled extensively researching the games for this new book and most of the new ones just aren't worth the effort."

"But they look as if they are," I said. "The casinos are offering new games that appear to give the players choices that have meaning, but in reality the games are heavily loaded in the casinos' favor."

"Like video poker," said KF.

"Now, wait a minute," said Alan Tinker. Video poker was a sore point with Alan Tinker. "Certain video poker games can be beaten."

"But you have to get a 40,000 to one shot to do it," said KF.

"Are you ahead?" I asked Alan Tinker.

"No," he said regretfully. "I haven't gotten my share of royal flushes."

"How many have you gotten?" asked AP.

"None," said Alan Tinker.

"None?" I said.

"I've played..." he took out his notebook and read slowly. "One hundred...ninety-three...thousand...four hundred fifteen hands..." he put the notebook in his pocket and looked up. "Not one."

"I don't trust the machines," said KF. "These casinos probably fix the play. All they have to do is fix the possibility of a flush...make it come up once every 200,000 hands and you get killed."

"I think that would be illegal," said Alan Tinker.

"Who's to know?" said KF.

"The programmers," said AP.

"The games are on the square. You can win on full payback machines," said Alan Tinker.

"But you haven't," said KF.

"No."

"KF," said AP. "You are a purist. You'll only place a bet on something that you can ascertain has a definite mathematical edge for you."

"True," said KF. "However, I don't trust the machines and I don't trust the casinos."

"It's not in their interests to cheat," said Alan Tinker.

"Don't be so sure," said KF. "On several occasions I think casinos have brought in mechanics to play my table when big money was being won."

A mechanic is a dealer who can control the distribution of certain cards in a hand-held game. He does this by subtly following the shuffle and placing the card he wants in reserve at the top. Then he deals seconds—that is, the second card in the deck until he decides to use the first card. He uses the first card to give himself a good hand or to bust someone who has been winning and betting big. (See appendix for Darwin Ortiz's book, *Casino Scams.*)

"I remember hearing that *snap!* when they dealt," continued KF.

"Some dealers just naturally snap their cards," reminded AP.

"So what did you do?" I asked KF.

"As soon as I lost three hands in a row or 10 percent of my win, I left and went to another casino," said KF.

"Better safe than sorry," said AP.

"I'm not a purist," I said. "I'll play slightly negative games like craps. I think if you are within a percentage point or so either way, you essentially have an even game. Then money management, good play, and luck all come into the picture."

"I agree," said AP. "In craps the 5-Count took us from losing to winning. Something as simple as not betting on every shooter."

"Never the big score," said Alan Tinker, who himself has started playing the Captain's way. "But you do protect yourself and I think it gives you a practical edge, although not a theoretical one."

"I still like knowing that I have the mathematical edge,"

said KF. "That's why it's blackjack for me. I don't even want to play an even game. Although I must admit, I would play craps the way you guys do but the game still confuses me."

"How can that be?" asked AP. "You have this great mind for blackjack and you get intimidated by craps?" KF nodded. "I think you just don't want to bother so you tune out when we talk about it."

"That too," agreed KF.

"But if you want a mathematical edge, you could play video poker and what's the name of that game—pai gow poker..." began Alan Tinker.

"You don't have that much of a theoretical edge at pai gow," I said.

"I'm telling you Alan, I don't trust those machines, and I know from what Frank told me that pai gow can only give you a marginal edge on a certain bet..."

"The banker," I said.

"So why bother playing when my blackjack edge is much better?" finished KF.

"But what about the other low house percentage games?" asked AP. "Are any of them worth playing, even if they are slightly negative?"

"Of course, "said Alan Tinker. "If you play them correctly. I agree that a percentage either way is essentially an even game."

"I think you also have to take the advice or at least seriously consider the advice of certain gambling sages," I said. "If an individual has been playing for decades and winning, or if an individual makes a good living from gambling, then this individual's advice should at least be entertained. There's no substitute for wisdom. Not even a computer."

"I think that what you have to remember about all the computer generated hands in blackjack or other games," said AP, "is that the likelihood of you playing the number of trials of a given hand that a computer uses for determining the proper play is...well, it is impossible. If you want to determine what the best strategy is for, say, hitting a 12 against the dealer's two in blackjack, then the computer runs a million or more hands of a 12 against a two. I'll never play a million hands of a 12 against a two."

"You have to play the best strategy," I said, "only because

the totality of your decisions over a gambling lifetime will give you a greater chance at winning if you do. But no one hand, played for a lifetime even, will fall exactly within the set probability. But maybe all of them put together will fall within a range that gives you the best chance for the risk involved. Did that make any sense?"

"Yes," said Alan, "and that's why craps can be beaten in the long run even though the computer and the math say it can't."

"Make it simple," said AP. "All you need are several shooters a year who have some control over the dice and you have upset the randomness of the game. If you haven't lost too much in the interim, then those shooters alone should give you a win."

"The 5-*Count* and proper money management," said Alan Tinker.

"That's why the Big Number strategy in roulette can work," said AP. "You are just betting a little at a time at different wheels until you get either a favorable fluctuation in randomness or a biased wheel."

"So essentially we aren't purists, except for KF," said AP. "But we are impurists only a little. We are venial sinners."

"Her religious upbringing," I said. "Notice the religious imagery."

"There's a religious element to gambling," said AP.

"Absolutely," I agreed, "there is an almost religious fervor to some gamblers. I sometimes think of Las Vegas as the Jerusalem of chance. A holy city."

"I'm certainly drawn to it," laughed Alan Tinker. "My ex-wife wanted to buy a condo in Israel. I told her I wanted a condo in Vegas. I haven't heard from her in years."

"I'm considering one, too," said KF. "It's just that Vegas is changing rather fast."

"Becoming a big city, like New York," agreed AP.

Alan Tinker looked at his watch. "Almost time for the tournament. Remember what I told you guys."

This was not only my first tournament but KF's too. Over the past few years we had watched Alan's phenomenal success at tournament play—he had finished first in a major Vegas tournament a couple of years before—winning a whopping $140,000. Since then he had finished second and third in two other major tournaments. In addition to his major tournament wins, Alan Tinker played every minor tournament he could find while he was in Las Vegas. He had won these on a number of occasions. Indeed, his tournament winnings were nothing short of staggering.

"You play against the other players," said Alan Tinker. "Get a lay of the territory at first. Then in the endgame—go all in. You are either going to win or lose every chip. Got it?"

KF and I nodded. AP was not entering the tournament. She just wanted to watch.

"This is exciting," I said. "I'm rarin' to go!"

"This whole thing is exciting," said KF.

"Us," said Alan Tinker, "against this city..."

"Against the whole casino industry," added AP.

"...is the most exciting thing in the world."

"A day in the life," said Alan Tinker. "That's an angle."

"A single day," agreed AP. "A single day—be it good or bad or indifferent—in your life as a guerrilla gambler."

"Just a regular day," said KF.

"It might put everything into perspective," said AP. "Let the readers see what your advice translates into in real life."

"So what day?" I asked. But I already knew what day it would be. Today. I was already up $350. I had a fresh memory of what we had talked about at breakfast. A part of the joy of what AP and I did was the sharing of the adventure with each other and with friends.

"I certainly want it to be a day when I finished ahead," I said.

"Most of the time we do," said KF.

"No, no, no," said AP. "I know what you're thinking. You want to end the day with a huge win. Show everybody not only the fun but the profits."

"Well," I said.

"And you want to look good," continued AP. She reads my mind all the time. "You don't want your readers to see you getting your head beat in with all the winning strategies that you're recommending to them."

"Give them the good and the bad," agreed Alan Tinker.

"Today," I said. "Today will be the day. I'll take notes as the day goes on and see if I can capture a typical day."

"Win or lose," said AP.

"I'm off to a decent start," I said. "We're up $350."

"The point of the chapter isn't really the win or the loss," said AP. "The point is the actual doing of it. The actual play, the conversations, the adventure. The process and not the result is the point of the chapter."

"Got it," I said. But deep down I knew that I would not have selected today if I were down $350 instead of up that amount. But I didn't say that to AP. I didn't have to. She already knew.

"Tournament time," said Alan Tinker.

The Rio tournament is fairly typical of small blackjack tournaments. There were three preliminary sessions at 11, 12 and one o'clock, followed by a semi-final round at two o'clock, and the final at three. All the entry fee money was returned in the form of prizes and thus the casino made no money from the tournament. This gave the player an even game—a game where skillful play could give you a long term edge. Of course, with a hundred or more people participating in the contest, the Rio was fairly assured of a profitable day since many would be gambling at the tables while waiting for their sessions or after they had been eliminated from the competition.

As luck would have it, none of us was seated at the same table for the first round. I was happy about that. I didn't exactly relish the thought of having to go against Alan Tinker the very first time out.

As we were approaching the table, Alan Tinker pointed to a group of six people, five men and a young woman.

"See them," he said. The three of us nodded. "That's a regular team. They're good. They play every tournament in town."

I scanned the faces of the five men, mostly late 50s early 60s, and the girl. I'm fairly familiar with the great blackjack players of Las Vegas—if not personally, at least by sight. I didn't recognize any of them.

"I don't know any of them," I said to Alan Tinker.

"They only play tournaments," he said. "It's a whole other world."

Of course, Alan Tinker was one of the masters of that world. Unlike KF, AP and I, Alan moved easily from the world of tournaments to the world of guerrilla gambling. Living part time in his condo in Las Vegas as he did, and being the personable and friendly type, Alan knew just about everybody.

The table and seat selection in tournaments is done by random draw and it just so happened that I was seated at the table with the girl (really, she couldn't have been more than 22 or 23 years old and from my current chronological vantage point that age constitutes "girls" and "boys") and five middle-aged men, one of them a teammate of the girl. I was on first base, that is, the first seat to the left of the dealer, and the girl was in center field—the middle position at the table. Her "partner" was sitting right next to her.

Each preliminary session of the tournament at the Rio consisted of 25 hands and each player received $500 in tournament chips to play with. The two with the most chips at the end of 25 hands moved to the next round. The buy-in for the tournament was $25. There were 108 participants. The winner would receive $1501.20; second place, $499.50; third place, $351; fourth place, $199.80; fifth place, $97.20; and sixth place, $51.30.

I followed Alan Tinker's advice and bet the minimum of $10 on the first round of play. (The maximum bet was $300). So did everyone else—except the middle-aged partner of the girl. He bet $50.

The dealer was showing a six, the "partner" had doubled on his 11 and caught a 10, the rest of us stayed.

The dealer busted. We all won. The partner was up $100.

He bet the $100.

He was violating everything Alan had said about tournament play. Indeed, he seemed to be violating everything I had read about tournament play. Yet he was supposed to be this great team player. Of course, I knew what he was doing. It was obvious. He was taking the chance of going out fast, getting a lead that was either unbeatable or would require the rest of us to bet big just to stay in the game. If he lost that $100, he would be essentially even with the table—as we were all betting the minimum. And he had a backup at the table—the girl.

With six hands remaining in the game, the Rio took a read of all our bankrolls. The "partner," betting big early, had caught a hot streak. He had $1,500 in chips. The girl had $730. I had $730. The others at our table had $300, $120, $90 and $30 respectively. Most of them had tried to catch the leader midway through the shoe and had failed.

I figured it was now or never, so I put up a bet of $130. If I lost that I would double up to $260, and if I lost that I would bet the table maximum of $300. Should I win that initial bet, I would keep pushing out whatever it took to beat the girl. I had no real hope of catching the "partner," as he was betting the table minimum of $10. It was not necessary to catch him either, as I only had to finish second to advance to the semi-finals.

The girl matched my bet of $130.

We all lost to a dealer blackjack.

I put out a bet of $260. The girl put out a bet of $10.

I lost. She won. I was now down to $340. She was at $610. Three of the other players had busted out.

I pushed out $300. The girl put up $200.

I got a blackjack. She won also. I had $790. She had $810. Three hands to go.

I put up $300. So did she.

We both lost—$490 for me—$510 for her. She still had me by $20.

Her partner was flat betting $10.

Two hands to go.

I bet the maximum of $300. So did she.

We both won. That was $790 for me and $810 for her.

Now it was her turn to bet ahead of me. She put out $300.

I put out $300.

I received a hand of 20 composed of two 10 valued cards.

She got a blackjack! The dealer had an eight showing.

Since I had to play my hand first, I did the only thing I could—I split my 10s. I now had $600 riding. If I won, I could beat the girl. Unless she doubled on her blackjack, a good move in some cases.

I received a 10 on my first 10. I could see the "partner" tense up. I received an eight on the second one. If the dealer had a 10 value card in the hole, that second hand would be a push and I would lose. The girl signaled that she would stand on her hand.

The dealer flipped over her hole card. A seven! I was still in the game. In fact, I was in a pretty good winning position! The dealer had 15 and, if she busted, I would beat the girl and advance to the semi-finals.

The dealer flipped over a card. An ace. I could feel my heart pounding.

"This is very suspenseful," I said to the girl. She ignored me. Now I really wanted to beat her! Come on dealer, I shouted in my head, another ace or a bust card! Come on baby!

The dealer turned over...a five. A damn five! The dealer had 21 and I lost *both* my hands. The girl gave a little cheer and her "partner" rubbed her back in congratulations. I congratulated her also. She nodded and smiled. She seemed quite nice, now that she'd beaten me.

The first thought that entered my head was: *Well, at least I'm still up $325 for the day*. I realized that this day could no longer be a typical day because I knew it was going to be a day that I was chronicling. This fact changed the nature of the day in a subtle way. I had a greater desire to be ahead than normal. My ego was now very much more involved with the results of the day—more than usual that is.

Alan Tinker and KF both advanced to the semi-final round, so their day now became structured around this tournament.

We made arrangements to meet at the Las Vegas Hilton at seven that night to eat at The Garden of the Dragon, one of our favorite Chinese restaurants.

"Let's get our match play coupons," said KF.

"Right," I said.

The Players Club International has a booth at the Rio and everyday Players Club members can get up to three match play coupons for craps and roulette. These coupons paid two to one on the even money bets this particular trip. So AP, Alan Tinker, KF and I picked up our coupons. We went to the craps table. KF bet his coupon and five dollars on the Pass Line as did I. On the other hand, AP and Alan Tinker bet their coupons and five dollars on the Don't Pass. Playing these three coupons this way at craps was an almost guaranteed win of $7.50 for each of us since the only outcome we could lose on was a 12 on the come out roll.

The 12 never showed.

Then we went to the roulette wheel. KF and I bet five dollars on black. AP and Alan Tinker bet five dollars on red. Here we could lose only on the green 0 or 00.

The green didn't show. So all of us had just won $15 using those coupons at craps and roulette. Alan Tinker and KF decided that they were going to go for a swim at Alan Tinker's condo before their next session of the tournament.

AP and I were heading downtown to play some blackjack and craps. However, before we did, I wanted to place a few Big

Number bets at roulette. While we had been playing our coupons, I had looked at the scoreboard above the roulette table and noticed that the numbers six and 33 had appeared three times each on the last 20 spins. I had pointed this out to AP.

"Yes," she said. "Not only are they Big Numbers but they're on the same slice—only one number separates them on the wheel, number 21. It's hit once."

"Let's bet all three—six, 33 and 21," I said.

"Thirty-eight spins," she agreed, "a dollar on each number."

I quickly calculated in my head that if I were to lose all 38 spins I'd lose $114. No problem. I'd still be up $211 and the day would still be young.

But it didn't work that way.

The first spin I bet on the 33 hit! I was now up $33 (You get paid 35 to one on a hit but I had three numbers working—two of which lost.)

And on the very next one—the 33 hit again! I was now up $66!

In the next half hour the six hit three times and the 33 hit five more times! (That was 10 hits altogether!) The 21 didn't hit at all. It was beyond belief. And I kept thinking, this is going to look great in my book! What a Big Number session! If this wheel isn't biased, no wheel is. I had never seen anything like it.

Nor had the pit.

Two pit people had come over to the table the second time the dealer had spun back-to-back 33s. First, they changed the dealer. A young lady took over for the young man. Her very first spin was—a six! Then she spun several times without hitting any of my numbers (I was still betting six, 21 and 33—that tiny slice) and then she hit 33!

At this point, the pit people whispered something to the dealer and one went over to the phone. We played exactly 38 spins. At the end of those spins, we were up $294. Now there was a regular conference at the table. The original dealer had returned and he was talking in hushed tones to the two pit people.

I heard him say: "All morning. A lot of doubles, too."

"I think they're going to shut this wheel down," said AP.

The female dealer was pausing as if waiting for instructions.

"Let's go," I said. And we did.

Since we were the only two playing, I never found out if they closed down the wheel or not.

It was now one o'clock. We planned to play for a couple of hours and then return to the Sahara for a swim and a nap. We would hit and run at several downtown casinos. Each day we had preselected several casinos, either downtown or on the strip, for an assault. Today it would be the Golden Nugget, the Four Queens, the Union Plaza and Fitzgeralds. Tomorrow would be the Mirage, the Sands, the Aladdin and the Imperial Palace.

Click, click: Heading for downtown on the highway I added $325 + $15 + $294 = ah, $634. And I expected to triple that downtown, where AP and I would hit and run at blackjack and place oddsman's bets at craps.

I was feeling great. This "day in the life" chapter would end with a decent win of around $2,000. My ego would be preserved.

Downtown Las Vegas is what most people visualize when they think of this city. It is a four block area of wall-to-wall casinos. Some of the best gambling joints are downtown—specifically Binion's Horseshoe, the Four Queens, the Plaza and the Golden Nugget. It has something for every level of gambler—you can play 25 cents craps or place a million dollar wager at Binion's. You have sawdust joints like the Pioneer and elegant yuppie heavens like the Golden Nugget. The night is awash in lights.

Of course, downtown Las Vegas, like downtown anywhere USA, has its share of derelicts, wackos, petty thieves and bums. And just out of the wash of lights, entirely surrounding the downtown gaming area, are rundown motels catering to transients, and disease-infested, toothless whores. A little farther to the north is one of the roughest, saddest neighborhoods in the Southwest.

Every so often downtown, you'll see the bedraggled backpackers; those men and, on occasion, women, bruised, scruffy, burned to a leathery brown, and raging as they come out of the hot surrounding desert. Vegas is a magnet for the demented and one should always be on one's guard—especially downtown. Just don't stray from those bright lights into the darkness of the surrounding dementia.

But in the bright and boilingly hot afternoon, downtown

doesn't quite have that other-worldly feel to it the way it does at night when it is the kingdom of kilowattage.

However, it was immaterial to me that day.

AP and I left our car with the valet at the Golden Nugget and entered downtown's most elegant casino.

The lobby of the Golden Nugget is small but done to perfection in reds, whites and golds. AP calls this place "the Yuppie Capital of Las Vegas," and indeed it is. While downtown denizens of Las Vegas often have the fumes of failure emanating from them (AP claims that she enjoys "smelling the sights" in some downtown casinos), the people who play or stay in the Golden Nugget, for the most part, have an identifiable air of success about them. They don't walk, they *saunter* through the casino. Everyone is dressed fashionably.

Once you pass through the lobby, a quick right leads you into the casino, a bright, clean, but always jam-packed place. The Golden Nugget has been offering single-deck blackjack games for quite some time now and on this visit much of the casino has them. AP and I split up. We will now walk slowly through the casino, ignoring each other for the next half hour, looking to jump in on games where no aces have come out in the first round (or where only one ace has appeared and there is a plus count). Occasionally, one of us might sit down to play a more extended game—if the dealer is dealing deeply enough. The Golden Nugget is one of the more paranoid casinos in Las Vegas when it comes to skilled blackjack players. Why? I have no idea. The place makes a fortune from all those sauntering people. Why should they care if a few expert players can make a little withdrawal once in awhile?

AP was at the pit where the "counter catchers" were. The "counter catchers" are a self-styled group in the pit closest to the bar who delight in backing off or sometimes banning card counters. They have that appellation stenciled on their clip board. AP loves to make a hit at the counter catchers' pit.

She was talking to one of the pit people ostensibly about deciding whether to play.

I could hear her from where I was standing.

"I don't know if I'm going to play," she said. "I got killed today."

"Rough day?" said the male pit person. AP smiled with those sparkling eyes and nodded.

Then she took out two $20 bills and placed them on the betting circle.

"Money plays," she said.

"Money plays," the dealer said. He then dealt to the three hands, AP's and two other women.

In Las Vegas and some other gambling towns, a player can still bet cash. Those of you who play in Atlantic City are not given that option. In Las Vegas, if you play with cash initially, you are still paid off in chips.

"Blackjack!" said the dealer.

"See that," said the pit person, "your luck has changed."

"I'm going to let it all ride," she said. That meant she had $100 on this hand. Even though I couldn't see her table—I was a pit removed from her—I could guess that three aces remained in the deck, the count was high, and the dealer was penetrating a little more deeply.

"Wow!" AP shouted. "Two blackjacks in a row! I'm quitting right now!"

"Why quit?" asked the pit person. "You're doing well."

I could see that the dealer was shuffling.

I was ambling behind some tables, one of which just finished dealing the first round. There were five people playing at this table and only one ace had come out. The count was plus four.

I bought in for $100 and put $40 on the betting circle.

I received a 17. The dealer received a 20.

The dealer shuffled. I placed a minimum bet of $5. I lost that and the count was low.

"Doesn't look like my table," I said to no one in particular as I got up. I pretended to be looking for someone. In reality, the table a few feet away was in its first round. No aces out, and the count was plus two.

"Give this a try," I said aloud and I went to the other table. I always talk out loud to myself when I'm hitting and running. I developed this little act after noticing how many truly degenerate gamblers talk to themselves. Everyone ignores you when you do that. The people who talk to themselves in casinos are usually consumed with gambling fever.

"Okay, come on now," I said to the cards in the dealer's hands, "let me win one."

I had a $40 bet up.

I lost it.

The dealer shuffled. I played the first round at the minimum of five dollars. Lost that.

I had lost $90.

When I had last looked, AP was up $150. Okay, so we're $60 ahead at the Golden Nugget, I thought to myself.

I started to walk slowly to the craps tables, holding an intense but relatively hushed dialogue with myself. At a blackjack table near the red dog pit, another good opportunity developed. There were two people at the table and they had each taken two hits apiece. The dealer had also taken a hit. Eleven cards has been played. No aces.

I mumbled as I fumbled with my wallet, "Hold up there, I'm getting my blackjack now."

I put $10 in chips and another $40 in cash on the table. I bet the $40 in cash. "Money plays," I said and then I mumbled, "What the hell." I received a 20. The two others players stood on their hands also. The dealer was showing a 10.

The dealer turned over his hole card—an ace—blackjack.

Was he going to deal another round? The deck was neutral but only one ace had come out. I placed my $10 in chips in the betting circle. The dealer dealt another round and...I received another 20 but...the dealer hit to 21!

This afternoon was starting feel like "one of those days." This "one of those days" is the gambling equivalent of someone hurting your feelings when you were a kid. You feel like you want to cry but you refuse to. You feel a little weak. You feel like a loser.

I got up from the table and shook the "one of those days" feeling out of me. Grow up, I said to myself, you lost a couple of small bets. Why are you panicking? Because this was "a day in the life" and I don't want it to turn into "one of those days."

I finished up my run at the Golden Nugget. I had lost $500. I estimated that my hit on Steven Wynn's first great enterprise was done with me holding approximately a two percent edge. Great. Tell that to my wallet. I've never found losing easy, but today it was especially annoying.

Well, maybe AP was continuing on a hot streak.

I'd find out in a little while. In a half hour, I would meet her at the Four Queens lounge and we would compare notes.

I left the Golden Nugget and walked along Fremont Street

to the Union Plaza (now called Gaughan's Plaza). One thing I don't think anyone can get used to is the furnace blast from hell that you experience when you leave a cool casino and hit the Las Vegas summer air. It takes your breath away—literally. People have been known to keel over and drop dead from it.

I remember my very first summer day in Las Vegas. It was my very first trip to the city. I was staying at the Maxim and I decided I'd walk to Caesars Palace and take a look around. The walk wasn't more than a few blocks—a quarter of a mile at most. It was approximately three in the afternoon. It was 112 degrees.

Now, fellow New Yorkers who had been in Las Vegas in the summers had all told me, "Don't worry, it's hot, but it's dry. It's not like it's 112 degrees with humidity. You won't find it too bad."

I didn't. After the initial blast, AP and I didn't think of the heat. We walked in a leisurely fashion and we were soon in Caesars.

"I know it's hot," I said to AP, "but it's not bad. I'm not even sweating."

Then I touched my forehead. It felt like I had been hit in the face with sand. I took away my hand and rubbed the particles between my fingers. Then I tasted. It was salt! Of course, I hadn't perspired. It was too hot and too dry to perspire—your water evaporated as soon as it hit the air, leaving behind salt. I licked my lips—salt.

AP and I found that we were ferociously thirsty about a half hour later. The walk back to the Maxim heard me saying, "Jesus, you don't even sweat! This is incredible! I have salt sticking to me everywhere. Put a little iodine on me and you can shake me over your French fries!"

We played for about an hour that late afternoon at the Maxim. AP and I both kept ordering glasses of ice water from the waitress.

"Just get a hose and connect it to the bar and bring it to me," I said once. "I'm so thirsty."

After our session that afternoon at the Maxim, AP and I returned to our room. We slept for three hours. The walk to Caesars and back had done us in.

So as I walked along Fremont Street, passing the Pioneer Club on my left with its now broken sign of the cowboy waving to the town, with the equally big sign of Sassy Sally sitting on the roof across the street to my right, I remembered that first visit to Las Vegas. AP and I had spent two straight months here. I was taking a break from writing. I had just finished a novel that I'd been working on for two years—a novel that has yet to see the light of publishing day—and I was in need of a long, long sojourn in a new clime.

When it was time to leave Las Vegas and return to New York to take up the hum-drum existence of scratching out a living from our creativity, AP had to sew our money into our clothes. It had been a remarkable, and a remarkably profitable, two months. On the plane (a red-eye to New York because I don't like taking off in the brutal heat of a desert day—planes don't seem to have the best of thrusts in hot weather and there is entirely too much mechanical straining to get into the air and over the mountains), I kept whispering into AP's ear—"Do you realize how much money we have on us? It's incredible." She would shush me and tell me to go to sleep. Eventually I did and all I could dream of was what an incredible two months it had been! The trip had been a gambler's dream.

Now, walking along Fremont, I was experiencing a gambler's dream of a different kind. A fear dream. I was afraid that when I hit the Union Plaza I would lose. I was worried about AP losing—she was at the Four Queens. I was afraid that I would have the chapter concluding my book showing me as a loser. I was sweating internally—although the dry desert heat would never know it. I wasn't playing with scared money. The chances of me losing my daily stake—$3000—were remote. Only once had I lost that much in one day. But even worse than playing with scared money, I was playing with a *scared self.*

Well, I didn't really have to write about today, now, did I?

Still, I had a "one of those days" feeling in my heart and soul as I entered the Union Plaza.

The Union Plaza is one of the biggest hotels downtown. It sits like an altar at the end of Fremont Street—at night, with it's entire front facade aglow, it is the single most spectacular sight in the whole downtown area. The hotel itself, its restaurants, shows, the very fabric of its feel, leaves you thinking its best days are behind it. It has a kind of Howard Johnson's elegance—a place past its prime.

But this summer it had a great two-deck blackjack game

and 10 times odds at craps. I entered the front lobby and turned left into the casino. I strolled the blackjack pit, placing an odd $40 bet or two at a given table. It was one of those days. I just couldn't win. Oh, I didn't lose every hand—fate wouldn't be so kind to me. Had I lost, say, 10 hands in a row, I might have quit for the day. But no, I would lose two or three, win one, lose two, win one, lose one, win one, lose three, win one. Lady Luck was sadistically whipping me like some deranged leather clad mistress of pain. And I was foolishly absorbing it. And remember this, I was only playing positive decks! Every hand I played, I had the edge!

Finally, down another $560 (I had lost $1060 thus far that afternoon), I decided to check out the craps tables. I wasn't going to stay long. Just place an oddsman's bet if I could.

I perused the table nearest the cashier. One old guy had a Pass Line bet of $5 up with no odds. I looked at the table. Three players had Come numbers working. That meant we were at least on the 4-Count. I stood next to the old guy.

"Mind if I place the odds behind your Pass Line?" I asked him politely.

I practically gave him a heart attack. He jumped. "What? What?" he said. I hadn't noticed it but in his other ear was a huge hearing aid. Great. It was one of those days. His wife was next to him and she shouted, "The man wants to put the odds behind your bet!" Then all eyes from the pit turned to me. The man seemed genuinely confused and I realized that if I stayed I would slow down the game. You never want to slow down a craps game. I smiled wanly and left.

Screw it, it was one of those days. So I headed for the Four Queens.

I wasn't going to play anymore this afternoon. It was 3:15. I was 15 minutes late.

AP was waiting for me in the lounge. She was sipping a glass of cranberry juice and watching a small, soft-rock band perform. I forget its name.

"Well?" I said.

"You first," she said.

I put the thumb down: "One of those days. Down $1060."

She put her thumb up: "Not one of those days. Up $430."

I did some quick figuring. "Are you ready," I said. "The world's greatest gamblers, the remarkable AP and her pathetic partner, are up—a grand total of, tadum! Four dollars!"

"A win's a win," said AP laconically.

"But we were up a little and now..."

"And now we're up a littler," said AP. "You know it's a roller coaster."

"I didn't want today to be a roller coaster," I said. "I'd have preferred to coast in with a nice win..."

"You wanted a huge win," said AP finishing her drink.

"I would have settled for a thousand," I said.

"Come on, you wanted five thousand," said AP.

"I would have been happy with two thousand," I said.

"So, we've got $4. That leaves only one thousand...nine hundred...and...ninety-six dollars to go," she said.

I snapped my fingers. "A snap," I said.

We each had a salad at the Carson Street Cafe in the Golden Nugget and by four o'clock we were back at the Sahara. AP went to the room to shower and work on her counted cross stitching (she also makes her own clothes—what can I tell you, the woman is multi-talented) and I went for a swim in the pool. When I got back to the room, AP had drawn the drapes and was in bed. There was a note on the phone in AP's graceful handwriting: "Producer will call and leave message about how the show went." It was five o'clock Vegas time; that meant eight o'clock Virginia time. In a half hour my play would be having its world premier. I showered and then joined AP for a nap.

My last thought as I drifted off to sleep was: "Please, don't let me lose that four dollars."

We slept till six. By 6:30, I was sitting down at a poker table in the Las Vegas Hilton being dealt my first hand of Texas hold'em. AP had joined Alan Tinker who was playing the Hilton's excellent two-deck blackjack game. As soon as AP and I had entered the Hilton, we had heard Alan Tinker's distinctive voice saying, "It's my lucky day, fellas! Let's put you on this hand too." I knew what this meant: Alan Tinker was in a high count, he was winning, and he was placing a bet for the dealers—probably to keep them dealing deeper into the decks.

So now as I was looking at a two and a 10 of different suits, I heard Alan Tinker say, "This was the way this game was meant to be played!"

Boy, he must be doing well, I thought, as I threw in my hand.

One half hour later, the four of us were standing in front of the Garden of the Dragon waiting for the Maitre'd to seat us. I hadn't even entered a hand in the Texas hold'em game. Luckily, I hadn't paid any blinds. I was still up $4.

"Good news," Alan Tinker had said when he saw me. "Dinner for four on me! Compliments of the Las Vegas Hilton." He had a comp for four. Neither Alan nor KF had advanced to the finals of the Rio tournament.

"What were you playing?" asked KF.

"Two hands of $50 to a $100 a hand, lower in bad counts," replied Alan Tinker. "By the end, I was on a roll. I originally started playing two hands of $15 and ended up at $50 to a hundred. Sometimes I went up to $200, in good counts. And no heat."

"What are you up?" asked KF.

"Five," said Alan Tinker, meaning $5,000. "Three here. Two spread around town. This has been one of those days!"

"And you?" I asked KF.

"Eight," he said. "Hundred. It's been a good day."

"Ah," I said. "It's been *one of those days* for me too."

"Good," said Alan Tinker.

"I'm up four—four BIG ONES," I said with meaning. "And here they are," I added as I took out my wallet and withdrew four singles.

It was good for a laugh.

At dinner, I ordered a bottle of Pouilly Fuisse. KF never drank—except for oceans of diet coke. Alan Tinker drank wine or mixed drinks on occasion. This night he ordered some Asian specialty drink—something that sounded like "Tornado-chi-wa-wa." AP would have a glass of the Pouilly Fuisse. If I ever wondered why I had gained weight, the reason was sitting there in the ice bucket looking at me.

But that night I didn't think of the weight I had gained living the good life. I was thinking about luck...and sipping my wine.

"I'm not lucky," I said.

"What do you mean?" asked KF.

"I mean, I don't really think I'm a lucky kind of person."

"Do you think of yourself as unlucky?" asked Alan, drinking his yellowish drink.

"No..maybe slightly...but I'm definitely not lucky," I said.

"How can you say that?" said KF.

"Because, well...take a look at my gambling. The only reason I win is because I'm great at it..."

"And very humble," said KF.

"You know what I mean," I said.

"Of course," said KF.

"I have to play perfectly...at all times...I can't afford one mistake...and I never have runs where *anything* I do turns out right...Alan Tinker here the other night starts playing like a wild man at craps at Binion's. Violates every rule. Bets every stupid bet at a certain point..."

"We were way ahead and I figured 'what the hell?' " said Alan Tinker. "I was feeling lucky anyway. I told you that when we went to Binion's."

KF shook his head. Alan Tinker sometimes violated all the rules of intelligent play. But he always seemed to do *the wrong thing* at the *right time*.

"But I don't seem to have those nights," I said. "Even on big winning days...it's more the accumulation of good play than a given quantity of good luck."

"Maybe, you just feel that way," said AP, "but the feeling is wrong. You can't do what you've been doing for years and be unlucky."

"I don't think I'm unlucky...I'm just not lucky," I said. I couldn't think of a better way to phrase it. "Take today. Of all the days, I wanted a win today because I was going to use today as my 'a day in the life' chapter. The day started off fairly well, too. I was already up a little before I decided to use today as an example of what we do and then we had an epic roulette session..."

"AP told me about it when I was playing blackjack," said Alan Tinker.

"What?" asked KF.

I told him about our Big Number session that morning at the Rio.

"Well, that was certainly good luck," said KF.

"I don't think so," I said. "I think I found a truly biased wheel. I know I didn't do a huge run of numbers and analyze them but the pit bosses were very concerned. I think that wheel was hitting the same numbers all night long. When I finally got to the table, they were watching the wheel carefully. I think I hit a biased wheel and won instead of having good luck and winning."

"Well, maybe, *finding* the wheel *was* the good luck," said AP.

"So you're not going to use today as your 'day in the life?'" asked Alan Tinker.

"I don't know," I said. "I should. I mean I should because this is just as typical a day as any other. Going from casino to casino—winning and losing. Fighting the good fight but... well, I don't want to look foolish. I have a $4 win right now."

"A win's a win," said AP. This is so true; trite, yes, but still so true. A win's a win. On a normal day, I would be happy to go to dinner up any amount of money. I would savor the win. But today was different.

"Look at the things you have," said KF. He pointed at AP. "How many men have a woman like AP? Men would kill to have her. Kill to have a woman like her in love with them."

"I still can't figure how you can love this guy," laughed Alan Tinker, pointing to me. Then he poked my rounded tummy. I sipped my wine and ignored him.

"He's the greatest man in the *whole* world," said AP sincerely.

One of the many wondrous personality traits of the beautiful AP is her ability to give a compliment—especially to me, especially in public, especially after all these years together. She sticks up for her man. Many another woman would have answered Alan Tinker's remark by saying, "I can't figure out why, either." But not AP. She was always in my corner. And, believe me, I'm not the greatest guy in the *whole* world...there is a guy in Europe...

"Now, if that isn't good luck, what is?" asked KF. KF had never married. He had been close on several occasions but he had never truly found Ms. Right.

"How many people get to give autographs?" said Alan Tinker.

"You have a play being performed right now in another part of the country," said AP.

"You're lucky. You just don't *feel* lucky but you *are* lucky," concluded KF.

After dinner, KF went back to the Sahara (he was also staying there) to catch a lounge act and then go to sleep.

"What's your pleasure?" asked Alan Tinker as we walked through the Las Vegas Hilton's casino.

"Binion's. Craps," I said.

"Good," said Alan Tinker. Then he winked at me. "I feel lucky tonight." And he rubbed his arm.

Alan Tinker often refers to himself as Golden Arm. He has no humility when it comes to playing craps and he will often announce to a whole table, "Don't worry, the old Golden Arm will be rolling now! Bet it up! We'll be the new owners of the casino in a couple of hours!" Of course, partially this is just Alan Tinker's exuberance and good humor; partially he believes he has a knack for rolling those dice; and partially it is true. Alan Tinker has had many good rolls when I've been with him. I was sure hoping he would have one tonight.

It was dark when we reached the Golden Nugget. We left our car with valet parking. Then we walked through the Golden Nugget, made a restroom stop (AP claims that the Golden Nugget's bathrooms are the cleanest in all of downtown), and headed across Fremont Street to Binion's Horseshoe.

The night was the usual explosion of light downtown but I didn't really notice it. I was intent on winning back my self-respect. AP had informed me on the drive downtown that I was to write about today—win or lose. That as a writer I owed it to the public—to my readers—to write the way things are, not the way I want them to be. And she had said that I was starting to whine and needed to, not in so many words for she is very tactful, *grow up!*

So I had to win tonight.

We met Alan Tinker by the Wheel of Fortune and headed for the craps tables. If you have never been to Las Vegas, then put Binion's on your must see (and AP says, "must smell") list. *It is the gambling joint of all gambling joints.* At the craps tables you will have people betting 25 cents standing shoulder to shoulder with players betting thousands of dollars per roll! You will have people who are scented and manicured standing next to people who seemingly haven't heard of indoor plumbing or hygiene. The place is dark, somewhat bluish with browns predominating; it is somewhat grungy, and it is *always* crowded. It's a throwback to the old days of oil and cattle and prospecting money. You can determine your own maximum bet by just betting it on the first hand or roll of the dice. I once saw a man carrying an armload of $100 bills—all neatly packaged—*an armload*! He'd bet the packets five at a clip. He never bet chips. He looked disheveled, unkempt, unconscious. He wandered through the casino, his armload of money ever ready. No one bothered him. In Binion's, the security guards are universally— BIG! Let me tell you, you never worry about a thief in Binion's. These guards would rip a thief's head off and eat it. That's how tough they look.

Unfortunately, Binion's has a somewhat checkered reputation with expert blackjack players, owing to nasty incidents (broken jaws—near-death experiences and the like) in past years. So even in the gambling joint of all gambling joints they don't want you to be *too good*. Despite that, it is the mecca of gambling for poker players wishing to test their mettle in the forge of combat against other expert players. It is the cite of the World Series of Poker. It offers dozens of single-deck blackjack games and 16 craps tables with 10 times odds. You haven't gambled until you've gambled at Binion's.

I've never stayed there so I don't know if the hotel rooms reflect the casino. From the look and smell of some of the players, however, the only thing you'd have to do to make their stay comfortable would be to put straw in the rooms. From what I've heard, in the past couple of years, the management has upgraded the restaurants, even adding several gourmet and Asian rooms. I don't know. I've never eaten there. I've never moved beyond the casino.

No matter. People go to Binion's to gamble. To bet armloads of money. And to win! And that's why I was there that night.

Alan Tinker, AP and I selected a table.

A shooter at the opposite end of the table was on his come out roll.

"Did he make a point?" I asked the dealer.

"No," said the dealer.

So I started the 5-*Count*. The shooter established his point and then sevened out two rolls later. I hadn't gotten into the action.

For the first 20 minutes, the table was ice cold—which was fine with me. The 5-*Count* was protecting me. Alan Tinker was also playing the 5-*Count* but I could see he was antsy to get into the action.

Finally, it was Alan Tinker's chance to roll. Violating all my rules, I decided to go with him right away, no *5-Count*, no *Supersystem*. I put a $3 Pass Line bet. AP frowned and shook her head. I ignored her. Alan rolled a seven. I was now up $7 for the day!

"Get ready, everyone," said Alan, rapidly fixing the dice. Most veteran craps players like to set the dice with certain numbers showing. If they can do it quickly, the casinos generally will ignore it and let you proceed. At Binion's, you have to do it like lightning or they'll shout, "Stop fixin' the dice, shooter!"

"Here we go, bayba!" said Alan Tinker as he rolled. (That's how he says it: BAY-BA!)

Another seven! Hey, I was up $10 now!

His next come out roll was a nine. I backed my $3 line bet with $30 in odds.

"Okay, bayba, right back with the nine," said Alan Tinker. He rolled. "Yeah, bayba!"

"Seven," said the dealer. "Seven out!"

Great, I thought. That's what I get for going up before the *5-Count*. Then AP whispered in my ear, "Play your game. If you're going to lose, lose the right way."

She was right. Even I, Mr. Iron Discipline himself, had started to tilt.

"Of course," I said.

It was my turn to roll. I put a Pass Line and a Don't Pass bet up simultaneously. The only number that could hurt me was the 12. I rolled a six. I didn't take any odds. It was only on the 1-Count. No odds would go up until the *5-Count*. On the 3-Count, I sevened out. I hadn't lost anything.

After an hour, at 9:30 pm, I was down $93 for the day. I had accepted it would be a losing day.

"After Alan Tinker's roll," I said to AP, "we leave—win or lose."

"Shooter on the come out," said the dealer.

"Let me have those dice, bayba! The Golden Arm is ready!"

The dealers smirked. Alan had been threatening good rolls all evening. He hadn't produced one yet. The dealers at Binion's can be a little jaded sometimes and they rode him a little.

"No one believes me?" asked Alan. He picked up four blue chips (at Binion's a blue chip is five dollars—almost everywhere else a red chip is $5) and threw them down: "Put the dealers on all the hardways. You guys start rooting and maybe we can all make some money," finished Alan Tinker. The dealers almost as one said: "Let's go and good luck!" For what it was worth, everyone at the table now wanted Alan Tinker to have the good roll he had been threatening all night.

"Here we go bayba!" yelled Alan Tinker on the come out.

"Eight. Eight the hard way!" shouted the dealer.

The dealers had just won $50 on that roll—$45 on the hard eight and the original $5 bet that was taken down.

In some Las Vegas casinos, the proposition bets in the center of the tables are working on the Come Out roll, unless you call them off, and this is why the dealers had won. In Atlantic City, it is the opposite, all proposition bets are off unless you call them on.

So Alan Tinker's point was eight.

I was not on the Pass Line. I was waiting for the *5-Count*. As AP had said: If I was going to lose, I was going to lose playing the right way.

Alan Tinker's next roll was—another eight! He had made his point.

"We're just beginning, bayba!" said Alan Tinker. "Off on those hardways bets on the come out."

"Dealer's bets are off," said the dealer.

He rolled his come out roll.

"Seven," shouted the dealer. "Winner seven!"

"New dice," said Alan Tinker. "These dice have too many sevens in them. They whispered to me."

The stickman pushed over the other three dice. Alan Tinker took two.

"Your center bets are working, fellas," he said.

"Dealer's bets are working," said the dealer.

I went up on the Pass Line and Don't Pass for $3 each.

Alan Tinker rolled.

"Six, the haaard-waaay!" said the dealer, genuinely enthused. The dealers had just won another $50!

It was the 4-Count so I didn't put any odds up. I put up a $3 Come and a $3 Don't Come bet simultaneously.

Alan Tinker's next roll was a five. And the *5-Count*. I was now in the game.

I put $60 on the table. "Odds on the five and six," I said. The dealer put $30 odds on each of my come numbers.

If Alan sevened out now, I would lose the $60 in odds but have the rest of my money returned (see the *Supersystem* in *Beat the Craps Out of the Casinos: How to Play Craps and Win!*). I would be down $153 for the day and I would go back to the Sahara and go to sleep.

But Alan Tinker didn't seven out.

"Five! Five! No field five. Repeater five!" shouted the dealer.

Since I had a Come and a Don't Come up, I won $45 on the five and the bet remained. (Just hit one more time, I pleaded with the fates, just one more.)

Alan started to roll again: "Another five, bayba!"

"Five! Five! No field fiiive!" shouted the dealer. I won another $45. If Alan sevened out now, I would be up $30 total for his roll ($90 win – $60 in odds = $30 profit) and down $63 for the day.

Alan's next roll was a four. I put the $30 down for the odds. I now had a total of $90 at risk on a combination of four, five and six. If Alan Tinker sevened out, I'd be down the original $93. (Come on Alan, just one number, I said to myself.)

"I love the four," said Alan Tinker. He picked the dice up. He rolled.

"Nine," said the dealer.

(Please, I said to myself, just hit one number.)

"Here we go, bayba!" and he rolled.

"Four—the haaaard-waaaay!" shouted the dealer. The other dealers looked quite happy. This was Alan Tinker's third hardway win for them!

I was just as happy. My $30 odds bet on the four returned $60. Since I wasn't on the Come and Don't Come, I got the original bet back too. That was $90. I was only down $3 for the day!

Now I became extremely religious: "Oh, God, please, one more time," I whispered to the wind.

I put down a Come and Don't Come bet of $3 each.

Alan Tinker set the dice.

(One more time. Please, God, one more time!)

"Bayba!" he shouted and rolled.

"Winna! Winna! Six! The easy way! Winna!" shouted the dealer.

"Yeah!" I shouted. The Pass Line odds bet had won me $36. I was now up $33. Of course, I would be risking $30 of it when he established his next point. But even if he sevened out immediately after his next come out—I would go back to the Sahara a winner. That's all I wanted now. Just to go back to my room, crawl into bed with the beautiful AP, and be up—even if it was only $3. A win's a win!

"Come out roll," said the dealer. "Same good shooter."

I placed a Pass Line and Don't Pass bet. Alan rolled.

"Nine, nine, the point is nine," said the dealer.

I put the $30 in odds behind the nine. Alan was getting ready to roll again. I was on the five and nine. I didn't place a Come and Don't Come bet because I wanted to make certain that I would go home a winner. Had I gone up on a third number, an immediate seven out would have left me $27 in the hole. I almost had to laugh at myself—sweating out this kind of money. But this $3 win had suddenly become as big in my mind as a $3,000 win.

"Five and nine, five and nine," I chanted in a whisper.

"Five and nine, fine and nine," chanted AP next to me.

Alan Tinker rolled.

"Five! Five! No field fiiivvve!" shouted the dealer.

"Yes! Yes! Yes!" I shouted.

Alan Tinker was laughing. I gave him the thumbs up!

I won $45 on the $30 odds be, plus the bet was returned. I was up $78 now. I placed a Come and Don't Come bet.

Alan Tinker fixed his dice.

I was off the five. But Alan Tinker still had a Come bet with odds on it. I looked at it. Damn, I thought he was betting blue—but he was betting green ($25) on the come with black chips in odds. I was so involved in my own struggle that I hadn't noticed that Alan Tinker was betting bigger than usual. How many black on his come bet? Two. He had $200 in odds. He was allowed another $50. I took two green chips and placed them on the table: "$50 odds on his five come bet!" Alan nodded his okay to the dealer.

The dealer swiftly scooped up the $50 and placed them on Alan Tinker's five.

"Five and nine, five and nine," AP and I chanted.

"Here we go, bayba!"

"Five and nine, five and nine," we chanted.

He released the dice.

"Fiiiiiivvvve!!! Repeater—FIVE! No field FIVE!" shouted the dealer.

"Yahoo! BAYBA!" I shouted or something equally inane.
AP hugged me.

My Come and Don't Come bets went up on the five. Alan
was off the five. He gave me my $50 plus my $75 win. I took
$30 and put the odds on the five Come. I was now up $133. No
matter what happened next, I would go back to the Sahara up
at least $103! (I was going to go up on three numbers if I could.)

"I'm just getting started," said Alan Tinker.

I put down a Come and Don't Come bet.

"Bayba!" shouted Alan Tinker.

"Seven! Seven!" shouted the dealer. "Pay the don'ts, take
the do's."

I turned to AP. "We're up $133."

"Good. A winning day," she smiled.

"That's the biggest $133 I ever won," I said.

Alan Tinker turned to me. "Let's call it a night," he said. "I just
won another $1,600. It's been a good day. No sense pushing it."

"It sure has, " I agreed. My $133 win seemed every bit as
huge as Alan Tinker's $6,600 day.

In our room at the Sahara, the message light was lit on the
phone.

"It's probably the producer," said AP, nodding towards the
phone.

"I'll get it in a minute," I said. "I don't want to ruin how I
feel right now if he tells me my show's a bomb."

"Let's get undressed," said AP. "Let's get comfortable."

We undressed in silence. AP put on her pajamas. She
looked so sexy, so inviting in those big, oversized pajamas she
had made. I stayed in my shorts and put on a lightweight
sweatshirt. Then AP shut the lights. She was standing by the
closed curtains.

"Come here," she said.

"I can't see," I said.

She opened the curtains. The light from the Vegas night
illuminated the room. I went to AP.

"Look out that window," she said. I did. I could see the
entire Strip ablaze in the distance to my left. The volcano at the
Mirage was spewing its flames into the sky.

"Beautiful," I said.

"Look at that town," said AP. I could see, directly ahead,
the twinkling lights of the houses for miles and miles.

"This is some city," I said.

"You have a wonderful life," said AP. "How many people live the kind of adventure you live?"

"And I won tonight," I reminded her.

"Tonight's win is irrelevant," she said.

"I realize that $133 isn't very much but…"

"I don't mean that," she said. "You could have lost the $3,000 daily stake, or won $10,000 if Alan rolled for two hours. All of that is irrelevant. Today is just one day. Write it truthfully and your readers will get a sense of what we do. It wouldn't matter to them whether you won or lost on one day. Believe me."

"I guess you're right," I said, and then sheepishly, "But I'm still glad I won."

"Your life is filled with wonderful things," AP continued, "wonderful people. You have wonderful children. Two sons who are a credit to you. You've been blessed with good parents. And you have had an impact on countless people in all the areas of life where you've used your talents. Few people can say that."

I looked out at the Strip. At the flames coming out of the Mirage's ersatz volcano.

"You know sometimes I feel that I haven't really done anything in my life. That I'm a failure," I said.

AP smiled. How could anyone not love someone who could smile like that?

"You are the greatest man in the world." she said.

"Well, there is that guy in Europe," I kidded.

"Only you," she said. "You have a wonderful life."

"With a wonderful wife," I added.

I kissed her. I have kissed this woman for years and years. I have kissed my beautiful AP a million million times.

And every kiss feels like that first wonderful kiss.

"Now," she said, "make the wake-up call. Get your message and let's go to bed. We have a long walk tomorrow morning."

AP got into bed.

I called the operator, told her our room number, and that we'd want a 5:30 wake-up call.

Then I called the message operator. The operator gave me the message.

I slipped into bed beside my beautiful AP.

I whispered in her ear: "It's a hit. The producer said the audience thought it was great." Even though I couldn't see her face, because her back was to me, I could just tell she was smiling.

I kissed the back of AP's neck and closed my eyes.

"I do have a wonderful life," I whispered. "Thank you."

More Recommended Books and Magazines

Las Vegas Behind the Tables and *Las Vegas Behind the Tables: Part Two* both by Barney Vinson. Gollehon Press, Grand Rapids, MI. (both $9.95) Vinson is a casino executive who can write. Wonderful stories about the Las Vegas very few people see. Both books are must reading for those of you who want to get a feel for the town and the people in it.

Gambling and the Law by I. Nelson Rose. Gambling Times Publishing, 16760 Stagg St. #213, Van Nuys, CA 91406. From taxes to cheating to everything you ever wanted to know about the legalities of wagering, this is the book for you. I. Nelson Rose is a gambling lawyer—as opposed to a lawyer who gambles—and he knows his business. Especially good book for card counters wanting to know what their rights are.

Gambling Scams by Darwin Ortiz. Lyle Stuart, Inc., Carol Publishing Group, 600 Madison Ave.,

New York, NY 10022. ($10.95) Wonderful book. Everything you want to know about dealers who cheat, players who cheat, casinos that cheat. Ortiz knows his scams. This is fascinating reading—can almost make you paranoid about playing.

Darwin Ortiz on Casino Gambling: The Complete Guide to Playing and Winning by Darwin Ortiz. Lyle Stuart, Inc., Carol Publishing Group, 600 Madison Ave., New York, NY 10022. ($10.95) Although this book does not have any information about most of the newer games, Ortiz's playing advice is solid. The best chapters are not the strategy ones, however, but his thoughts on probability and luck, the places to play, junkets and comps and the like.

Probabilities in Everyday Life by John D. McGervey. Ballantine Books, New York, NY. ($3.95) This book is just plain interesting and not too heavy on the math. Tells you about the odds for and against just about everything—from gambling to wearing a seat belt to flying in a plane to getting hit by lightning.

To Gamble or Not to Gamble by Walter Wagner. World Publishing, New York, NY. ($9.95) This book is probably out of print but my guess is that most libraries will have it. It is a sharp attack on the evils of gambling and the author has an almost religious fervor in his approach. This is the flip side of the fun. Details the chilling facts behind compulsive gambling. Of course, Wagner sees no cause to play games whatsoever and to him people who enjoy gambling must have something seriously wrong with them.

Casino Games by John Gollehon. Gollehon Press, Grand Rapids, MI. ($4.95) John Gollehon is good reading because he is practical in his advice. However, this book is somewhat outdated and doesn't cover the new games and the new options on the old games. It's worth making Gollehon's acquaintance because his ideas are solid.

Gambling Theory and Other Topics by Mason Malmuth. Self-published, Las Vegas, NV. ($24.95) You have to enjoy mathematics to really get into this book. However, Malmuth is an interesting and often arresting theorist. He challenges some of the rogue blackjack experts and exposes what he considers to be the follies of most gambling writers—especially concerning money management, something he considers to be silly. He lays a groundwork for approaching just about every game. He needs an editor badly but the book is good.

The Only Game in Town: An Illustrated History of Gambling by Hank Messick and Burt Goldblatt. Thomas Y. Crowell Company, New York, NY. ($12.95) This is a coffee table book from the mid-70s but it is well worth searching for. Gives you the history behind many of today's games. Great old photographs!

The Complete Illustrated Guide to Gambling by Alan Wyckes. Doubleday and Company, New York, NY. ($9.95) This is a BIG book and was first published in the early 1960s, so you'll have to search for it. Has every game (up to that time) carefully covered. Wonderful photographs. The world has changed since the publication of this tome but it is still a very riveting read for those of you who are interested in all phases of gambling, its history and lore.

Inside Las Vegas by Mario Puzo. Grosset and Dunlap Publishers, New York, NY. ($14.95) Mario Puzo is a great writer and this is a great book about his personal Las Vegas. Wonderful photographs complement a superb writing style. This fabulous book is no longer in print but try to find it. I loved it.

Fools Die by Mario Puzo. G.P. Putnam's Sons, 200 Madison Ave., New York, NY 10016. ($12.50) This is quite simply the best novel I've ever read using Las Vegas and gambling as a backdrop for the human condition. Most fiction concerning gamblers and gambling is ultimately preachy or unrealistic. The Las Vegas that Puzo writes about is so, so real. The man is a master.

Beat the Casino by Frank Barstow. Pocket Books, Simon & Schuster, 1230 Avenue of the Americas, New York, NY 10020. ($4.50) I like Frank Barstow. I like him because he doesn't let the theorists get in the way of his common sense. His book is enjoyable reading. Barstow has unusual advice on the games that he covers. This book is a good read and is quite original. You might not agree with all of Barstow's advice but nevertheless he makes compelling cases for certain approaches to various games.

Extra Stuff: Gambling Ramblings by Peter Griffin. Huntington Press, Box 28041, Las Vegas, NV 89126. ($11.95) Peter Griffen is at once brilliant and fun. He knows how to write and analyze—two sometimes disparate talents. He and Frank Barstow should be put on opposite sides of a craps table and told to hurl chips at the count of 10! Good reading.

Magazines and Newspapers

Casino Player Magazine. Published monthly by ACM Marketing Inc., 2524 Arctic Avenue, Atlantic City, NJ 08401. First rate, glossy magazine that covers all aspects of the casino scene. Leans towards the Atlantic City and Caribbean beat but has good information about Las Vegas too. Runs approximately 60 pages an issue. Covers entertainment end of casino business as well. Twenty dollars for a yearly subscription and $4.95 per issue.

WIN Magazine. Published by Gambling Times, Inc., 16760 Stagg St. #213, Van Nuys, CA 91406. Another first rate, glossy magazine that generally comes out monthly (will occasionally skip a month here and there). Covers all aspects of casinos and gambling but has a distinct west coast flavor and will cover the California card room scene. Also contains fiction by notable writers. Averages 80 pages or more. Forty-four dollars for 12 issues and $4.95 per issue.

The Sports Form. Published weekly by Dirson Enterprises, Inc., Box 93116, Las Vegas, NV 89139. Newspaper format and loaded with interesting articles and columns. Covers the sports scene heavily but has quite a bit of information on casino games as well. A great buy but is only distributed to newsstands in Las Vegas so out of towners have to subscribe. One of the best buys on the gambling scene. Single issue $1.75. Subscription is $98 for one year.

Gambling Book Clubs, Gambling Book Publishers, Gambling Book Stores

You should be able to order the books you are interested in directly from the publishers. The publishers listed here are those whose primary inventory revolves around gambling titles. Obviously, most mainstream publishers have some books on gambling but this list contains only those who specialize in the area. Write them and ask for a book list. In addition, this list contains those select bookstores and book clubs that also specialize in gambling and gambling-related titles. With the exception of a couple of obscure and out of print books, you should be able to get every book I recommended somewhere on this list.

Gambler's Book Club and Book Shop
GBC Press
630 S. 11th Street
Las Vegas, NV 89101

Paone Press
Box 610
Lynbrook, NY 11563

Pi Yee Press
7910 Ivanhoe Ave. #34
La Jolla, CA 92037

Huntington Press
Box 28041
Las Vegas, NV 89126

Gambler's Book Store
Box 14827
Las Vegas, NV 89114

Gambling Times Publishing
16760 Stagg St. #213
Van Nuys, CA 91406

Gambler's General Store
800 South Main St.
Las Vegas, NV 89101

The Gambler's Bookstore
99 North Virginia St.
Reno, NV 89501

Atlantic City News and Books
101 South Illinois Ave.
Atlantic City, NJ 08401

Gambler's World
1938 E. University Drive
Tempe, AZ 85281

Rocky Mountain Gaming Books and Supplies
1931 Sheridan Unit 5
Edgewater, CO 80214

RGE Publishing
414 Santa Clara Ave.
Oakland, CA 94610

CompuStar Press
1223 Wilshire Blvd.
Santa Monica, CA 90403

Research Services Unlimited
6920 Airport Blvd. #117-111
Mobile, AL 36608

Lenny Frome Publishing
5025 S. Eastern Ave. #16
Las Vegas, NV 89119

GLOSSARY

The Language of Gambling

Ace: The highest card in poker, the die with one dot, and another name for a dollar.

Aces and Eights: In poker, this is considered the "dead man's hand" because it was the hand being held by Wild Bill Hickok when he was shot. Also, the name of a version of a table game in honor of Wild Bill.

Ace high: A hand in poker containing odd cards, the highest of which is an ace.

Ace poor: A lower than average number of aces remain in the unplayed cards.

Ace rich: In blackjack, the composition of the remaining deck has more aces proportionally than normal.

Aces up: A hand in poker containing two pair, the higher of which are aces.

A Cheval: French for the split bet in roulette.

Across the board: A bet on all the numbers (4,5,6,8,9,10) in craps.

Act: The persona adopted by some card counters to give the impression that they are not skilled or expert players.

Action: The amount of money you wager over a given period of time. Used as a basis of judgment for comps.

Action player: A player who bets big and for long periods of time. Sometimes used as a euphemism for stupid player.

Ada from Decatur: Archaic craps term for the eight. Sometimes known as *Annie from Arkansas*.

Agent: A person who works with a cheat.

Aggregate limit: The maximum amount paid out in a casino keno game.

All-King Ticket: Individual keno numbers are circled and are to be played in all possible combinations.

American Wheel: Roulette wheel that has the 0 and 00 grooves.

Anchor man: The player who sits to the right of the dealer and is the last to act on his hand. Sometimes referred to as a third baseman.

Ante: In poker, chips or cash put up by the players before the dealing of the hands.

Any-craps: A bet at craps that the shooter will roll a two, three, or 12 on the very next roll. A Crazy Crapper bet and not recommended.

Any-seven: A bet at craps that the next number rolled by the shooter will be a seven. A Crazy Crapper bet and not recommended.

Back line: A bet on the Don't Pass that the shooter will lose. Any bet that is placed against a shooter.

Backliner: A person who places a wager on another player's betting square.

Backlining: Placing a wager on another player's betting square. Sometimes known as piggybacking.

Backing the bet: Placing the odds on the Pass Line and Come bets. One of the better bets in the casino.

Back to Back: In stud poker, a pair consisting of a hole card and the player's first up card. Also known as *wired*.

Back-in: In poker, to enter the betting after first passing or checking. Technique used to build the pot with raises.

Backtrack: The outer, stationary rim of the roulette wheel where the ball is spun.

Bad Rack: Casinoese for a player who doesn't pay his gambling debts.

Bank: The person who covers the bet in a game. In most casino gambling, the bank is the casino itself. A row of slot machines.

Bank hand: The second of the two hands dealt in baccarat. One of the better bets in the casino.

Bank roll: The total amount of money a gambler sets aside to gamble with.

Bar: The banning of an individual from playing in a casino. Used against cheats and expert players alike.

Barber pole: A bet consisting of different colored chips all mixed together. Trick often used by card counters to cover the amount of money they are betting.

Bar the 12 or 2: In craps, the wrong bettor is not allowed to win on these numbers. They are pushes.

Base dealer: A dealer (card mechanic) who deals from the bottom of the deck.

Basic strategy: In blackjack, the best possible play of any given hand based on the dealer's up card and the two cards you possess. In other games, the best play available.

Basic ticket: In keno, the same as a straight ticket. Contains only one wager.

Beard: Someone who places bets for a cheat.

Beat: To win money from someone by cheating.

Behind the line: Placing the odds behind your bets on the Pass Line and Come. This is one of the best wagers in the casino.

Best Buys: Created by the Captain. To buy the four and/or 10 for $39, paying a $1 commission. To buy the five and/or nine for $38, paying a $1 commission. This radically reduces the house's otherwise stifling edge on these bets.

Bet blind: To bet without seeing your cards.

Bet the pot: In poker, betting an amount equal to the amount in the pot.

Betting against the dice: In craps, a wager where you are betting against the shooter and for the seven.

Betting with the dice: At craps, a bet that the shooter will make his point. A bet against the seven showing.

Bevels: Dice that have been shaved on some corners to favor certain numbers.

Bias: The tendency of the game to favor either the dealer or the player for prolonged periods.

Biased wheel: A roulette wheel that has an imperfection which shows up by certain numbers appearing out of all proportion to their probability.

Big Bertha: Those giant slot machines placed at entrances and exits to lure the unwary gambler.

Big Number: A wagering procedure at roulette to find biased wheels, where you look for numbers that have hit several times in a short interval.

Big or Small: A bet in sic bo that the next shake of the dice will be either big numbers or small numbers. The best bet in this game.

Big Player: In blackjack play, the member of a team that bets the big money on the high counts.

Big Six and Big Eight: One of the worst bets at craps. A wager where you bet that the six or eight will appear before the seven. Pays off at even money. A Crazy Crapper bet.

Big Six Wheel: Also known as the wheel of fortune. Carnival game for suckers that has made its way into casinos.

Bird Cage: Another name for chuck-a-luck. The cage-like contraption that holds the dice.

Black action: A bet made with a black ($100) chip.

Black bet: A wager at roulette that the next number will be black.

Black book: The list of excluded persons that every casino in Vegas contributes to. Contains the names and photos of known cheats and card counters.

Blackjack: A natural—10 value card and an ace. Pays off at three to two.

Blacks: Chips valued at $100.

Blind: In hold'em or other poker games, an ante put up by one or two players. Rotates with each hand.

Blower: The air machine used to select the keno numbers. Blows numbered ping-pong balls into a shoot.

Bluff: In poker, the attempt to take the pot by making the other players think you have a superior hand.

Board: The tote board that shows the winning keno numbers.

Body-time: For purposes of comping, how much time your body is at a table. Some of this time will not be risk-time.

Bombing for a blackjack: Scanning technique for determining a better than average chance for getting a blackjack.

Bon: The eighth highest hand in pai gow.

Book or book a bet: To cover somebody's wager. The casino books most bets.

Bot: The 14th highest hand in pai gow.

Bottom track: The slanting, stationary inner area of a roulette wheel down which the ball slides into the grooves.

Boxcars: In craps, the number 12.

Boxman: The person who sits at the center of the craps table and supervises the game.

Box numbers: The numbers four, five, six, eight, nine, 10.

Break: To go over 21 in blackjack. Sometimes referred to as busting.

Break down a bet: Separate chips by various denominations. Used by dealers to accurately pay off bets.

Break the deck: To shuffle the cards before continuing play.

Brushing: Substituting cards or dice into a game.

Buck: Another name for the black-white disk used in craps to indicate the point. Also name for button to indicate the designated dealer in casino poker. When President Truman said, "The buck stops here," he was not referring to money but to the deal of the cards!

Bull: Another name for the ace in poker.

Burn a card: To bury a card at the beginning or during a blackjack round. Used as a device to prevent card counters from getting an edge.

Burred dice: Somewhat scratched dice, where certain sides will tend to catch on the felt of a table.

Bury a card: Place a card in the middle of a deck.

Bust: To go over 21 in blackjack. Same as breaking.

Bust Out Joint: A casino that cheats the players.

Buy bet: To buy the point numbers four and 10 by paying a five percent commission.

Buy-in: Exchanging cash for chips at a table. The original amount of cash exchanged for chips in the beginning of a player's action.

Cackling the dice: To pretend to shake the dice in your hand. In actuality, the dice remain fixed in order to control the roll.

Cage: The cashiers area of a casino where chips are exchanged for cash.

California aces: Name given to the four jokers in California aces.

Call: In poker, to see a bet by putting in the same amount as the previous bettors.

Call bet: A bet made verbally without any chips being put on the table. Most casinos will not accept call bets anymore.

Caller: In baccarat, the dealer in charge of the game. In keno, the person who announces the winning numbers.

Camouflage: To play in such a way as not to alert the casino that you can count cards at blackjack.

Cancel button: The button in Video Poker that allows a player to cancel the previous choice(s) made.

Cancellation betting system: A betting system using a series of numbers that cancels numbers after a winning bet and adds numbers after a loss. Also known as the *Labouchere system*. Not recommended.

Capping a bet: Adding more chips to a bet that has already won. Also known as *past posting*.

Capping a deck: Adding cards to the top of the deck after the shuffle.

C&E: The abbreviation for craps-eleven. A Crazy Crapper bet that the next roll will be two, three, 11, or 12.

The Captain: The greatest and most innovative craps player in history.

Card clumping: The tendency of groups of cards to stay together for prolonged periods in shoe games because of insufficient shuffling by the dealer.

Card Counting: Keeping track of the cards that have been played in blackjack to determine whether you or the casino has the advantage. The only way to win at blackjack in the long run.

Card Mechanic: A skilled manipulator who can control the cards as he or she shuffles. Technique used strictly for cheating.

Carre: The French term for the corner bet.

Carousel: The name for an area containing a group of slot machines, usually of the same type, serviced by an individual cashier.

Cash out button: In Video Poker, the button that allows you to receive the coins that a machine has credited you with.

Casino advantage: The edge, usually shown as a percentage, that the house has over the player.

Casino Host: The person responsible for seeing that high rollers are treated with the dignity and graciousness their wallets merit.

Casino Manager: The person responsible for seeing that the games of a given casino are handled properly.

Catch: The number or numbers selected by a keno player that correspond to the numbers selected by the caller and show on a board during a given period of play.

Center field: The stickman's name for the nine in craps. The center betting position in a blackjack game with seven betting squares.

Change person: Individual who changes currency for coin in the slot areas.

Chasing losses: Increasing your bets in order to recoup what you've lost. Not a good way to play.

Check: In poker, to pass without wagering.

Check rack: The tray that holds the chips for a game.

Checks: Another name for chips.

Chit: The 15th highest hand in pai gow.

Chong: The seventh highest hand in pai gow.

Choppy game: A game where neither the house nor the player has been winning consistently. Opposite of a streak.

Clocking: Keeping track of the results of a particular game.

Cocked dice: Dice that land on a chip or against the wall and are slightly askew. Often requires the pit boss to decide which numbers have come up.

Color up: To exchange smaller denomination chips for larger denomination chips at a table.

Cold dice: Dice that aren't passing or making numbers.

Cold table: Any table where you are losing.

Colonne: French word for column bet.

Column bet: In roulette, a bet on one of the columns of 12 numbers on the layout.

Combination bet: In roulette, a bet with one chip on two or more numbers.

Combination ticket: In keno, a bet on a number of different propositions.

Come bet: Similar to the Pass Line bet, a wager that the next point number rolled will come up before another seven is thrown.

Come Out roll: The roll that establishes the shooter's Pass Line point.

Come point: The come number that must be repeated before a seven is thrown.

Commission: The percentage that the casino takes out of winning card hands or for buy bets in craps, usually five percent.

Comp: The "freebies" that casinos give out for certain levels of betting.

Condition: The type of bet on a keno ticket as indicated by a player's notation on the right hand side.

Corner bet: In roulette, at bet that four numbers in a given segment of the layout will win. Also known as a *square bet* or a *quarter bet*.

Counter Catcher: The individual hired by a casino to catch card counters. Pejoratively known as the "catcher-dog."

Couplet: The bet in sic bo that two dice will have the same numbers showing. Not recommended.

Crapless Craps: New game where the two, three, 11, and 12 become point numbers.

Crap out: To roll a two, three or 12 on the come out roll.

Craps: The numbers two, three, and 12.

Crazy Crapper bets: The Captain's term for all the bad bets in craps.

Credit button: On slot and Video Poker machines, the button that allows the player to play winning credits and not coin.

Credit line: The amount of credit a player is allowed by a given casino.

Credit manager: The person in charge of determining casino credit for a player.

Crew: Personnel who man a craps game. Also name for the group of high-rollers who play with the Captain.

Crimp: To bend a card for later identification.

Crossroader: A casino cheat.

Croupier: French for dealer in roulette.

Cull: To sort cards out of a deck for later use as a dealer shuffles.

Cut card: The card that indicates the shuffle point in a shoe game.

Cut the deck: To divide the deck before dealing. Usually done by a player.

d'Alembert betting system: Increasing one's bet by one unit after a loss and decreasing it by one unit after a win.

Day: The third highest ranking hand in pai gow.

Day gow: The 18th highest ranking hand in pai gow.

Day shift: The casino work shift that usually runs from 10 am to 6 pm.

Daub: To cheat at cards by placing a small amount of paint or ink on a card for purposes of later identifying it.

Dead ace: Loaded dice that tend to land with the one face showing. Any dice that have the one face loaded to show are called *dead dice*.

Dead hand: In poker, a hand that has been discarded or can no longer be made.

Dead table: A table that is manned and ready for action but has no players.

Deal button: In Video Poker, the button that is pushed to get the machine to "deal" the cards.

Dealer: The casino employee who staffs the games offered.

Dealing seconds: Dealing the second card in the deck until you need the first card to either make a good hand or break a player's hand.

Derniere: French term for last as in columns or dozens bets at roulette.

Desperado: A gambler who plays foolishly, usually chasing his losses.

Deuces: The two in cards and the two on the dice.

Devil: A term for the seven in craps. "The devil jumped up!"

Dice: Cubes with six sides, numbered respectively one through six.

Dice faces: The bet at sic bo that the next shake will result in a given face on one of the three dice.

Dice tray: The small tray that holds the dice that are not being used. Sometimes known as the *dice boat*.

Die: One cube, the singular form of dice.

Discard rack: The plastic, upright receptacle for cards that have already been played in shoe games.

Discretionary removal: The ability in place betting to call off or remove your bets. Odds bets are also discretionary.

Do bet: To bet with the dice and against the seven.

Doey-Don't: Betting both Pass and Don't Pass or Come and Don't Come simultaneously. An element of the Captain's *Supersystem*.

Don't bet: To bet against the dice and for the seven.

Don't Come: A bet at craps that the next point number rolled will not be repeated before a seven is thrown. One of the better bets in the casino.

Don't Pass: A bet at craps that the shooter will not make his point before the seven is thrown.

Double down: In blackjack, to double the size of your bet and receive only one card. You can also double for less than the initial wager.

Double exposure: Blackjack game where both of the dealer's cards are dealt face up.

Double odds: The right to place a free odds bet up to double the original Pass Line or Come bet. One of the best bets in the casino.

Double progressive slots: Two different progressive slot jackpots on the same machines, each growing independently. Jackpots alternate based on the pull of the handle or press of the button.

Double up system: This is also known as the Martingale family of wagers. Player attempts to get all his previous losses back by increasing (doubling) his previous bet.

Double zero: Another term for the American roulette wheel. The area of the American roulette wheel that contains the 00.

Douzaine: French word for dozen bet.

Down with my odds or bet: Telling the dealers at craps to return your bet.

Dozen bet: A bet at roulette that one of 12 numbers in sequence will win.

Draw: In Video Poker, to receive new cards. In baccarat or poker, to receive more cards.

Draw button: The button on a Video Poker machine that allows a player to receive another card.

Drop: The casino term for the total amount of money and markers wagered at the tables.

Drop box: Where the money is dropped after a player cashes in. Usually located under the table.

Dumping: A casino table that is losing money to the players.

Duplicate ticket: The receipt for a regular keno ticket given to a player after he places his bet. Also known as an *outside ticket*.

Early surrender: Rarely found rule in blackjack that allows players to forfeit half their bet, even if the dealer has a blackjack.

Easy way: In craps, the numbers four, six, eight, and 10 made without doubles.

Edge: Having the advantage in a game.

Eighty-six: The same as barring someone from playing in the casino.

Eldest hand: The player to the dealer's immediate left.

En plein: French term for the straight up bet in roulette.

En prison: Found in European casinos in roulette. Player is allowed to keep his bet playing on the next spin if the 0 should show.

Even bet: A wager in roulette that one of the even numbers will win.

Even up : A bet that has no mathematical edge for either side.

Even money: A bet that pays off at one to one.

Exposed card: A card inadvertently shown during the play of a hand.

Eye in the sky: The cameras, usually in bubbles, located throughout the casino that videotape the action.

Face cards: The king, queen and jack. Also known as *picture cards*.

False Cut: A cut of the cards that leaves them in the same order that they were in before.

Fair game: A game where neither the house nor the player has an edge.

Favorable deck: A deck whose remaining cards favor the player.

Fibonacci betting system: The progressive betting system as follows: *1,2,3,5,8,13,21,34,55,89* and so forth, where each bet is a combination of the two previous numbers.

Field: Uncircled numbers on a keno ticket that are to be played with king numbers.

Field bet: A wager at craps that wins if the number two, three, four, nine, 10, 11, or 12 is rolled. Shooter loses on a five, six, seven, and eight. Not recommended.

First base: The seat at the table immediately to the dealer's left.

First basing: Attempting to see the dealer's hole card when he checks for a blackjack.

5-Count: The revolutionary system developed by the Captain to avoid horrendous rolls of the dice, stretch the amount of time your money gives you at the table, and position you to take advantage of hot rolls.

Five number bet: Can only be made on the American roulette wheel. Wager is that 0, 00, one, two, or three will hit. The worst bet in roulette. Also known as the *Beast with Five Numbers* or *the House Special.*

Flat bet: Bet that is paid off at even money in craps. Also, any player who bets the same amount hand after hand.

Floorman: Individual responsible for supervising several tables in a pit.

Fluctuation in probability: Numbers appearing out of all proportion to their probability. A short sequence of repeating numbers. A mathematical term that means good or bad luck depending on whether the fluctuation is in your favor or not.

Flush: In poker, five cards of the same suit.

Fold: In poker, to drop out of play.

Foo: Ninth highest hand in pai gow.

Four flush: Four of the same suit. A four-flusher was someone who attempted to win a pot by declaring a flush when he only had four of the same suit.

Four of a kind: Four cards of the same rank.

Four straight: Four cards in sequence.

Free odds: Wager placed behind the Pass Line bet or the Come bet that is paid off at the true odds.

French wheel: The European roulette wheel that only has the 0 and not the 00 number.

Front line: Another name for the Pass Line in craps.

Front loader: A blackjack dealer who unknowingly shows his hole card as he places it under the up card.

Front money: Money previously deposited with the cage and used by the player to draw markers against.

Full house: A poker hand consisting of three of a kind and two of a kind.

Full odds: Whatever the maximum odds allowed on a given craps table.

Fun book: Coupon book used by casinos to encourage play. Can be used to get an advantage at certain games if two players pool money and bet opposite sides. Also, contains discounts for drinks, food, etc.

Gaffed: Any gaming device that has been rigged.

Gambling stake: Amount of money reserved for gambling. Same as *bankroll*.

Gee Joon: The highest ranking hand in pai gow.

George: A good tipper.

Ghost: A stop on a slot machine reel that is blank.

Glim: A small, concealed mirror used to cheat at cards.

Golden arm: A shooter who consistently has good rolls at craps.

Goose: A transparent tube for selecting keno numbers.

Gor: The fifth highest hand in pai gow.

Gow: The 13th highest hand in pai gow.

Grand Martingale: A wagering system where you double your bets and add one extra unit after a lose.

Graveyard Shift: The 2 AM to 10 AM working shift in a casino.

Greens: Chips valued at $25.

Grifter: A scam artist.

Grind: Derogatory term for a low roller. A small money player.

Grind down: The casino wining all of a player's money due to the advantage it has on bets.

Grind joint: A casino that caters to low rollers.

Grind system: Increasing one's bet by a unit after each win. Also, any system that attempts to win small amounts frequently against the casinos.

Guerrilla gambling: The combination of smart play and hit-and-run tactics to beat the casinos at their own games.

Gutshot straight: In Video Poker, a straight that can only be made by drawing a single card. Same as an *inside straight*.

Hand: A player's cards in a card game. Also, the entire series of rolls in a craps game by one shooter.

Hand held game: A blackjack game, usually single and double deck, dealt from the hand and not from a shoe.

Hand mucking: A casino dealer who palms and then substitutes cards into a game at the appropriate time.

Hard hand: A blackjack hand that cannot use the ace as an 11.

Hard way bets: A bet in craps that the shooter will roll the four, six, eight, or 10 as doubles before a seven shows. A Crazy Crapper bet.

Hardway hop: A bet that the shooter will roll a particular total as doubles on the very next roll. A Crazy Crapper bet.

Head to head: To play against the dealer with no other players in the game. Sometimes referred to as *face to face*, or *heads up*.

Heat: Surveillance by the casino of a suspected card counter. Or pressure put on a card counter to leave before being banned. Also known as *steam*.

Heel a bet: Putting bets in the same space slightly askew to distinguish one type from another. For example, the odds on a Come bet are placed on top of the original bet but slightly askew.

High card: A jack, queen, king or ace.

High hand: In pai gow and pai gow poker, the hand that must be higher.

High-Low: A bet at craps that the next roll will be a two or a 12. Also, different spelling for the counting system Hi-Lo in blackjack. Also, the bet in roulette that the next spin will be either a high number or a low number.

High-low pickup: A cheating method at blackjack when the dealer picks up the cards in high-low alternating order.

High Roller: A player who plays for large stakes.

High Roller system: A method of betting for large stakes developed by the Captain that reduces the house edge and allows excellent comps without the normal risk. Would include the *best buys*.

High pair: A pair of jacks, queens , kings or aces.

Hit: To receive another card on your hand in blackjack.

Hold: The actual amount that the casinos take from their games.

Hold Button: In Video Poker, the button that allows you to keep certain cards.

Holdout shoe: A shoe that has been tampered with to allow the dealer to deal seconds.

Hole Card: The second card dealt, face down, to the dealer in blackjack. Any face down card.

Hole card play: Any method used to get a glimpse of the dealer's hole card.

Hop: A bet in craps that the next roll of the dice will be a certain combination. A Crazy Crapper bet.

Horn bet: A one roll bet that combines the two, three, 11 and 12.

Horn High: A horn bet where one of the totals has one more unit riding on it than all the others.

Horrendous rolls: Rolls where the shooter sevens out within a few rolls after establishing his point number.

Hot: A player who has been winning.

Hot and cold system: A wager on the side that won previously. Another name for the streak method of betting.

Hot dice: Dice that have been passing and making numbers.

Hot shooter: A shooter having a good roll at the craps table.

Hot table: A table where the players have been winning.

House edge: The mathematical edge that the casino has on a given bet.

House odds: The payoff that reflects the casino's tax on your winning bet.

House person: A dealer who is unusually concerned with the casino's profits. A dealer who enjoys watching the players lose. A dealer who identifies with the casino.

House ticket: A special keno ticket that only holds for one casino.

Hustler: A gambling cheat.

Inside bet: A bet made on the central, numbered portion of the roulette layout.

Inside numbers: In craps, the numbers five, six, eight, nine.

Inside straight: A straight that can only be completed by one card on the inside. Example: 4-5-*-7-8.

Inside ticket: The ticket upon which the keno player writes his bet and that he hands in to the casino. Also known as an *original bet*.

Insurance: A side wager at blackjack for up to half the original wager that the dealer has a blackjack when he has an ace showing.

Impair: French for the Odd bet in roulette.

Irregularity: A departure from the standard procedures at a given game.

Jacer: In pokette, the name for the two aces and two jokers appearing on a spin.

Jackpot: A grand payout, either on a machine or at a table game.

Joker: A wild card that can usually be used as a substitute for any card in the deck. Usually resembles a court jester.

Juice: The five percent commission that the house charges on buy bets in craps. Also known as *vig* or *vigorish*.

Junket: A trip arranged, organized and subsidized by a casino to bring gamblers to play at the games.

Junket master: The person in charge of a junket.

Kelly Criterion: A betting system utilizing the knowledge of a player's advantage at any given point in the game. The player bets the proportion of his bankroll that represents his advantage.

Keno counter: The place where wagers are submitted and winnings collected.

Keno lounge: Where the game of keno is conducted by the casino. Usually set apart from the rest of the casino.

Keno runner: The casino employee who collects keno tickets from players in different parts of the casino and hotel.

Keno writer: The individual who collects players' tickers, issues duplicate tickets, and pays off the winners.

Kibitzer: An individual who is not playing at a given game but is giving unwanted advice.

Kicker: In poker, an extra card, usually a high card, that is kept with a pair.

King number: A single number circled on a keno ticket that is to be played with other numbers circled.

King ticket: A keno ticket that contains one or more king numbers circled that are to be played in combination with other numbers circled.

Labouchere system of betting: The player adds to a written series of numbers after each loss and subtracts after a win. Also known as the cancellation system.

Ladder man: The casino employee at baccarat who sits on a high chair and watches the game.

Law of Repeating Numbers: The Captain's tongue-in-cheek term for his observation that numbers tend to repeat.

Lay bet: A wrong bet on a number at craps that is paid off at true odds after the casino extracts a five percent commission.

Laydown: A bet. Also, someone who quits in the middle of a game.

Laying odds: For the wrong bettor to make an odds bet on the Don't Pass or the Don't Come.

Layout: The design imprinted with the various bets at a given game.

Level one system: Any card counting system that uses +1 or –1 as the value of the cards that are counted.

Levels: Honest gaming equipment and personnel. As in: "This game is on the level."

Liberty Bell: The original slot machine created by Charles Fey.

Limited Bankroll System: The name of the craps system for individuals who can't afford the Captain's *best buys,* or who do not wish to play the *Supersystem* or *5-Count* Pass and Come. Also known as the Low Roller System.

Line bet: A bet in roulette that one of six particular numbers will win.

Little Joe: In craps, a roll of four. Also called *Little Joe from Kokomo*.

Locationing: The ability to memorize a group of cards so that when one of the group appears the player knows which cards will follow.

Long end of a bet: The side of a bet that must pay off more than it collects.

Long run: The concept that a player could play so often that probability would tend to even out. That is, you would start to see the total appearance of numbers approximating what probability theory predicts. A long run player is one who plays a lot!

Look: The 12th highest hand in pai gow.

Loose machine: A slot machine or video poker machine that is paying off more than other machines of its type. A machine that is winning for a player.

Low hand: In pai gow and pai gow poker, the second hand.

Low pair: In poker, any pair that can't open the betting. Also, in Video Poker, any pair that doesn't win money on the payout schedule.

Making a point: Having your Pass Line number repeat before the appearance of a seven.

Manque: The French term for low at roulette.

Mark: An individual who has been or is going to be cheated. A sucker.

Marker: The check a player fills out before receiving casino credit at a table. A promissory note or I.O.U.

Martingale system of wagering: Doubling one's bet after a loss in an attempt to make back all your losses and a small win.

Match play: A casino promotion where players are given special chips that they can bet. They are paid off in regular casino chips on a win.

Mechanic: Anyone who can manipulate and control either dice or cards.

Mills machines: The first slot machines to use the fruit symbols and to offer a jackpot.

Mini-Baccarat: Baccarat played on a regular blackjack table and for lower stakes.

Money at risk: Money that has been wagered and can be lost.

Money management: The methods a player uses to conserve his bankroll from ruin.

Money not at risk: Money that is on the layout but that you cannot lose. For example, during a come out roll, the odds portions of Come bets.

Money Plays: The call that alerts the dealer and the pit that you are betting cash and not chips.

Monster roll: A craps roll that is long and where many numbers and points are rolled. The dream of every craps player. The "Arm" from *Beat the Craps Out of the Casinos* is known as the Queen of the Monsters for the epic rolls she regularly produces.

Mooy: Sixth highest ranking hand in pai gow.

Mucker: Anyone who uses sleight of hand techniques to cheat at cards or other games.

Multiple coin machine: Slot and Video Poker machines that require more than one coin for maximum payouts.

Multiple-deck game: Blackjack played with more than one deck which gives the house more of an advantage over the player. Also, any shoe game with more than one deck.

Multiple hands: To play more than one hand at blackjack.

Nail: To catch someone cheating. "We nailed him."

Natural: A perfect hand. In blackjack, an ace and a 10 card. In baccarat, an eight or a nine. In California aces, two aces. In super pan nine, a nine. In craps, a seven or 11 on the Come Out roll.

Negative count: A count that favors the casino.

Negative progression: Any system of wagering where you increase bets after a loss.

NG: The 16th highest hand in pai gow.

Nickel: A five dollar chip—usually red.

No action: A call made by a dealer that the casino will not cover a particular bet or that a particular deal or roll doesn't count.

Noir: A French term for black at roulette.

Non-seven mode: A roll in which a rhythmic roller is positioning and rolling the dice in such a way that the seven doesn't appear.

N.S.G.N.G.R.: The Captain's tongue-in-cheek rule that you should never get upset if you can't guess correctly. Stands for *No Second Guess No Guess Rule*.

Nut: The total amount of money needed to run a casino or the total amount of money an individual needs to succeed at what he is doing.

Odd bet: A bet at roulette that one of the odd numbers will hit on the next spin.

Odds: The bet that pays off at true odds in craps. Also, the likelihood of a given event happening.

Off: To remove a bet from play at craps for one or more rolls. Means no decision will affect that bet. Place and odds bets can be called off.

On: A call that your bets are working or at risk on the next roll.

One armed bandits: The term given to slot machines.

One roll bet: A bet that will be decided on the very next roll of the dice. All one roll bets are Crazy Crapper bets and should be avoided.

One roll hardway: The next roll will be a four, six, eight or 10 made with doubles.

On the square: A game that is honest.

Open: In poker, to make the first bet.

Openers: The cards that qualify a player to open.

Original ticket: The ticket upon which the player records his keno numbers and that he hands in to the casino.

Outside bets: One of the two to one or even money bets at roulette. They appear on the outside of the layout.

Outside numbers: The box numbers four, five, nine and 10 on the craps layout.

Outside ticket: The keno player's receipt for his original ticket. Also known as *duplicate ticket*.

Paddle: The tool used to push the money into the drop box.

Paint: A picture card. When a player says, "Paint me," he is asking for a picture card.

Painter: A name for an individual who cheats at cards by daubing them with a small amount of paint. Also known as a *Picasso*.

Pair: A French term for even in roulette. In poker, two cards of the same denomination.

Palm: To conceal money or chips in one's hand.

Parlay: To double one's bet after a win.

Pass: A win by a shooter at craps, either on the Come Out roll or by making his point. Also, in poker, a player who checks on his betting round.

Passe: A French term for high in roulette.

Passers: Dice that have been loaded to favor the shooter.

Pass Line: A wager with the shooter that he will make his point.

Past Posting: Placing a winning wager *after* a decision has been reached. Usually done by capping a bet.

Pat Hand: Any hand in a card game that does not require getting additional cards.

Patience system: A grind method of playing whereby the player waits for a certain number of decisions before placing a bet. The Captain's methods of play all require a certain amount of patience.

Pawn: Any numbers marked in the field of a king ticket in keno.

Pay line: The line upon which a player is paid at slots. Generally corresponds to the number of coins played.

P.C.: The house edge expressed as a percentage.

Penetration: How deeply a dealer deals into a deck or a shoe at blackjack.

Penny Ante: A game played for small stakes.

Pilgrim's progression: The Captain's method for getting more money on the table during a hot roll. To be used in the High Roller System.

Pinching: Illegally removing chips from one's bet after an unfavorable decision.

Ping: The 10th highest hand in pai gow.

Pit: An area consisting of a number of gaming tables.

Pit boss: The individual in charge of a pit.

Place bet: Going directly up on a number. The house pays the bet at house odds and not true odds.

Player hand: The first of two hands dealt at baccarat.

Plus-Minus system: Another name for the Hi-Lo system or High-Low system of card counting. Cards are given a +1 or a −1 value.

Point: The number (four, five, six, eight, nine or 10) which the shooter must repeat before a seven is rolled in order to win on the Pass Line at craps.

Positive count: A count that favors the player.

Pot: The total amount of money at stake in a deal.

Pot limit: The betting limit is fixed by the size of the pot.

Power of the pen (or pencil): The ability to issue hotel comps to players on the part of some casino executives.

Premiere: A French term for first in roulette.

Premium players: A casino term meaning big bettors or players with big credit lines.

Press: To increase the amount wagered, usually by doubling it, after a win.

Price: The total sum wagered on a keno ticket. Also, the house percentage on a given bet.

Producer: Casino term for a player who loses often and for large sums. This individual is a producer of profits for the casino.

Progressive jackpots: The grand prize offered on certain kinds of slot and Video Poker machines that keeps growing as more and more money is played. Grows until it is hit by a player.

Prop: Another name for *shill*. A person employed by a casino to play a game to generate action. Most often used in baccarat and poker.

Proposition bet: Bets in the center of the craps layout. These are all Crazy Crapper bets and should be avoided. Also, any bet that is a longshot and carries a heavy house edge.

Push: Casinoese for tie.

Pushing the house or *pushing the casino*: The term coined by the Captain to describe a player in the act of getting a better game from a casino than advertised. For example, the *best buy* bets have radically pushed the casinos.

Quarter bet: A wager at roulette that one of four numbers will be hit on the next spin. The same as *corner bet* and *square bet*.

Quarters: Chips valued at $25. Also known as *greens*.

Rabbit ears: The two transparent tubes into which the keno balls are blown.

Race: An archaic term for a keno drawing. In the past, keno numbers also had the names of horses on them. Also known as *racehorse keno*.

Rail: The high border that encloses a craps table where the players keep their chips.

Rail bird or rail thief: Name for the individual who steals chips from other players at craps.

Raise: In poker, to increase the amount previously bet by another player.

Rake: The commission the card rooms take out of a pot.

Rating: Evaluating a player's play for the purpose of comps.

Rating card: The card used for rating a player.

Razzle: A version of lowball seven card stud.

Red bet: An even money bet at roulette that the next hit will be a red number.

Reds: Casino chips worth $5.

Reel: One of the loops inside a slot machine upon which the symbols are painted.

Reel window: The glass display area that shows the reels.

Replay ticket: A duplicate keno ticket that is played a second time because a player wishes to bet the same numbers again.

RFB: Complimentary room, food and beverage.

Rhythmic Roller: A shooter who by chance or design gets into a non-seven mode. Usually a shooter who rolls the dice the same way time after time.

Rich deck: In blackjack, a deck that has many 10 value cards remaining to be played.

Riffle: Splitting the deck in two and shuffling both sections into each other.

Right bettor: A player who bets with the dice and against the seven.

Risk-time: The amount of time you are at a table with your money at risk.

Rouge: A French term for red at roulette.

Royal flush: An ace, king, queen, jack and 10 of the same suit.

Ruin or element of ruin: Losing your bankroll. The probability of losing every penny of your bankroll.

Rule card: The card that shows the rules for a given game.

Running count: In blackjack, the raw count that has not been divided (or multiplied) by the number of decks remaining.

Running the shoe: A player at baccarat who is in the midst of dealing a streak of bank wins.

Rush: A quick winning streak.

Scanning: In blackjack, the quick perusal of the cards that have been played for the purpose of determining advantage.

Section shooter: A roulette dealer who tries to hit certain areas of the wheel on a given spin.

Section Shooting: Attempting to have the ball hit a certain section on the roulette wheel.

Section slicing: Dividing a wheel into sections based upon which numbers have been hitting for the purpose of discovering biases.

Scam: Any scheme to defraud a casino or player.

Scared money: Money a player can't afford to lose. Also known as *perspiration pennies*.

Session: A given period of play at a casino. Usually terminated at a predetermined time, or at a certain level of wins or losses.

Seven out: For a shooter at craps to roll a seven before repeating his point number.

Shaker: The container that holds the three dice in the various Asian games.

Shift boss: The individual in charge of the casino during a given work shift.

Shill: An individual employed by the casino to play games that are being underplayed.

Shoe: The box that holds the decks for a card game.

Shoot: To roll the dice.

Shooter: The person who rolls the dice.

The short end: The side of a bet that has to pay off less than it will win.

Short odds: Less than the true odds payoff of a bet.

Short run: The limited amount of time during any given session when probability theory will seemingly be skewered by streaks or fluctuations.

Short shoe: A blackjack shoe that has had cards advantageous to the players removed.

Showdown: In poker, the final betting of the players who remain, followed by the showing of the cards.

Shuffle tracking: Watching as the cards are being shuffled to memorize and later locate groups of cards.

Shuffle up: Technique used to thwart card counters. Dealer will shuffle after every deal or when a player enters a game and bets big money.

Side bet: A second bet, in addition to the normal bet, on a proposition at a table game.

Side pot: In poker, a pot in addition to the main pot.

Single-deck blackjack: The best game in the casino if the rules are standard.

Single odds: The ability of a player to place an amount equal to his Pass Line or Come bet in odds that will be paid off at the true odds for the number.

Single Zero Wheel: French or European roulette wheel that only has one 0.

Sixain: The French term for a six number bet at roulette.

Six number bet: A single bet that one of six numbers will hit on the next spin.

Sleeper: A winning bet at craps that the player has forgotten about. Quite often the player will leave a table and the bet will remain until it is lost or some player or dealer takes it.

Slot arcade: A casino devoted exclusively to slot machines.

Slot floor: Areas devoted to slot machines in a casino.

Slot mix: Slot machines of different denominations and of different percentages in the slot area.

Slug: A group of cards that have been prearranged in a given order and inserted into a deck. Any group of cards inserted whole into a deck. Also, a piece of rounded metal inserted into a slot machine that mimics a coin.

Snake eyes: The two at craps.

Snapper: An archaic term for a blackjack. A *red snapper* is a blackjack composed of two red cards.

Snowballs: Dice that only have the numbers four, five and six.

Soft hand: Any hand at blackjack where the ace can be used as an 11.

Soft players: Unskilled players who are easy to beat.

Split: To make two hands from a pair at blackjack.

Split bet: At roulette, a single bet that one of two particular numbers will hit on the next spin.

Spook: A player who gets the dealer's hole card in blackjack and relays that information to his accomplices.

Spooking: The process of discovering the dealer's hole card at blackjack.

Spooning: Sticking a spoon into a slot machine to get it to pay off.

Spot: The number on a keno ticket that has been Xed out for betting purposes.

Spread: The difference between the minimum and maximum bets a player makes.

Square bet: In roulette, a bet that one of four particular numbers will hit on the next spin. Also known as a *quarter bet* and a *corner bet*.

Squares: A game or player that is honest. "This game is on the square."

Stack: A group of 20 roulette chips.

Stacked deck: A deck that has been prearranged.

Stand: To keep the cards you have. Not to draw any more cards.

Steaming: A player who is visibly upset and is playing recklessly at a table.

Stickman: Crap dealer who uses the thin stick and pushes the dice to the shooter.

Stiff: In blackjack, a total of 12 through 16. Also, not to tip a cocktail server.

Stops: The various points where a slot reel might become stationary.

Straight: Five cards in sequence.

Straight flush: Five cards of the same suit in sequence.

Straight slots: Slots that have an unvarying payout.

Straight ticket: A keno ticket that has only one wager and that involves the selection of from one to 15 different numbers.

Straight up bet: In roulette, a bet on one number.

Street bet: A bet in roulette that one of three particular numbers will hit on the next spin.

The Strip: Las Vegas Blvd. Three miles of casinos.

Sub: A secret pocket in a dealer's uniform where he deposits chips he's stealing.

Surrender: A blackjack option where the player may give up half his bet. Player loses full bet if the dealer has a blackjack, however. Sometimes known as *late surrender*.

Supersystem: The method of play developed by the Captain for long term play at craps. Divided into the *classical* and *radical* supersystems.

Sweat: Casinos who are upset by players winning are said to *sweat* out their games. Also, a player who is losing and is worried.

Swing Shift: The shift that runs from 6 PM to 2 AM.

Table games: Any game in a casino that is played at a table.

Table hopping: Moving from table to table in a casino.

Take the edge: Giving yourself an edge at a game—usually by cheating.

Take down: To recall a wager before a decision.

Taking the odds: To put the odds behind a Pass Line or a Come bet.

Tapped out: To lose one's entire bankroll.

Teen: The second highest hand in pai gow.

Teen gow: The 17th highest hand in pai gow.

Telegraph: To unwittingly give away your hand or your next move.

Tell: An unconscious signal that a dealer gives when peeking for a blackjack. Any unconscious signal that allows you to know what a player has.

Third base: The position to the dealer's right at blackjack. Player acts on his hand last.

Three faces: In sic bo, the wager that the next shake of the dice will result in the three faces selected.

Three flush: Three cards to a flush.

Three of a kind: Having three cards of the same denomination.

Three straight: Three cards to a straight.

Tight machine: A slot machine that is not paying back a good percentage. A machine that a player is losing at.

Tit: The 11th highest hand in pai gow.

Toke: A tip to a casino employee.

Toke hustler: A dealer who tries to get the players to tip him.

Tom: Casinoese for a poor tipper.

Topping the deck: Palming cards.

Totals: The wager in sic bo that the next shake of the dice will result in a given total.

Tough out: The Captain's term for a skilled player who doesn't beat himself.

Transverale: The French term for the triple or trio bet at roulette.

Trio bet: A single bet that one of three numbers will be the next to hit at roulette.

Triple odds: The placing of three times one's original bet in odds behind the Pass Line or Come bets.

Triplet: The wager in sic bo that the next shake will result in three of the same faces appearing on the dice.

True count: The adjusted count that reflects the count per remaining deck.

True odds: The actual probability of an event happening.

Twenty-one: Another name for blackjack.

Two-faces: In sic bo, the wager that the next shake of the dice will result in two specific faces appearing.

Twenty-two: Another name for California aces.

Two pair: A hand consisting of two separate pairs.

Underground joint: An illegal casino.

Unfavorable deck: A deck or shoe in blackjack that favors the casino.

Up card: Any card that is dealt face up.

Vic: A sucker. Short for victim.

Vig or vigorish: The casino tax on a bet. Also known as *juice*.

Virgin principle: The superstition that a beginner will have luck. Also known as *beginner's luck*.

Wager: Another term for bet.

Wash: One bet cancels out another bet. Also, the process of mixing fresh cards together on the top of the table without lifting them.

Way ticket: Several bets of the exact same type in keno.

Weight: Loaded dice.

Wheel: Casinoese for roulette.

Wheel chips: Special chips used only at roulette.

Wheel head: The portion of a roulette wheel that contains the numbered grooves.

Wheel of fortune: A carnival game that has found its way into the casinos. A bad bet.

Wheel roller: A roulette dealer.

Wild card: A card that can be used for any other card in a game.

Wired: In poker, having a pair composed of one face up card and one hole card.

Wonging: Hit and run style of playing in high counts only. Named after blackjack author, Stanford Wong.

Working bet: A bet at craps that is at risk.

Wrong bettor: A player who bets against the shooter and with the seven.

Yun: The fourth highest hand in pai gow.

Zero: The numbers added to the roulette wheel to give the house the edge. Also, a loser.

Index

Frontier, 250-51
Full House, 136
Full-pay poker machines, 210-14,
　221, 244

Gambler
　a day in the life of, 247-84
　books for, 285-88
　magazines/newsletters for,
　288
Gambler's Book Club, xi, 14
Garden of the Dragon, 263, 273
Gaughan's Plaza, 269
Glossary, 293-332
Golden Nugget, 265, 266-68, 272,
　276
Grand Martingale strategy, 28
Gros, Roger, xi
Groveling, 230

Haggerty, Julie, 15
Hard hands, 38
Heads and tails, 179
Hi-Lo counting system, 55
Hickok, Wild Bill, 165
Hickok's aces and eights, 166-67
Hickok's six card, 165, 223
　Foxwoods variation, 166-67
　payoff schedule, 165-66
　playing procedures, 165
High bet, 25
Highest card, 136
High rollers, 127-28, 224
Hilton, 263, 272-73
Hit, 39

Impair, 25
Imperial Palace, 265
Inside bet, 19, 23-24
Insurance, 48, 70
Insure, 40

Jackpot rules, 50
Jacks-or-better poker machine,
　210-11
Joker wild poker machine, 213-
　14

Keno, 13, 159-61, 223
Knowledge, 3

Late surrender rules, 49
Law, books on, 285
Law of Three, 128
Layout
　baccarat (American), 89
　California aces, 173
　craps, 100, 102
　pai gow poker, 187
　players, 19
　red dog, 175
　roulette, 19, 20
　sic bo, 162
　super pan nine, 168
Lies, big, 2-7
Line bet, 24
Loose player, 147
Lost in America, 14-15
Low bet, 25
Low rollers, 127-28, 224-26

Mammon, Mary, 194
Mann, Howard T., *xi*
Manque, 25
Martingale, 241
　mini- for baccarat, 96
　strategy, 28
　wagering system, 68-69
Maxim, 269
Mechanic, 256
Microprocessor slot machines,
　200-201
Mini-baccarat, 92, 220
Mini-Martingale, 96, 241
Mirage, 265
Money management
　bankroll requirements, 238-46
　theory, 235-38
Multi-level count, 55
Multiple action blackjack, 51, 52
Multiple-deck basic strategy, 41,
　42, 43-44
　Martingale wagering system,
　68-69
　variations in, 58-60